MONEY, it's all about Money
It should be about **MORALITY**

Philosophy,
Economics,
& Ethics

GREGORY THAIN
Editor Paul Phillips

Money, it's all about Money
It should be about Morality

ISBN 979-8-3492-0201-8 PBK
Available in Hardcover, eBook and Audio

March 2025

Published and Distributed by
Alliance of Independent Authors, Inc. in conjunction with **Moral Money GLD.**
Sarasota, FL 34276
www.allianceofindependentauthors.com

Editor Paul Phillips
Economics Artem Shitkov
Website: www.moralmoney.co
Jan 2nd - Oct 29th, 2024

Disclosure: All figures are in dollars; we use euro to dollar exchange at 1.05 and UK pound to dollar exchange at 1.25.

This book is dedicated to my family and friends

Many thanks to Paul Phillips for editing
Artem Shitkov for reviewing the economic information
John Varnom and Ben Aris for some early thoughts
Nick Kenwrick-Piercy for reviewing as we went along
James Thain for sorting out the charts

Thanks also to the team behind:
Katya, Sarah, Nick, Poppy, and Magnolia

Cover design by
Olga Gusarova-Tchalenko

CONTENTS

Author's Note

This book is a reflection on the need for a better way forward for the human race. A new more robust morality to guide us and frame our decisions. Because if we don't very quickly find a better way we will end up in a very bad and dark place.

We all have faults. I admit to many. I also recognise I write from the inside and as part of the elite I'm critiquing here. But that does give me access and understanding.

We need to ask ourselves over and over, what is right for all of us, not just me? For the 'We' and not just the 'I'.

Every day in newspapers, on television and online we see things happening that horrify us. Many of these things show us that there is no universal desire for democracy, freedom, independence, equality and decency as we have always understood them.

The global debt crisis of 82/83, book burnings on our streets, Black Wednesday in the UK, 9/11, the banking collapse of 2007/08, Covid 19 and its consequent lockdowns, Ayatollah Khomeini's return to Iran and Putin's invasion of Ukraine are just a few of the events that have shaken our faith in our governments, their weak responses, in the status quo, and, yes, maybe in democracy itself.

This book is my attempt to make some sense of how we got here, but more importantly to map a way forward.

Gregory Thain
30th January, 2025

Introduction

Among the themes in this book, one focus is the speed at which things are changing, and about how that change is accelerating at ever faster rates. As much as we have updated, we have been constantly overtaken by events, many of which we were predicting.

Our main theme, though, is the need to create a more moral and ethical world. And, again, the speed with which a rules-based order is being ripped up as we struggle towards publication has been breathtaking. If we refer to a specific event, it will date even as we write. So, we have not done that. Let's just focus on our message.

We are at a turning point,[1] technologically and geopolitically. The convergence of artificial intelligence, genetic engineering, and the renewed race for space exploration is poised to reshape our world in unprecedented ways. Geopolitical tensions, climate change, and economic disparities further amplify the urgency of this moment. We stand on the precipice of a new era, one that demands a fundamental re-evaluation of our values and priorities.

Life as we know it is going to become very different, and relatively quickly. Over the past 1,000+ years, change has taken a long time. It has mostly been a protracted and multi-generational process.

And then, over the past 100 or so years, progress sped up. It took just 30 years to overthrow 5,000 years of horse culture, replacing the horse with automobiles.

Then came flight, air travel, jet speed; radio, film, television; humans in space, on the moon, rockets to Mars; room-sized computers, desktop computers, smart hand-held devices; and genome mapping.

Most of that, and a lot more, in the last 80 years.

But if we thought things moved quickly in the 20th century, life is about to become very challenging, and much quicker than all of us are prepared for, in this 21st century.

Because everything[2] - business, social interaction, medical advancement, scientific development and change, in every person's life - is speeding up dramatically.[3]

And spearheading this change will be Artificial Intelligence and GAI-AI, (Generative artificial intelligence).[4] AI's potential to automate tasks, analyse vast datasets, and even to create original content will disrupt industries, redefine jobs, and challenge our understanding of what it means to be human. GAI, with its potential to surpass human intelligence, raises even more profound questions about the future of our species and the ethical implications of creating such powerful entities.

If you are over 80 - and 167m people are[5] - even if you were born in a G7 country, the likelihood would have been still quite high in 1945 that your house had neither connection to electricity nor the comfort of an indoor toilet.

If you are now over 60, you started your business life without a computer, and cell phones were just a dream.

If you are over 40, the iPhone, launched June 29, 2007, in the USA, has been with you for less than half of your life - only 17 years. But it has dramatically changed our lives, both business and personal.

Physically, things on many levels have improved. There are hundreds of thousands of items and experiences we can purchase today - online, without even leaving our homes - that had barely been dreamed of 50 years ago.

Some politicians might even suggest you have never had it so good.

But?

We currently have a war in Europe; conflict involving Israel which threatens to encompass at least the whole Middle East; any of which may evolve into WW3. Plus, conflicts in Syria, Yemen, Iraq, Libya, Afghanistan, Myanmar, and the Philippines, Sahel region,

Ethiopia's Tigray region, to name a few. A future conflict between China and America is highly possible.[6]

One of the problems of our modern world is our access to so much information and news. Whereas in the recent past you might only have been looking at a newspaper daily, or listening to the news on radio at 9pm, we are now swamped with so many stories that we have become immune to their effect. There is too much data: a murder, a bomb, a terrorist event, children dying from lack of food - we have become anaesthetised to the impact of the most miserable of stories. We do not have the processing power to analyse and make sense of it all. If we aspire to rise above the animal, the tribal, I suggest we need to think about or acquire a better sense of morality.

Child poverty is a good example. The assumption is that this is something only affecting the Third World. But child poverty in G7 countries is frightening and growing.[7]

As Will Hutton[8] has put it very clearly: we need to think about the **We** not the **I.**

Human Life has always been a permanent process of change. From caves to houses. From foraging to farming. From footsteps to the wheel, to flight, and soon rocket ships.

Since we have messed up so much on earth, we must ask, before we go into space, what is best for all, not just for me. The driver or motivation should not be: how can I obtain more power, money, wealth; but how can I contribute as an individual, as a family, as a community, to create a better world for everyone? We frequently hear President John F Kennedy's inaugural speech quoted: "Ask not what your country can do for you. Rather ask what you can do for your country."[9] We hear it. But we've forgotten what it means. As citizens, we have become increasingly passive, and the more passive we become, the more we will be at the mercy of the state, the unelected, the dictator.

The idea behind this book is to spell out some targets that we need to aim for, to start the path to a better life for everyone. For the **We** not the **I**. There are quite a few books, many of which we refer to or mention, that discuss the generalities. But there are few clear targets and ideas that aim to create a better life for everyone.

Now we are on the verge of a Space Revolution, whose exploration and exploitation are increasingly backed by companies with almost no accountability. The drive into space will certainly create the next, the Fourth, Industrial Revolution.

But where will that leave most ordinary people? Almost half of the world's wealth (46.1% of it) is currently owned by 1% of its population. At the very top of that 1% are the globe's billionaires - roughly 3,000 of them - who control 3% ($14.2T) of our total wealth.

The turnover and power of the world's biggest companies is also a real concern. Amazon, for example, has a current market capitalization of $1.85 trillion which is getting very close to the total GDP of Canada, a G7 country, at $2.1T. In fact, Amazon's value is greater than all, but the top 12 countries of the world ranked by GDP.

Size gives power and essentially that power is unaccounted for, and each day more wealth is syphoned off to the very few. Our society is very fractured and huge gaps have grown between the haves and the have nots.

The task of this book will be to expand upon some of these issues, to discuss the details of how the issues have arisen, and their consequences. But also, to offer and explore some concrete solutions to create a more equitable universal society.

Do the systems we currently have inspire you as structures capable of dealing with humanity as it faces the swiftest and most powerful changes we have ever seen?

The good news is that we are all living longer. But as the population ages we will need higher taxes to provide the care required, and no one, no politician, is prepared to say this. And where will those higher taxes come from? Will they come from taxing the top 10% properly, particularly the billionaires and the elite? Or will governments try to squeeze the poor further? I would suggest that we must consider what is good for us all, what is the grown-up response? Because in many ways we have not grown up. We remain only a short step from the original savage cave.[10] Indeed, in Afghanistan, 700 families, bereft of home and work by constant war, are now back living in caves.[11]

We should all be aware of how close our civilisation is living to the edge of the cliff. We have an absolute need for a better morality, a grown-up morality. Or, as a civilisation, we will simply implode, moving to a very dark future.

Footnotes – Introduction

---

[1] Note 1, Appendix 1 for previous turning points.

[2] Note 2, Appendix 1 for some ideas on changes that will happen in the next 10 years

[3]"The world around us is changing at unprecedented speed" Konstantin Kisin - An immigrant's love letter to the west https://ourworldindata.org/technological-change

[4] https://en.wikipedia.org/wiki/Generative_artificial_intelligen

[5] The 2023 World Social Report by the United Nations, the estimated global number of people aged 80 or over in 2021 was 155 million. This number is projected to triple by 2050, reaching approximately 459 million

[6] For the reason read Technofeudalism: What Killed Capitalism Hardcover – 28 Sep. 2023

[7] The USA is showing that 14% of all children are affected by poverty. In the United Kingdom 4.2 million children were living in poverty in 2020 and this figure is growing. In Canada, 1.2 million children are living in low-income households. In France around 18% of children were living below the poverty line. In Germany. The figure is 13.8%, in Italy 20.3% and even in Japan 13.9% of children were living in relative income poverty. These figures are generated by different methods and different assumptions, but they show a very frightening trend

[8] Will Hutton, This Time No Mistakes; 2024 - a book about capitalism and democracy and how the degraded forms they have taken have diminished the lives of its citizens

[9]https://www.jfklibrary.org/learn/education/teachers/curricular-resources/ask-not-what-your-country-can-do-for-you

[10] We were living in caves during the Palaeolithic Era, which ended around 10,000 years ago

[11] https://www.bbc.co.uk/news/world-asia-28583933

CHAPTER 1

Where are we now?

Life as we know it will soon be very different. And sooner than you think.

Business life for many of us started without computers.[1] They only appeared in offices in any meaningful way after 1981.[2] Mobile telephones were only a dream in the 80s, becoming a status symbol in the early 1990s,[3] before the work-friendly Blackberry launched in 1999.

At the time of writing the iPhone had been with us for just 17 years, since 2007, but it has dramatically changed our business and personal lives. (And I think to most people it seems like it has been here forever).

So work and personal communication/interaction has changed massively and rapidly over the last 40 years.

But now we have AI which will speed things up further. Life will be turbocharged. We are living at a time where we will see further dramatic change in the development of the world as we currently know it. Three years from now, or maybe a little later, unmanned spacecraft will be reaching Mars.[4] By 2030 or shortly thereafter manned spacecraft will be landing there.

In the late 15th century, Columbus set off to reach America. (Well, he thought he was going to China!). Following Columbus's first discovery of America early in the 16th century, Juan Ponce de León explored Florida in 1513. Also in 1513, Vasco Núñez de Balboa crossed the Isthmus of Panama and discovered the Pacific Ocean. Ferdinand Magellan sailed around the tip of South America, across the Pacific to the Philippines, through the Indian Ocean and back to Europe between 1519 and 1522 - more than the time it will take to go to Mars and back, currently forecast as between 18 months and two years.

Why the history lesson? Because, just as with Columbus, after the first Mars landings there will be a flood of future explorers into space. And the August 2024 revelation that 'an ocean-sized reservoir of water' has been discovered 'deep in the crust of Mars', will only serve to heighten the enthusiasm to get there.[5]

In the next 20+ years there will be plans for spacecraft to explore moons, asteroids and planets. Investors in these exploratory voyages will be hoping for the discovery of new sources of gold, silver, diamonds, rare metals and precious materials as yet unknown. Or maybe grabbing the territory for the country from which the spacecraft originated.

Space exploration will have the advantage of driving the world's economy as many race for new wealth and new power. Costs of extraterrestrial travel have significantly reduced and will continue to do so. Saturn 1, which made its maiden voyage in 1961, cost $864m (£10bn adjusted to current values). By contrast, Starlink is currently costing $1.1 million per satellite. The Falcon 9 launcher has a reported launch cost of $67M. It can simultaneously launch 60 satellites.

It's 150 years since the Second Industrial Revolution began in 1870, peaking in 1914. Interrupted by the First World War, it was characterised by rapid technological and economic growth. Some of the key developments of the Second Industrial Revolution include: widespread adoption of electricity and the internal combustion engine; the development of new industries such as steel, chemicals, and petroleum; the rise of mass production and assembly lines; the expansion of railroads and telegraph networks; and the growth of urbanisation and consumerism.

This Second Industrial Revolution which was powered by oil (the First being powered by coal) had a profound impact on the world, transforming economies, societies, and cultures. It also led to several new social and environmental problems such as pollution, poverty, and inequality. There were very few people thinking about a better morality, or a better way of racing forward, a few individuals, like Robert Owen[6] of New Lanark Mill, being rare exceptions.[7]

The Third Industrial Revolution is the one we are currently living through: the communications technology era, where corporate power and wealth have ended up residing in the hands of fewer and fewer individuals, who are richer and more influential than any humans who have ever lived.

And before we draw breath on the Third Industrial Revolution, we are now facing another. The Fourth Industrial Revolution could be dubbed 'The leaving of earth', or the First Space Revolution. (Powered by solar, wind, geothermal, nuclear).

Untold and unimaginable wealth awaits. But to whom will it belong?

At the same time, the new South Sea Bubble, the new Tulip Mania of the 2030s,[8] will be The Galaxy Bubble, an irresistible investment opportunity where a few will make spectacular returns, but the majority may lose their money. Companies like Asteroid Mining Corporation, Lunar Industries, and Mars Colonial Transporter are already attracting billions in investment, promising untold riches from the extraction of rare earth metals and other valuable resources. However, the risks are immense, and the potential for a speculative bubble that could leave many investors with nothing but empty promises is very real. There are already over 10,000 companies in the USA, and many more in China, India[9] and elsewhere, offering you shares to invest in different variations of the First Space Revolution. Many of them will fail. But some will make huge profits. A recent funding round has valued SpaceX (Elon Musk's venture) at over $100 billion, making it the most valuable privately held space company. Meanwhile, although not publicly traded, estimates suggest Blue Origin's (Jeff Bezos) valuation could also be in the tens of billions of dollars. Relativity Space (Tim Ellis and Jordan Noone) is also not publicly traded, but recent funding rounds have valued Relativity Space at over $4 billion.[10]

Will the profits from discoveries that flow from these ventures benefit the entirety of mankind? Or will history repeat, with fabulous wealth accruing to just a few individuals?

Space X is planning a Mars mission. Blue Origin is eyeing lunar missions. Northrop Grumman is developing technology for planetary exploration. And Sierra Nevada Corporation is working on reusable spacecraft. These are just a few examples.

But while our new heroes and explorers are escaping our current world, we are in disarray and very unclear about our direction and morality. Because of advances in technology, we were able to watch on our televisions, in real time, as aeroplanes attacked the World Trade Centre in New York on September 11, 2001.

After the first iPhones appeared in 2007, world events could be followed on handheld devices as we moved around towns and cities, and it became possible for us to phone or text each other and spread the word about earth-shattering events, again in real time. The Arab Spring - a widespread revolt against despotic leaders in the Middle East - was organised and encouraged by widespread use of social media on smart devices. In 2020, live video of thousands of Chinese trying to flee Wuhan woke the world up to a novel and dangerous coronavirus which came to be called Covid-19. On June 24/25, 2023, there was almost another revolution in Russia which we were all able to track on the internet and on our iPhones as soldiers supposedly marched towards a new revolution in Moscow.

By now, we are used to getting our news up to the minute. No waiting, as we had 100 years ago, for the newspaper to arrive days, weeks or even months later.

Technology and the access provided by the Internet means that going forward everybody in the world is able to access information and knowledge.

Yes, there is fake news, fake propaganda, and governments - with all their resources - spinning their 'official' slant on reality.

But we have access to a lot of basic information, and it is up to us to develop the critical faculties to determine what is real and what is not; what is true and what is a lie. In our *education* chapter, we discuss how the teaching of critical thinking is crucial to developing our sense of reality. Meanwhile, some governments are turning off people's internet access. But I believe we will soon be able to access the Internet without government control. Elon Musk's company SpaceX has already launched over 7,000 satellites as part of its Starlink project.[11] The purpose of this project is to provide high-speed Internet services to all people around the world, especially in remote or underserved areas. If this does not work, people will still find a way. Briar is one option.[12] Briar builds on FireChat, which was used during the unrest in Hong Kong 2019/20, allowing mobiles to connect to other mobiles without Wi-Fi. Even after the Chinese (Hong Kong) government turned off internet access, people could still talk to each other.

There is no doubt in my mind that this world can provide a good life and a safe life for the entire eight billion of us, and those still to come. If that is what we want. Do we have the moral strength to push for this? There is enough money circulating in the world for everyone to earn a decent living. There is more than enough wealth for everyone to be comfortable. We have enough food in developed countries to feed the world. We throw a lot of it away,[13] while in emerging countries people are starving.

With a world income in 2022 of approximately $103.3 trillion which represents just under $18,782 per person annually, why are many millions subsisting on $2-3 a day?

Why do we have so much grief and suffering, growing income for the rich, and dire wealth inequality? The simple answer is that the elite, those at the very top of our society, are taking far too much of the pie.

We currently live in a global society where the rich continue to get richer and the poor stay fixed or are pushed increasingly further to the bottom to look up with increasing envy, anger and diminishing hope. Inequality is bad and it is getting worse.

This growing wealth gap between rich and poor is the first fundamental problem we must tackle. I hope we all can agree that the gap between the rich and the poor must and should decrease.

In the 1980s, for instance, the richest 10% of the population in OECD countries earned seven times more than the poorest 10%. That gap has now increased to 10 times.[14]

It is difficult to provide specific figures because wealth distribution varies greatly country to country and internally within countries. In fact, internal distribution is increasingly becoming an issue. Recently, John Burn-Murdoch showed that the average income for the UK - if you exclude London - was the lowest in all of the G20 Countries.[15] So if you live in the UK, but not in London, you are one of the poorest people in Europe.

Current World Income 2023

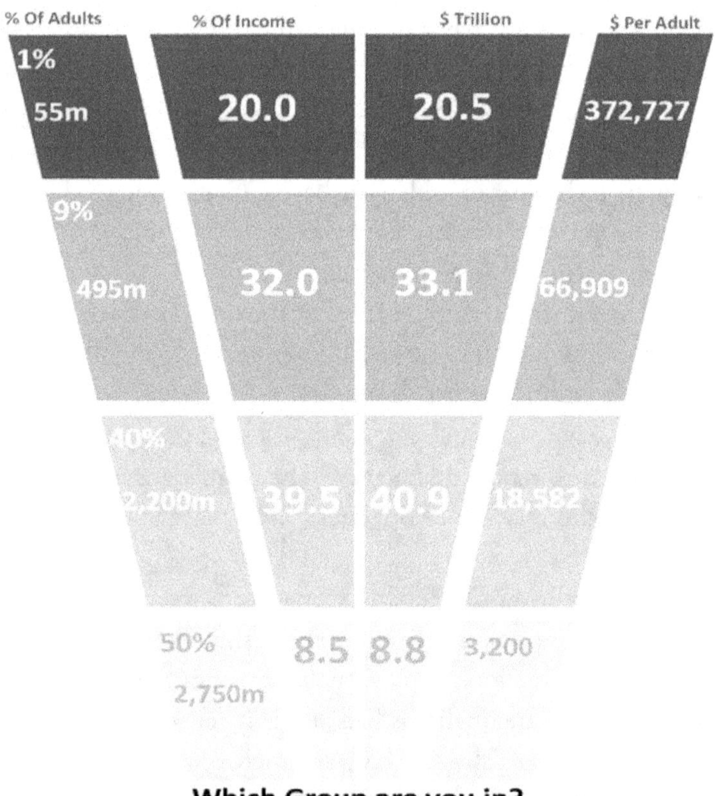

Which Group are you in?

These figures are based on IMF & World Bank data aggregated. This chart shows how much various sectors of the global population earn annually. Top left, reading left to right: 1% of global population, 55m adults; has a 20% share of annual income; total $20.5trn earnings; at an average $372,727 each.

However, an even greater concern should be that, globally, the top 1% of the world's adult population holds more than three times the wealth (46.1%) compared to the bottom 90%. That is: 55 million adult individuals hold $200.4 trillion, while 4.95bn inhabitants of our planet 'share' $63.11 trillion. Another shocking statistic: the top 10% of the world's adults have 85.5% of global wealth. The bottom 50% of the world's adults have only 1.8% of total wealth. (See this graphically demonstrated in the chart on page 9).[16]

In many countries, the top 1% of the population has seen a significant increase in their wealth in recent decades, particularly since the introduction of 'quantitative easing' (the printing of new money, on demand, by governments, designed to get us through the disastrous effects of the 2007/2008 banker and bank failures). Meanwhile, the bottom 50% has seen a slower rate of growth, or even a decline in their limited wealth. Such extreme wealth concentration in the hands of a few raises questions about the fairness and sustainability of current economic systems. It confirms that wealth is not distributed equitably. Meanwhile, opportunities for upward mobility have become severely limited and cycles of poverty for a vast majority of the world's population are perpetuated.

This level of inequality will inevitably lead to social unrest, political instability, and a sense of injustice among those who feel excluded from the benefits of economic growth. And especially now that internet access for everyone makes information on injustice available in an instant. This undermines any democratic principle. The wealthy elite are now exerting an increasingly disproportionate influence over our political processes and decision-making to their own benefit.

These trends are contributing to accelerating income and wealth inequality. This is highlighted in the following sources:

- World Inequality Lab shows that the gap between the top 10% and bottom 50% of earners has almost doubled in many countries [World Inequality Lab

Report, https://wir2022.wid.world/www-site/uploads/2023/03/D_FINAL_WIL_RIM_RAPPORT_2303.pdf

- Institute for Fiscal Studies (UK): This analysis uses charts to show rising income inequality in the UK, with the top earners pulling further ahead. https://ifs.org.uk/articles/income-and-wealth-inequality-explained-5-charts

- The World Economic Forum: Highlights how the COVID-19 pandemic exacerbated existing inequalities, with the wealthy benefiting more from government interventions. https://www.weforum.org/agenda/2021/12/global-income-inequality-gap-report-rich-poor/

The increasing gap between rich and poor creates numerous economic, social, and political issues. We need to look at income and total wealth for both. The gap is growing, but even worse is the increase in wealth for the super-rich - the world's 3,000 billionaires and those who are multi-millionaires.

The richest 0.01% of the global population earn 3.5% of global income and hold 11% of global wealth. This share has risen significantly over the past few years - in 1995 it was 7% - while the poorest 50% of the global population earn 8.5% of global income.[17] So the richest 550,000 adults have more than the bottom 2,750,000,000.

On average, an individual from the top 1% of the global income distribution earns $372,727 per year, whereas an individual from the poorest half of the global income distribution averages $3,200 per year, $8.77 a day.

Global wealth inequalities are even more pronounced than income inequalities.

The poorest half of the global population barely have any wealth at all, possessing just 1.8% of the total between them, the total being

$434T. In contrast, the richest 10% of the global population have 85.5% of all wealth. On average, the poorest half of the global population owns $2,905 per adult. This suggests a total lack of resources and financial security for a large portion of the world's population. This figure includes individuals living in extreme poverty, struggling to meet their basic needs for food, shelter, and healthcare.

Current World Wealth 2023

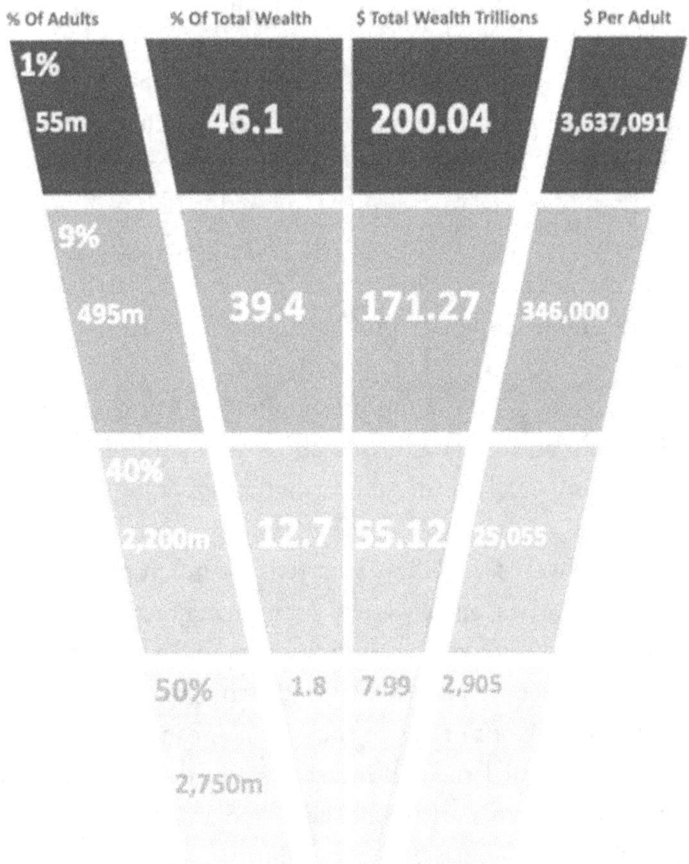

Half of the wealth of the world is owned by the top 1% of population. The bottom 50% owns only 1.8%. Total world wealth is $434.42T. This chart shows how much wealth four sectors of the global population have. Top left, reading left to right: 1% of global population, 55m adults, has 46.1% of global wealth; a total of $4.2T; at an average $3,637,091 each.

The top 1% of our population own $3,637,091 on average, with the next 9% having $346,154. This underscores the concentration of wealth among the elite. A very small minority of individuals hold a disproportionate amount of global assets, including financial investments, real estate, and business ownership.

Could we create a more reasonable and moral system? Should we insist on a better morality? I believe this is very urgent, because now everyone knows the reality, even if it's only instinctively. And if we do not seek to begin to implement the needed change and make improvements for the future, just as with climate change, we ignore the need at our own peril. We must all ask ourselves what we have done that has made people's lives better; what have we contributed to making the world a better place? Because real change is going to come from many small actions by many of us. Since this is not a problem that is going to be solved by action from governments alone, can it be made better by everyone of us making changes ourselves, considering our own morality and our own position? There are so many different problems, but they all link. They are interrelated.

I realise I am talking from the point of view of a privileged European, someone who has reasonable wealth and is inside the top 0.01%. So, can I really understand what's happening in the rest of the world? [18]

My only answer is, I can try. I started in a much poorer segment of society. I have travelled widely. I ran a major market research company, created a lot of the early big data and was very involved with analysis of people and trends over many years. I have tried to see the extremes at both ends of society. You can agree or disagree with my view, but if I succeed in getting you thinking and acting, maybe something can start to change. Change will come if enough of us take small and consistent steps. But first those at the top have to accept that there needs to be a reduction in their own wealth and income.

This book is not just a recitation of the world's problems. It also contains suggestions and solutions. We too often hear that there is no further money available for public sector workers; there is no money available for medical services for the poor. In reality we are being lied to, as the UK's new Labour Government has just demonstrated, committing £1bn a year extra to fund a 22% pay raise for junior doctors who had been striking for 12 months while the previous failed government told voters there was no money.

There is, in fact, plenty of money in the world. But the elite, who fund politicians around the world, are keeping the money for themselves and their own kind.

The alternative to acting now is to ignore the increasing poverty and accept that violence, and revolution will be the only solution for many. If you want to live in a liberal democracy, you need to make it better. **The gap between a moral democracy and dictatorship must be clear, not marginal**. If we look forward, the world is going to be very different. But we are very bad at looking forward even though sometimes the future may not be too far away. As I have already said, everything is speeding up, so we need to start taking action.

Soon, there is going to be very little actual labour. Machines will increasingly take over all production work, even in agriculture. The remaining jobs will be much more focused on the arts and entertainment, understanding and communicating with AI, mental health counselling, and massive opportunities for individuals to create their own artisan businesses. Plus taking care of the elderly, who require human interaction rather than machine interaction. When we get to this stage, and it will be soon, I hope the rational amongst us will look at the logic of a basic (universal) salary for everyone. We have a choice between levelling up or letting the rich continue to get richer.

Why are we where we are? For millennia, the world has been fundamentally tribal. Our countries, our institutions, our likes and dislikes are built in many cases on our membership of a tribe. Until we can rise above the tribal and consider ourselves as thinking moral humans, citizens of one earth, we are not going to see a great deal of progress.

We are all equal, whatever the tone of our skin, our sex, attitudes, or persuasions. But it seems we are going backwards. Various factions are dividing society into smaller and smaller cliques, based on skin colour, sexual orientation, gender choices, or religion. These cliques are moving their adherents to the extreme right or extreme left, with associated lobbies creating hate and division where we need care, support and cohesion. We could look at these developments as a return to primitive tribalism.

We need to look at our tribal past and the problems we have inherited from it.

Violence and warfare have always been used as a means of obtaining or maintaining leadership in tribal societies, together with creating and hoarding wealth.

Throughout history, tribes and communities have engaged in conflict with one and another, killing over resources, territory, and power.

How many of our current world leaders are in effect maintained in power, or elected to power, using the gun, the backing of their military and police/secret service? We will discuss how democracy is under attack, something those of us in the developed world, and the West in particular, have increasingly taken for granted during the past 120 years. Democracy has to date only really taken hold in roughly half of the United Nations' member States and is now on the slide. Which means that countries run by despots, controlled by guns, are on the increase.

The leaders of these countries are effectively continuing to use violence and the techniques of the bully to grasp the power, wealth and money that they want. Throughout the past century, there have been instances where leaders have come to power through military coups, revolutions, or other undemocratic means. Examples include Adolf Hitler in Germany, Benito Mussolini in Italy, Francisco Franco in Spain, Joseph Stalin in the Soviet Union, and more recently, leaders like Robert Mugabe in Zimbabwe, Saddam Hussein in Iraq, and Bashar al-Assad in Syria.

Not all tribal societies relied on violence and warfare as a means of obtaining or maintaining leadership. Occasionally the methods used to select tribal leaders - which varied greatly between cultures and were influenced by the tribe's social structure, cultural beliefs, and environmental challenges - were benign. In a few tribal societies, leaders were chosen through non-violent means such as elections, appointments by a council of elders, or based on demonstrable leadership ability.

However, power has increasingly drifted to the elite in each country, selecting the leaders/rulers from their own group to protect their own wealth. Or the military, because they were not included in the benefits of the elite, decided they would seize power. Or leadership continues to be hereditary with no reflection on ability or suitability.

But the past also feeds on the lack of education among the masses. So, the most common methods of selecting leaders were:

Hereditary succession: Leadership passed down from generation to generation within a certain dominant family or clan.

Tribal elections: Leaders elected by tribal members through a voting process or consensus decision-making. But voting was usually limited to older men or family leaders.

Appointment by a council of elders: Leaders chosen by a group of respected elders within the tribe who made decisions based on their wisdom and experience.

Demonstrating leadership ability: Leaders selected based on their ability to lead and make effective decisions in a crisis or other important situations, especially military. Win the war and kill all our enemies and you have a good chance to be our chief, leader, king!

Spiritual or supernatural means: in some cultures, leaders were selected based on a claimed spiritual connection to the tribe's ancestors or gods, or through supposed supernatural means such as divination or prophecy.

But these past power grabs relied on a lack of education among the majority, those who could be easily convinced that power should be retained by a few on the basis that either they had been appointed by the gods or were linked to supernatural beings.

I would suggest that we are now past this stage in our evolution, but the picture does not look good. In many countries it is still the bullies, those with excessive wealth, guns or control of the media who are the ruling elite.

Every citizen should have a vote or a say in how and who we want to manage our lives. Good education is essential for everyone to make a good choice. But good education - one that prepares us for the world we will inhabit - is in short supply. It is probably the most important thing we should address immediately.

If everyone is provided with a good education, we may move over time towards better solutions for managing our affairs.

But how do we provide everyone access to the same education when the wealthy purchase the better teachers, the better schools, the better environment, for their children and grandchildren?[19] We have recently seen a few ambitious parents in the USA arrested for bribing top universities[20] to give places to their already privileged children.

The United Kingdom's proposed move to tax private education is certainly a positive step. It is in line with the majority of G20 countries, all of whom tax private education, except for Saudi Arabia.[21]

We also need to consider very strongly what we teach in our schools/education systems. Are we really preparing people for their future lives?

Why does education not discuss in more depth how we should behave to each other? Why is AI not on the curriculum? Or Space?

With equal and good education for all, we might be able to start asking ourselves tough questions such as: what is a State?

What should be the real or potential role of politicians?

How should the world's Civil Services be managed?

What is a just and fair legal system?

How do we ensure companies behave ethically?

Should pharmaceutical companies be allowed to maximise their profit at the expense of us all?

Can it ever be right to price the poor out of healthcare access?

In the past, some of these questions would have been considered as part of every important discussion about something called *ethics*. Today ethics is a branch of philosophy, and not much discussed outside of academia. Mostly we come across the word when someone has clearly behaved outside the norms of acceptable behaviour. Their behaviour is described as 'unethical', which is to say they have done something which the mass of society finds unacceptable, even reprehensible.

So, we know the word. But we don't generally understand the concept. If we are to move forward as a civilisation, we need to reintroduce the concept of ethics[22] into general education, and talk a lot more about the **We** and not the **I**.

For more than a century, we have been satisfied that religious studies - in the West, primarily the study of Christianity - were enough to imbue pupils with a sense of right and wrong. We also had, at the end of the first and second world wars, teachers who had been through those wars and survived and had real experience and values based on those experiences. But those teachers and those values have long faded from view. Lessons learned have also mostly faded. In an increasingly secular world (specifically the liberal democratic West), doubt has crept in, and the idea of the existence of 'moral relativity' has muddied the waters.

We are no longer comfortable making judgements about right and wrong. Yet, at the same time, we become more and more judgemental - witness 'cancel culture', the supposed moral superiority of being 'woke', and the current blazing row about how many sexes there are, which throws into question the very definition of 'female', and the rigidity of the science of biology. All of which makes a case for the reintroduction of ethics as a concept into general discourse, but particularly into the education curriculum.

In Classical times, ethics consisted of shrewd advice on how to live happily, avoid unnecessary troubles, and advance one's career. Ethics also proposed broadly based ideals of conduct, such as: that rulers should treat people justly and judge impartially between their subjects; that they should aim to make their people prosperous; and that those who have bread should share it with the hungry. Humble and lowly people must be treated with kindness. As the ancients used to say, one should not laugh at the blind or at dwarfs![23]

Socrates says: 'the good is like the sun'. The sun gives light and life to the earth, the good gives knowledge and virtue to the sentient world. It is the cause of goodness in people and actions, and it also is the cause of existence and knowledge. Socrates believed that the pursuit of and love of good itself (rather than any good thing) was the chief aim of education and (especially) of philosophy.

So perhaps we do need to spend a little more time again looking at Ethics.

We must also look at the structure of countries and states. What makes your country? Why should a country exist? Can a country simply be a group of people who want to live together with the same ethos and attitude to life?

Many of the existing 195 countries of the world were created by conflict and formed with arbitrary borders relatively recently, imposed without any real consultation of the people affected.

Here are some thoughts from philosophers about Statehood:

"A state that does not protect its citizens from external and internal danger, that does not ensure them the enjoyment of their rights, or that does not fulfil its duties towards them, is not a state." - Immanuel Kant (1724-1804)

"A country is not a mere territory; the particular territory is only its foundation. The country is the idea which rises upon that foundation; it is the sentiment of love, the sense of fellowship which binds together all the sons of that territory." - Giuseppe Mazzini (1805-1872)

"In a just society, the rule of law replaces arbitrary power, and the dignity and rights of the individual are protected." - Aung San Suu Kyi (b1945)

We can see from these thoughts that cynicism about nationalism is not new, and nor is idealism. Aung San Suu Kyi might be seen as having a foot in both camps - her words are pure idealism, her actions not always matching her words. Her Buddhist faith and her popularity with the Buddhist majority in her country put her at odds with Myanmar's Muslim Rohingya minority.

Friedrich Nietzsche (1844-1900), on the other hand, was simply cynical - "The state is the great fiction by which everybody tries to live at the expense of everybody else" - as was William Ralph Inge (1860-1954) who said: "A nation is a society united by a delusion about its ancestry and by a common hatred of its neighbours."

Some thinkers emphasise the importance of protecting the rights and dignity of citizens. I would suggest that a country is (or needs to be) an area populated by a group of people who either share or are tolerant of each other's heritage, habits, attitudes and opinions. Emigration and immigration put these tenets to the test from time to time, so we expect or hope each country will be governed by individuals who respect the rule of law, but also respect the freedom of its citizens to live their lives free from undue pressure from government or from each other. Without respect for the rule of law, from government and citizens alike, and tolerance of each other's differences, trouble is guaranteed, as the 2024 riots across the UK demonstrated.

The Kurds, a large ethnic group spread across the Middle East, have no such rights and dignity because they lack their own independent nation due to a confluence of historical and geopolitical factors, plus the territories they inhabit have oil. They provide a classic case history of the difficulties of creating a nation state and, even more, how such a state might thrive in a world on the move. Following the collapse of the Ottoman Empire after World War I, the Treaty of Sèvres initially proposed an independent Kurdistan. This was never ratified, and the Kurds became the world's largest ethnic group without their own state. But as we say in the title of this book 'it's all about money' and this sums up the situation: 'Where's the money from the oil under the ground?' is much more important for some than the desires and dreams of the people.

The countries containing Kurdish populations have viewed Kurdish nationalism as a threat to their territorial integrity, so Kurdish cultural identity and political aspirations have been suppressed. And while a desire for self-determination unites many Kurds, there hasn't always been unified leadership or a singular vision for an independent Kurdistan. But now the Kurdistan Region of Iraq enjoys a degree of autonomy, with its own parliament and president. However, it remains part of Iraq. There are also Kurdish-controlled areas in Syria functioning with a level of self-governance. There are also Kurds in Turkey and Iran. For there to be an independent Kurdistan would require these four countries - Turkey,

Syria, Iraq and Iran - to give up territory and for borders to be redrawn. This, however, gives us a different set of problems, because in the current world, migration and movement of population is a major and increasing problem that must be solved. What sense does it make to create another country when its population might later wish to move elsewhere? It is natural for all people to wish to move to a better location that is safer and gives security and hope to their family. Twelve million people, half of Syria's population, have been displaced by their country's 13-years of civil war.[24]

One solution here is to take the view that we are one world and one people and the sooner we can move towards removing all the barriers to international social cohesion, the better it will be for all of us as individuals. This was certainly a trend we were already seeing with the development of the single European market.[25]

But recently, the trend seems to be towards populist politics and imposing barriers that cut off hope and access for the disadvantaged of the world.

This is almost certainly due to the declining standard of politicians themselves. We will look at their role in the world going forward and how we continually fail to attract individuals who at least appear to be working for the good of all of us. Politicians tend to come mostly from the elite upper-class. Most have been to university, in the USA often Ivy League, and in the United Kingdom a significant proportion traditionally have been the product of the top two private elite schools, Eton and Harrow. Nine other expensive private schools have further fed the governing elite. Often the primary role of private schools appears to be to protect the elites, provide good quality breeding stock and protect their status quo.[26]

Politicians need to care more about improving the lot of the citizens and voters, plus each and every individual they represent, and less about their own wealth, social media approval and speaking engagements.

Do we need a new philosophy, a new way of living? Are we moving towards Aldous Huxley's Brave New World, or a rewrite of Orwell's 1984? Given the dystopian nature of Huxley's book, in stark contrast to the optimism of its title, neither is desirable. But power is being further concentrated in a few hands, much more so than in the past, and companies are growing larger because there are no limits now to worldwide dominance and worldwide trade.

Perhaps we need an International Antitrust Law, such as that introduced in America as long ago as 1890? Senator John Sherman and colleagues recognised the danger of companies growing so big they could inhibit or even squash competition.

In 1911, when Standard Oil had become the largest petroleum company in the world, the Sherman Antitrust Act allowed the American government to split it into 43 smaller companies. The US Supreme Court had ruled it was an illegal monopoly. In 1974, AT&T was similarly forced to split some of its telephone services into seven regional operating companies.

How many monopolies do we have today? In the 2000s, Microsoft, in both the USA and the EU, and Google in the EU were forced to make some minor changes. Surely Google, Microsoft, Apple, Meta and Amazon are, in many ways, monopolistic?[27] This question was partially answered in August 2024 by American judge Amit Mehta who concluded: "Google is a monopolist, and it has acted as one to maintain its monopoly." The US Justice Department's case was that 'Google's domination of search was the result of freezing out potential rivals, rather than because it offered the best service'. Judge Mehta ruled that Google had spent $26bn to ensure it was the default search engine on smart devices and web browsers.

Google, of course, will appeal. But this judgement - which took four years to reach and will rumble on for years more - begs the question as to why there has been no previous action to limit the power and size of such companies. Essentially the leaders and owners of these companies are part of the new elite ruling our world. Our current politicians/lawyers and decision makers would be going against their own tribe, fighting the elite group to which they belong, affecting their own income and multiple associated benefits, if they decide to take a more moral approach. Few people in 2010 would have placed a bet on the fresh-faced, apparently empathetic, leader of the UK's Liberal Democrat Party 2007-2015, becoming a shill for

Facebook. But there he was, Vice-President, Global Affairs and Communications, until January 2025.

Being kind, perhaps our politicians don't see the world that is coming. A world where we no longer need to worry about making things. The sweat, toil, heat and fire of the factory and the steel mill will be taken on shortly by robots. According to the World Economic Forum, up to 85 million jobs could be lost to automation by 2025.[28] A study by the McKinsey Global Institute, says up to 800 million jobs could be lost to automation by 2030. The study found that the industries most at risk are manufacturing, transportation, agriculture, and retail.[29]

Robots are already being used in manufacturing to automate tasks like welding, painting, and assembly. They are also being used in logistics to automate tasks such as picking and packing orders, loading, and unloading trucks, and driving delivery vehicles. As they become more capable, they will be able to automate even more tasks in the logistics industry. And from being 'capable', we will quickly progress to sophistication. With increased sophistication, robots will be able to automate even more tasks, putting more and more manufacturing jobs at risk. According to the World Bank, the world's workforce breaks thus: 50% services, 26% agriculture and 24% industry. Where is going to be safe?[30]

It's easy, and only natural, to imagine this is a long way off. But In 2023, Amazon had over 520,000 robotic drive units in its warehouses around the world.[31] These robots are used to pick, pack and move products around the warehouses. Amazon also has a variety of other robotic systems in its facilities, including sort centres and air hubs. Dave Clark, Amazon's senior vice president of worldwide operations says: "We're not replacing people with robots. We're collaborating with robots to make our jobs more interesting and rewarding for our employees."

But I will remind you that the motorcar is barely 140 years old. The normal date given for the first motor car is 1886. This is the year that German inventor Carl Benz patented his Benz Patent Motorwagen, a three-wheeled vehicle powered by a gasoline engine. The first flight of an aeroplane is given as December 17, 1903, the date that the Wright brothers, Orville, and Wilbur, made the first successful controlled, powered flight of a heavier-than-air aircraft at Kitty Hawk, North Carolina. What you think is only a dream of the future, will happen very quickly. It took only 30 years for the motor car to displace 5,000 years of horse culture. Within 66 years of the first aircraft flight, humans were standing on the moon. Development is accelerating at an unprecedented rate.

What other developments are in our immediate or foreseeable future? One example: farming will increasingly be carried out automatically and driven by AI and drones.

We will soon move to Renewable Energy everywhere, taking power from the sun, the wind, and geothermal heat from the world's core; but probably not fast enough to stop much of the long-term damage we are currently doing to our world. The dramatic weather events of the last few years make this very clear.

Recently, July 14, 2023, was one of the hottest days ever across whole regions of southern Europe. The Intergovernmental Panel on Climate Change (IPCC) Sixth Assessment Report, released in 2021, states: 'It is unequivocal that human influence has warmed the atmosphere, oceans and land.' The report also states that 'human-induced climate change is already affecting many weather and climate extremes in every region across the globe'. The World Meteorological Organization's (WMO) State of the Global Climate 2022 report found that 'the past eight years have been the eight warmest on record' and that 'the frequency and intensity of extreme weather events have increased'. The United States Environmental Protection Agency (EPA) states that 'climate change is already having a significant impact on extreme weather events in the United States', and that 'these events are expected to become more frequent and severe in the coming decades.

Extreme weather events have increased in recent years:

Heatwaves: the number, intensity, and duration of heatwaves have increased in recent decades. For example, in 2021, North America experienced its hottest summer on record, with temperatures reaching over 50 degrees Celsius in some places.

Heavy precipitation: The amount of heavy precipitation has increased in many parts of the world. For example, in 2021, Europe experienced its deadliest floods in centuries. People died in Spain and southern Germany after severe flooding during 2024.

Droughts: The frequency and intensity of droughts have increased in many parts of the world, including the United States, the Middle East, and Africa.

Tropical cyclones: The intensity of tropical cyclones has increased in recent decades. For example, in 2019, Hurricane Dorian devastated the Bahamas, with sustained winds of up to 295 kilometres per hour.

So, we have elements of chaos occurring alongside the coming technological developments. How will all this progress and chaos affect the mass of people?

The masses need not only more education, but better education, better medical care and better food to enable us all to live longer and more fulfilling lives. If we look at the list of the key factors in measuring quality of life, it is concerning that many of the indicators have changed in the wrong direction in recent years. The difference between those at the top, the majority of the rest of us, and the abjectly poor has grown.

It may be time to ditch GDP as an indicator of national health, and switch to an index that measures quality of life - Gross National Happiness[32] rather than Gross Domestic Product. Treating civilians as little more than units of productivity has had its day, and life will continue to deteriorate for the majority unless we change our attitude to what really matters, which also requires us to address morality at national and international levels. The chart below is a list of key factors to measure if we want to demonstrate that quality of life is improving.

There will be many individuals over 100 years old in the future. Currently 0.3% of the population in America are over 100,[33] a figure that has doubled during the last 20 years and is forecast to continue to grow. In France, it is expected that 50% of all women born in 2024 will live to be over 100.[34]

Key Indicator	2023 Figure	2030 Forecast	Source
Infant Mortality Rate(per 1,000 births)	27	20.0	WHO
Life Expectancy at Birth	72.98	77.1	UN
Gross Domestic Product per capita ($)	18,381	23,000+	World Bank
Human Development Index	0.732	0.750+	UNDP
Poverty Rate (% of population living on <$2.15/day)	8.20	5.0	World Bank
Access to Education (literacy rate %)	86.30	90+	UNESCO
Gender Equality Index	0.686	0.750+	UNDP
Access to Clean Water and Sanitation (% of population with access)	74	85+	WHO/UNICEF
Income Inequality (Gini coefficient)	0.63	0.55-0.60	World Bank
Unemployment Rate (%)	5.40	4.5-5.0	ILO
Healthcare Access and Quality Index (HAQ Index)	No standard global index exists yet	Development of standardised index is in progress	WHO
Hunger and Food Security (prevalence of undernourishment%)	9.20	6.0	UN/FAO
Environmental Sustainability Indicators	Varies significantly by country	Significant reductions needed to meet climate goals	IPCC

But who will be in control, and how will they raise the money required for increased medical budgets, and to fund everyone's pensions?

Pension ages are set to rise everywhere, despite violent protests in France. In the United Kingdom the pension age is set to increase to 68. In the US it is due to increase again to 68 by 2037, having been raised to 66 in 2020. In Canada it was due to increase to 67 by 2023, but currently this is on hold. In Australia and Japan there has already been an increase of the retirement age to 67. How long until pensions start at 70?[35] Every country needs higher tax or higher tax revenue to be able to pay pensions to populations that are living longer.

But as the mass of people are pushed and pulled by progress and environmental concerns, power remains in the hands of the banks, financial funds, the largest corporations and the elite from a few Ivy League universities. In some countries, power also still resides with dictators, religious leaders and/or the military.

Everything else is blowing in the wind. Politicians have the real ability to make things worse, to focus on their own survival and that of their elite tribe, to cause everything but progress. If we want to make things better, we need to change a lot. And that is what this book is about - change: which things need to change; and how to change them.

For a start, we need to tax the very top earners in a much more effective way;[36] to establish guidelines for future corporate remuneration that are equitable; and to control the power of the financial institutions. We also need to recognize people's social benefit to society, not just their monetary benefit; make education truly equal and accessible for all; accept that historically most wealth and income has been created by being a member of the elite, which has not been equitable; and then look at inheritance, which is a by-product of the inequitable earning power of the elite.

Limiting the power of mega companies or splitting their power should also be added to our list. As should consideration of future ownership in space, whether of bits of space itself (similar to the earth's oceans), specific planets, asteroids or moons, or the precious materials that will be mined. To avoid more conflict here on earth, it is essential we agree to some ground rules before leaving Earth. Plus: create a political system that benefits citizens as a whole and limits the possibilities of corruption and damage by politicians; create the means whereby wealth can be redistributed; understand that violence and revolution is a likely response to inequality, a cry for a better life. And finally, end the aristocracy and the elite being a self-perpetuating group that essentially works for itself. Quite a list, but let's look at the issues in more detail in the chapters that follow.

Chapter 1 - The 10 key points

1. Accelerating Technological Advancements: The pace of technological change is increasing exponentially, with major breakthroughs occurring at an unprecedented rate.

2. Space Exploration as the Next Frontier: The exploration and potential colonisation of space will drive the next industrial revolution, offering vast new resources and opportunities for economic growth.

3. Flaws in Global Governance: The current system of global governance is inadequate, characterised by power concentration, growing inequality, and a lack of accountability.

4. Widening Gap Between Rich and Poor: The disparity between the wealthy elite and the rest of the population is increasing, leading to social unrest, political instability, and a sense of injustice.

5. Education as a Key to Empowerment: Education is crucial for individual empowerment and societal progress, but access to quality education remains unequal, perpetuating existing inequalities.

6. The Need for Ethical Reflection: The concept of ethics must be reintroduced into education and public discourse to address the moral challenges posed by technological advancements and societal changes.

7. Political Systems Favouring the Elite: The current political system often prioritises the interests of the elite over the needs of the majority, necessitating reforms to ensure greater representation and accountability.

8. AI and Automation Impact on the Workforce: The rise of artificial intelligence and automation will disrupt the job market, requiring new approaches to work, income distribution, and skills training.

9. Climate Change and Environmental Concerns: Climate change and environmental degradation pose serious threats to the planet, demanding urgent action and sustainable solutions.

10. Shaping a Better Future: The future presents both opportunities and challenges, and it is our collective responsibility to create a more just, equitable, and sustainable world for all.

Footnotes – Chapter 1

[1] 1981: The IBM PC is introduced, making personal computers affordable and user-friendly for businesses of all sizes.

[2] When I was 27

[3] The History of Mobile Phones by the BBC. Cell Phones became popular in the early 1990s.

[4] Experts believe that humans could be flying to Mars as early as the 2030s. The journey is long and dangerous. The Martian environment is harsh and unforgiving. However, the potential rewards are great, and the prospect of exploring a new world is driving us forward. The challenges that will need to be addressed before humans can fly to Mars: Distance: Mars is 140 million miles (225 million kilometres) from Earth. This means that it would take a spacecraft about six to nine months to travel to Mars, and another six to nine months to return to Earth. Gravity: Mars has only about one-third the gravity of Earth. This means that astronauts on a Mars mission would experience muscle loss and bone density loss. They would need to exercise regularly and take medications to mitigate these effects. The food and water: Astronauts on a Mars mission would need to bring their own food and water, or they would need to develop ways to grow food and purify water on Mars. The resources are available: We have the financial resources and the industrial capacity. Governments and private companies are investing billions of dollars in space exploration, and there is a growing public interest in Mars missions. The determination is there: Humans have a long history of exploring new frontiers, and we are not about to stop now. We are driven by a natural curiosity about the universe, and we believe that exploring Mars is essential to our future.

[5] https://www.bbc.co.uk/news/articles/czxl849j77ko

[6] Robert Owen, who managed the Mills from 1800 to 1825, did a great deal to improve living and working conditions, and New Lanark became famous as a model village, with no child labour, progressive education, and free medical care, among other benefits

[7] Note 3, Appendix 1 has further similar social experiments

[8] https://www.britannica.com/money/Tulip-Mania

[9] Note 4, Appendix 1 for additional Space companies.

[10] Initiation Report: Relativity Space - Manhattan Venture Partners | Tomorrow's IPOs Today™

[11] Note 5, Appendix 1 for details of Starlink project

[12] Briar is an open-source, decentralised messaging app that allows users to communicate directly with each other without relying on the internet or cellular networks. This makes it a valuable tool for people in areas with limited or no internet access, or in situations where the internet is censored or blocked. Briar is still under development, but it has already been used in several real-world situations, such as during protests in Hong Kong and Puerto Rico. In these cases, Briar allowed people to communicate with each other and share information even when the internet was unavailable. Some of Briar's key features: Briar messages are not stored on a central server, so they are more secure and private than messages sent through traditional messaging apps. Briar can be used to communicate even when there is no internet connection. This is because Briar messages are relayed directly between users' phones. Briar messages are encrypted with end-to-end encryption, meaning only the sender and recipient can read them. Briar's code is open source, so it can be audited by anyone to ensure that it is secure and private. Briar is a powerful tool for secure and private communication, and it is especially useful in situations where the internet is unavailable or censored. As Briar continues to develop, it is likely to become even more widely used.

[13] Note 6, Appendix 1, additional information on food waste

[14] https://www.oecd-ilibrary.org/social-issues-migration-health/income-inequality_9789264246010-en

[15] Note 7, Appendix 1 has details of low-income UK

[16] Sources of information, world inequality report/database, Oxfam, Credit Suisse Global Wealth Report

[17] World Inequality Report 2022: https://wir2022.wid.world/

Oxfam Inequality Report: https://www.oxfam.org/en/research/inequality-kills

[18] Note 8, Appendix 1 for details of the author's background

[19] The UK Labour Party has proposed changes to the taxation of private education, aiming to generate revenue for state schools. The proposed changes include adding VAT to private school fees: Currently, private schools are exempt from charging Value Added Tax (VAT) on their fees. Labour proposes to add VAT at the standard rate of 20%, potentially raising £1.3bn-£1.5bn per year. Removing business rate relief: Private schools currently receive an 80% discount on business rates in England and Wales.

[20] In March 2019, the Federal Bureau of Investigation (FBI) unsealed indictments against 50 people, including wealthy parents, college coaches, and test administrators, in a nationwide college admissions bribery scandal dubbed "Operation Varsity Blues." The scheme involved wealthy parents paying millions of dollars to William "Rick" Singer, a college admissions consultant, to help their children get into top universities, such as Yale, Stanford, Georgetown, and the University of Southern California (USC). This involved paying test administrators to inflate their children's SAT and ACT scores and creating fake athletic profiles for their children. In total, Singer and his associates are alleged to have collected over $25 million in bribes from wealthy parents. It led to several arrests, including those of actress Felicity Huffman and fashion designer Mossimo Giannulli, who pleaded guilty to paying bribes to get their daughters into USC.

[21] Note 9, Appendix 1, tax for education.

[22] https://plato.stanford.edu/entries/ethics-ancient/

[23] Ancient Wisdom Collections: The statement aligns with the themes found in wisdom texts from various cultures, like the ones mentioned earlier: "The Instruction of Amenemope" (Egypt) or "The Maxims of Ptahhotep" (Egypt)

[24]https://reporting.unhcr.org/operational/situations/syria-situation#:~:text=In%20its%20thirteenth%20year%2C%20the,forcibly%20displaced%20across%20the%20region

[25] Note 10, Appendix 1for transnational markets worldwide

[26] Note 11, Appendix 1 for educational background of politicians

[27] Note 12, Appendix 1 for more details of monopolistic-type behaviour

[28] 85 million jobs could be lost to automation by 2025, World Economic Forum's *The Future of Jobs 2020* report.

[29] https://www.weforum.org/reports/the-future-of-jobs-report-2020/

[30]https://docs.google.com/document/d/1FxN8dXAfgjwfwaA4gGp6H3A_tZRXsJadErHt8pS81II/edit#:~:text=https%3A//ourworldindata.org/grapher/share%2Demployment%2Dagriculture%2Dindustry%2Dservices

[31] There is no official forecast from Amazon regarding the exact number of robots they will be using by 2030. However, Cathie Wood, the founder and CEO of ARK Investment Management, has predicted that Amazon could have more robots than human employees by 2030. Wood based her prediction on the following: Amazon's current rate of robot deployment: Amazon is reportedly adding about 1,000 robots per day to its fulfilment centres. The ratio of robots to employees: Currently, the ratio of robots to employees at Amazon is about 1:3. Wood believes this ratio will shift towards robots surpassing human employees by 2030.

[32] https://ophi.org.uk/gross-national-happiness

---

[33] According to the Population Reference Bureau, there were an estimated 89,739 centenarians (people aged 100 and over) living in the United States in 2021. This represents about 0.03% of the total US population. The number of centenarians is expected to grow in coming years, reaching an estimated 1.2 million by 2050.

[34]According to a study published in the Lancet medical journal, girls born in developed countries today can expect to live to an average age of 100.2 years. This is a significant increase from the average life expectancy of 76.6 years for girls born in 1900. The study's authors attribute the increase in life expectancy to several factors, including Advances in medicine: Medical advances such as the development of antibiotics, vaccines, and new treatments for diseases have helped to reduce mortality rates at all ages. Improved nutrition: People in developed countries today have access to a more nutritious diet than people did in the past. This has helped improve their overall health and reduce their risk of chronic diseases like heart disease and diabetes. Better sanitation and hygiene: Improvements in sanitation and hygiene have helped reduce the spread of infectious diseases. Reduced smoking rates: Smoking is a major risk factor for many diseases, including cancer, heart disease, and stroke. Declining smoking rates in developed countries has helped improve life expectancy.

[35] China: The pension start age in China is currently 60 for men and 55 for women. However, the government has announced plans to raise the retirement age to 65 for men and 60 for women by 2035. India: The retirement age in India is currently 60 for men and 58 for women. However, the government has announced plans to raise the pension start age to 65 for both men and women by 2023. Russia: The retirement age in Russia is currently 65 for men and 60 for women. However, the government has raised the pension starting age gradually in recent years, and it is now expected to reach 65 for men and 60 for women by 2028.

[36] Jeff Bezos, Amazon CEO: Bezos paid about $6.5 billion in federal income taxes in 2021. This is equivalent to an effective tax rate of about 1.4%. Elon Musk, Tesla CEO: Musk paid an estimated $11 billion in federal income taxes in 2021. This is equivalent to an effective tax rate of about 3.4%. https://www.theguardian.com/us-news/2022/apr/13/wealthiest-americans-tax-income-propublica-investigation

CHAPTER 2

Freedom, Personal Freedom for Everyone

What are we looking for? A more just world. A more moral world. A world where ethics are understood and practised. A world where the unethical is punished, not just criticised.[1]

Kant said, "Freedom is the ability to work from reason, not desire".

To achieve these aims, and to work from reason, we would need to force, not wait for, the next step in our economic evolution. If we really are going to be free and move forward, it needs to be a move forward for everyone. The inequality that exists in the world today is devoid of morality as we understand it and is utterly unjust. To make the world a better place, one where society does not destroy itself, we need to do everything we can to instil a better sense of the ethics that guided the ancient Greeks.

This suggests everyone must accept change. But for the richest 1% - those who own 46.1% of the world's wealth - there will be the most change.

What am I really proposing? As a first step - and it's very simple - with more proposals to come: that the richest 1% of the world should be forced to stop scouring the world for accountancy and legal loopholes to reduce and avoid tax. This would require International Law to multilaterally legislate that no country can promote itself as a place to hide money. To those who might react with scepticism to this concept, something similar has already been achieved with Corporation Tax.[2] So why not all other taxes?

Then we should simplify tax codes worldwide to the extent that tax avoidance becomes impossible. To keep it simple, you keep tax very simple. You agree on a rate, and you do not have any exemptions or exclusions or special cases. Because it is the rules and regulations that emerge from complex tax codes that the elite are able to exploit to avoid payment.

With all this in place, the rich will pay the tax they owe on the earnings they make, no exceptions, on pain of certain jail if they default; and they will pay their taxes on the same basis as the rest of us. I would also suggest that the rich start donating (tithing) immediately some of their currency wealth (1% per annum would be a reasonable start, as detailed later in this book).

The point of this exercise is to start building a fund that will pull the poorest of the world out of their desperate state, and to begin the work of establishing education, medical help, sufficient food (of sufficient quality) and a decent living wage as practical human rights, as opposed to the current theoretical handwringing, with little action, which has been going on for my entire life.

Simplification of tax codes, and collection of due taxes would, I will demonstrate, raise $trillions. Other measures I will propose will raise $trillions more.

At the top of the international money community sit an estimated 3,000 billionaires, and 62.2m dollar millionaires. That is 1.12% of all adults, which I acknowledge being part of.

The best data we currently have regarding how much the richest really have, including the billionaires and millionaires, shows that the top 55 million adults (1% of the global adult population of 5.5 billion people) control over 46.1% of the world's wealth. The bottom 50%, 2.75 billion adult humans, have only 1.8% of the world's money pile. That is: 2.75bn people 'sharing wealth' of $8T, or around $3,000 each when 55m people control $200+T or

$3,637,000 each - 1200 times more per person than those in the bottom half.

This top 1% needs to accept a new regime of paying due tax on their earnings and tithing a percentage of their wealth for those less fortunate. The 46.1% of global wealth controlled by these 55m individuals is $200.04T. If they were to donate, say, 1% of their wealth each year over a period of 10 years - 10% of their wealth in total - that alone would amount to over $20T moved to the poorest.

Just for a sense of perspective, $20T amounts to more than 10 years' worth of gross domestic product for the bottom 100 countries in the United Nations membership of 193 nation states.[3] So, in addition to paying due taxes, we are now looking at amounts of money that would help bring everyone on the globe to the dining table. This small tithe - tiny, really, at 1% per year - has the potential to transform life for all humans.

In his recent book, *This Time No Mistakes*, Will Hutton talks about changes in the United Kingdom, and makes a suggestion, that works well for our purposes in this book if we simply remove the word 'Britain': "The task is to find a philosophy and programme that will allow (British) capitalism to be managed successfully, to create a paradigm shift in investment and productivity, while simultaneously promoting fairness and social cohesion in ever-more-turbulent times."

At present, the emphasis is generally on autonomy, from the Greek 'to self-legislate'. Autonomy of the State, which was what Brexit was about, and autonomy of the individual. No politician has perhaps been more maligned than Margaret Thatcher for allegedly saying "There is no such thing as society". There are layers of irony in the reaction to this out-of-context quote, not least that her critics, who maul her for apparently suggesting it's every man for himself, are the same people supporting the cult of 'individualism'. In fact, Margaret Thatcher was saying - in context - that society does not exist of its own volition, but is an entity created by the community involved. In other words, unless individuals recognise a greater good, and a greater need, and act accordingly, we are all left to our own devices. This is what Mrs Thatcher said: "Society as such does not exist except as a concept. Society is made up of people. It is people who have duties and beliefs and resolve. It is people who get things done."[4] In this, she is not straying too far from the philosophers who created the bedrocks of democracy.

It's very clear that we need to control our desires and share more, to legislate our own habits and spending.

We all want freedom of association, freedom of belief, freedom of speech, freedom to express oneself, freedom of the press/internet, freedom to choose how to live, freedom of religion, freedom from bondage or slavery.

Freedom means securing for everyone an equal opportunity for life, liberty, and pursuit of happiness. If we really want freedom to develop and grow, we need to set a better example, especially in the developed countries. We need to show that our model is a much more moral and beneficial model, that being part of our society means everyone has a reasonable life.

The foundation of morality, the guiding principles that govern our behaviour, has been the subject of philosophical debate and societal discourse for centuries. Its essence has been shaped by various cultural traditions, religious beliefs, and social norms. While there is no single universal moral code that applies to every individual or society, certain fundamental principles resonate across cultures and epochs, providing a framework for a new era of ethical conduct.

Throughout history, various thinkers have contributed significantly to the evolution of our understanding of morality. John Locke, the English philosopher, emphasised the inherent rights of individuals, arguing that all people are born free and equal: "We are born completely free, we are naturally free, we are free to act within the laws of nature." Locke's concept of individual freedom and social contract laid the foundation for modern democratic societies. Of course, nearly 500 years after Locke's birth, humans are now able to see that nature itself is selfish, ruthless and uncaring about the beings it hosts on our planet: animal, vegetable or mineral; all are subject to Earth's whims, be they volcanic, tectonic, orogenic, or climatic. We can see it's necessary to bring more recent human experience to broaden and leaven the philosophies of the ancients.

Philosophers also indulge in language that puts their thoughts beyond the common man. Immanuel Kant, the German philosopher, proposed a 'deontological' approach to morality. The word 'deontological' is beyond the experience and therefore the understanding of at least 99.9% of the global population. But we can, most of us, understand the explanation that this strain of thought emphasises the inherent rightness or wrongness of actions regardless of their consequences. Put simply, an action or decision you take may impact others negatively, but you do it because it is the right thing to do. Kant called this a 'categorical imperative', which most of us would recognise in common lingo as 'do unto others as you would be done by'. We would all be better off if we acted only on principles that we would wish to be universal laws.

So, if tomorrow, by some glorious consequence of international agreement, we gained the ability to access 30%+ of the wealth of the top 1% (remember, they control 46.1% of global wealth) and put it to work lifting the lowest 50% (remember, they share a mere 1.8% of global wealth) out of their poverty and raise their education standards, that would very obviously negatively impact in reality to a small extent the top 1%. Can we agree that that would, nevertheless, accord with Kant's deontological theory?

Locke, Kant and other philosophers have been influential in shaping ethical decision-making across various disciplines. Franklin D. Roosevelt, the 32nd President of the United States, championed the concept of four essential human freedoms: freedom of speech and assembly, freedom of worship, freedom from want, and freedom from fear. These four, encapsulated in his speech to the American people in January 1941, were intended to prepare the American people to enter WW2, in defence of these same freedoms. Within the year, Japan's attack on Pearl Harbour made the case more forcefully. Nevertheless, Roosevelt's four freedoms have since become a cornerstone of human rights discourse and the pursuit of a more just and equitable world.

The more contemporary, and still living, philosopher Lars Svendsen maintains that the conditions for a good life are best realised in a liberal democracy, where the four freedoms (and others) are self-evident. But in the 21st century, we appear hard pushed to agree on what is a liberal democracy. Most generally, the word 'liberal' is intended to indicate that a state's power over its citizens should be limited by law and that 'democracy' is intended to mean that citizens should have power over their state (rather than the other way round).

These ideals have become corrupted. To take the UK as one example, the Liberal Democrat Party has moved to the left of the Labour Party, so that the very word 'liberal' has lost all political meaning. As for citizens having power over their state, during the Macmillan government of the late 1950s and early 1960s, the UK state had 57 rights of entry to the home of citizens. By the time Labour left office at the end of its tenure between 1997 and 2010, the State had 1200 rights of entry to our homes.[5]

So, we have reached a crossroads at which the expression of individual demands is creating schisms in the very society we claim to desire while, at the same time, we have lost individual power to the State. We are, surely, going to have to learn to control our desires, to legislate our own habits, sharing and spending, all in a common good?

We all want those freedoms described. But when the freedom we wish for ourselves impinges on the human rights of others, we have taken the concept too far, into the realms of unforgivable selfishness. Ensuring freedom means ensuring for everyone an equal opportunity for life, liberty, and the pursuit of happiness. Freedom of choice brings with it a responsibility to allow others the same.

If we don't start doing this we will end up with a world where the dictator, the emperor and the thug again rule our lives, and we won't have that power over the state that comes with true democracy. The state will remain in the hands of the elite. Unless we have better education, a more even starting point, basic subsistence, and food for everyone, power will remain in the hands of the elite. If we allow that to continue, other aims such as cessation of fighting amongst ourselves, fairer distribution of wealth and distributing income on a more moral basis will remain just an ideal that cannot be achieved. Control of your life chances will remain in elite hands.

Education is key and can play a pivotal role in shaping individual moral development and fostering a more ethical society. But we have to take politics out of the classroom. Schooling should provide a platform for imparting moral values, encouraging critical thinking, and nurturing empathy. But for critical thinking to be truly developed in our youth, it is important to teach **them *how* to think, not *what* to think**. By engaging students in discussions about ethical dilemmas, promoting ethical role models, and instilling a sense of social responsibility, education can contribute to the cultivation of moral citizens. Integrating ethical education into school curricula is essential for shaping the moral compass of future generations. Critical thinking skills are crucial for making informed ethical judgments. By teaching students how to evaluate sources of information, analyse arguments, and consider different perspectives, we can empower them to make sound ethical decisions in their personal and professional lives.

Critical thinking can also promote a sense of empathy, the importance of which cannot be overstated in cultivating moral consciousness. By encouraging our young to understand the perspectives and experiences of others, we can foster a sense of compassion and promote prosocial behaviour. This can help to reduce prejudice, promote understanding, and create a more inclusive society.

And then there's the question of who we allow to make our laws, to govern our countries, and how we hand them those powers, albeit temporarily. The exercise of power has a profound impact on societal morality. Power wielded responsibly and ethically leads to positive social change. Power unchecked or abused fuels corruption, undermines ethical standards, and leads to harmful consequences for individuals and society. What we have not fully realised is that each one of us can make a difference because of the internet. Social media allows everyone a voice, and everyone can fight what is wrong.

And what do we do with this new power? We complain, we gossip and criticise, and we censure and cancel those with whom we disagree. Holding those in power accountable is essential for upholding moral standards. But if our own behaviour lacks a moral standard, our voice becomes redundant. The choices we make online can betray our lack of education, lack of critical thinking, lack of empathy, and a small-minded vengeful nature. Or they can be part of uplifting the collective thinking of the human race. We each have to ask ourselves which path would we rather follow?

If we choose the small-minded and vengeful route, societal mechanisms such as independent judiciaries, decision-making, and public consensus will remain beyond our control. Constructive voices, raised in unison, can help ensure that power is exercised in a just and ethical manner. If you shout out every time something is wrong, if you intelligently critique your leaders and those making poor decisions, if enough of us do these things, we will make a difference. Encouraging ethical leadership is crucial for fostering a more equitable and moral society. By promoting integrity, accountability, and respect for human rights among those in positions of power, we can create a culture of ethical governance that benefits all members of society.

But we don't promote integrity by being mean and vicious in our language; and we don't promote morality by calling people names and attempting to cancel them.

This is why we need an agreed new set of shared human ethics. In an increasingly interconnected world, the need for a shared global morality has become more pressing. As we confront global challenges such as climate change, pandemics, and economic inequality, a shared ethical framework can provide a common ground for collaboration and cooperation.

The concept of universal human rights serves as a potential foundation for a global moral code. These rights, already enshrined in international agreements and national constitutions, uphold fundamental human values such as dignity, equality, and freedom.[6] What we lack is a collective global will to enforce these rights in every country. We are keen to recognize the diversity of cultures and moral perspectives of different countries, cultures and faiths. This leads us to make excuses for countries like Russia, China and North Korea which stamp all over what we in the West consider basic human rights. Then again, we blame ourselves for the poor behaviour of other nations in whose past we may have played a significant part. We need to cast aside what is seen as the collective guilt of previous generations and work harder to identify shared moral principles that can guide our actions towards a more just and equitable world. By promoting dialogue and understanding across cultures, we can bridge moral differences and foster a more humane global community. Most of all we need to show that the democratic liberal system is better; so that the systems managed by dictators, thugs and guns will change internally because their citizens can see the benefits of a better, more moral society.

All this is made all the more necessary by the rapid advancements in technology that have brought about new challenges and opportunities for ethical reflection. If we cannot agree on a set of moral and ethical rules by which to live on Planet Earth, how are we going to behave in Space? Social media platforms, artificial intelligence, and other technologies have the potential to shape our moral values and influence our behaviour, and we should be taking full advantage of the opportunities they provide while we are still earthbound.

Navigating the ethical implications of technology requires careful consideration and ongoing dialogue. We have already seen the potential for technology to exacerbate social divides, erode privacy, and amplify harmful behaviours. Promoting responsible and ethical use of technology is essential for safeguarding our moral values and protecting the well-being of individuals and society. By developing ethical guidelines, educating users about responsible digital citizenship, and holding technology companies accountable, we can ensure that technology serves. On this endeavour, there is no time to be lost.

Chapter 2 - The 10 key points

1. The Illusion of Freedom: True freedom, both personal and societal, is often limited by systemic inequalities and power imbalances.

2. The Need for a Moral Society: A more ethical and just society is urgently needed, one that prioritises collective well-being and social responsibility over individual wealth accumulation.

3. Critique of Power Structures: Traditional and emerging power structures perpetuate inequality and prioritise their own interests, necessitating a shift towards a more equitable distribution of power and resources.

4. Education's Role in Moral Development: Education should play a crucial role in shaping moral values, encouraging critical thinking, and fostering empathy, contributing to the development of ethical citizens.

5. Accountability for Those in Power: Leaders must be held accountable for their actions and exercise power responsibly and ethically, ensuring that decisions are made in the public interest.

6. A Shared Global Ethic: In an interconnected world, a shared global morality based on universal human rights and values is essential for addressing global challenges and fostering cooperation.

7. Ethical Use of Technology: While technology offers transformative potential, it's crucial to navigate its ethical

implications and ensure responsible use to prevent harm and promote social well-being.

8. Striving for the Four Freedoms: Roosevelt's Four Freedoms remain aspirational goals for a just society, but their full realisation requires addressing systemic inequalities and promoting greater social justice.

9. The Power of Information and Social Media: The internet and social media empower individuals to expose injustices, hold the powerful accountable, and advocate for change, but they also present challenges in terms of misinformation and manipulation.

10. Rethinking Capitalism and Wealth Redistribution: Capitalism, while the dominant economic model, needs to be reformed to ensure a fairer distribution of wealth and opportunities for all. This may involve measures like progressive taxation and increased social safety nets.

Footnotes – Chapter 2

[1] "The Morality of Power" by Michael J. Sandel is a book that explores how power can be used to promote or undermine morality. "The Ethics of the Internet" by Luciano Floridi is a book that examines the ethical challenges of new technologies, such as social media and artificial intelligence. "The Case for Universal Human Rights" by Amartya Sen is a book that argues for the importance of developing a global morality based on human rights.

[2] https://www.weforum.org/stories/2024/02/oecd-minimum-tax-rate/#:~:text=More%20than%20140%20countries%20have%20committed%20to%20implement%20a%20new,of%2015%25%20on%20corporate%20profits.

[3] As per the United Nation's own forecast for 2022

[4] https://www.margaretthatcher.org/document/106689

[5]https://assets.publishing.service.gov.uk/media/5a7e02bde5274a2e8ab45422/Powers_of_Entry_Review_27_November__2_.pdf

[6] Note 13, Appendix 1 for further information/list re civil and political rights

CHAPTER 3

The Power of the Financial Institutions

Money is the lubricant that makes everything move and everything possible. And yet, as W.G. Langworthy Taylor noted as far back as 1905, 'Financial wealth consists in promises and nothing else'.[1] Taylor was being literal. Even the cash in your hand is only a promise. It says so right there on your dollar bill: 'This note is legal tender'; and on your £10 note, underneath the Bank Of England insignia: 'I promise to pay the bearer the sum of £10 on demand'. The notes themselves are worthless but for the backing of their respective Central Banks.

And the money you can see, the money you can hold in your hand, money that has been printed and minted, represents a mere 8% of the entire nominal amount of 'money' circulating through the financial institutions around the world. This means that the money which isn't minted and circulated - roughly 92% of total estimates - requires even more of an act of faith by banks, governments, corporations and society at large. And we face a future very soon with only digital/electronic money. Of the 193 member states of the United Nations, 130 are now exploring a Central Bank Digital Currency (CBDC). These 130 countries represent 99% of global GDP.[2] Central Bank Digital Currencies (CBDCs) are a new form of digital money issued directly by central banks. With 130 countries exploring CBDCs, their potential impact on the global financial landscape is significant.

CBDCs could revolutionise financial inclusion by providing the unbanked - those with access only to the cash in their pocket, or the cash their employer owes them - with access to secure and efficient financial services. CBDCs could also streamline payment systems, making transactions faster, cheaper, and more secure, while enhancing monetary policy tools for central banks. Additionally, the transparent and traceable nature of CBDCs could significantly deter illicit financial activities like money laundering.

However, the rise of CBDCs also raises significant concerns. Advocates for privacy worry about the potential for increased government surveillance and control over individuals' financial transactions. The traditional banking system could be disrupted as CBDCs may bypass commercial banks, potentially impacting their profitability and stability. The development and implementation of CBDCs will be heavily influenced by powerful stakeholders, including governments, financial institutions, and tech giants. Their interests may not always align with those of the broader public, raising concerns about potential biases in the design and use of CBDCs. For instance, some wealthy individuals and corporations might lobby against features that enhance tax transparency or limit their ability to move assets discreetly. Striking the right balance between innovation and safeguarding individual rights will be crucial. The future of money is always going to be 100% digital, but it is essential to ensure that this future is equitable, secure, and respectful of individual freedoms.

Ironically, the very reasons these concerns are raised may also provide a benefit of their own, because one area where CBDCs could have a profound impact is taxation. The ability to automatically deduct taxes from CBDC holdings, track transactions in real-time, and program automatic tax payments based on specific rules could revolutionise tax collection, making collection more efficient and potentially reducing tax evasion.

Still, the fact remains that, as things are, central banks, financial institutions, bankers, and financial markets control the world's money. To a lesser extent, politicians can have some influence, but they and we are largely at the mercy of the global money machine.

The US dollar has dominated since the end of the Second World War, when it replaced UK Sterling as the world's reference currency. The UK, of course, was impoverished by its efforts to repel Nazism, and had to lean on America for help post-war. The succession to dollar dominance was determined by these events.

Increasingly the US dollar is used as a weapon to keep the rest of the world in line. If you don't cooperate with the USA, you will suffer sanctions. You will struggle to run your economy, sell your goods, and feed your population. To transfer money between countries, paying for what your own country needs, will be made increasingly difficult unless you comply. Donald Trump's threat regarding tariffs as he prepared for his second term as President only goes to highlight this.

It's worth repeating, even this early on, that money increasingly has very little real worth or tangible value. Keep in mind that among the major currencies of the world, only 8% of the money has been printed and is in circulation.[3] The balance is effectively additional zeros put on an Excel or Central Bank spreadsheet.

And the more recent tendency when faced with global problems is to print/produce more money to pay the bills. But in printing more money, or adding to it electronically, you further reduce its worth (theoretical as it may be) and money's value declines further. Electronic money, created electronically, is very much the trend. Think of the advantages, from a government point of view. No longer will you be able to store the money under the bed, or in the cupboard, or at the end of the garden. All this will make a cash economy much harder. Everything will be trackable and traceable. Every tax office will be able to take their share of your money directly.

Every ruler in the history of our planet has at some time been beholden to their bankers.[4] Unfortunately the historic option of 'killing the bankers' is not currently available in most territories. So, the financial sector will grow. It is already big. As a sector it is 7.4% of the American economy. The power of the Big Banks is well spelled out in the following link, https://longreads.tni.org/state-of-power-2019/global-finance

A major concern must be the extent to which our governments will continue to print or manufacture money, the so-called 'quantitative easing' which was supposed to see us through the crisis of 2007/08, and again during Covid lockdowns. On many levels, quantitative easing is simply an admission of governments' failure to manage their economies correctly.

Printing more money will normally cause both inflation and periodic attempts to tackle the consequent debt, which leaves a government with less money to spend on public services. It also frequently leads to increases in the lending rate, which disproportionately affects the poorest as they pay the highest interest for their borrowing,[5] if, indeed, they can borrow anything at all. Another strategy governments can employ is to suppress salary increases in the public sector. Again, this damages the poorer sectors as they have less negotiating power. And suppressing salaries further widens the gap between rich and poor. It is a fact that in every crisis, even those caused by bankers, the rich benefit and the poor suffer.

Part of the solution we will explore in this book is to see how much money can be raised by ensuring the global top 10% pay tax in the same way and at least at the same level as the rest of us. The problem with that is that governments, individual politicians, and administrations across the globe need to commit to tackling the same people who are often funding their careers. With everything going digital, it will actually be easier and easier to trace tax fraud.

A proposal spelled out on page 173 of *Adults In The Room*,[6] to tax Greek tax avoiders and non-payers in 2015, could be a model we might see more of in the future. It was proposed that 45% of the money Greece's top earners had hidden would be taken, but first they would be given an opportunity to declare their untaxed income and pay only 15%, effectively an amnesty for past sins. This never happened as it was stopped by the elite. AI can already analyse your bank account, your tax returns and your spending patterns to clearly show if you should be paying more tax. In the future, such tax will just be taken directly from your bank, with penalties if required. In short, it is going to become harder to avoid tax.

In 2022, the United Kingdom government completely messed up its economy, resulting in Prime Minister Liz Truss lasting just 49 days in post. Over this period billions of pounds were lost due to the actions of the Conservative government. But, again, those who suffer most are the poor and those Individuals whose job it is to care for us and look after our quality of life. Junior doctors, teachers, nurses and lower paid public sector workers - whose numbers, as a percentage of the workforce, have grown significantly over the past 25 years - will always feel the brunt of austerity measures. In 1997, these 'quality of life' employees accounted for 12.6% of the UK workforce, while by 2022, they accounted for 17.2%. This is due to several factors, including the ageing UK population, the increasing prevalence of chronic diseases, and the expansion of the healthcare and education sectors.[7]

These are factors beginning to affect all developed countries. Salaries have been decreased aggressively by governments, reasoning that we had no ability to pay salary increases. Surely these jobs, key to our social society, should at a minimum keep pace with inflation? But the conversation never moved to being about where the money came from and who should pay. Doctors and nurses around the world have just worked spectacularly through the Covid pandemic. We should be thinking about how the richer members of society can fund the poorer and how we value and reward the social contributions made to our quality of life, to achieve a reasonable increase in the salaries of doctors, teachers and nurses.

Bankers' salaries by contrast never seem to decline,[8] even when they perform poorly. No one seems to question what bankers really do, and greed is seen as good.[9] Bankers are playing with your money, both personal and corporate. Plus, the money which is managed by your investment companies and pension funds.

Yet there is almost zero will to hold bankers to account for their decisions made with your money and their often-poor performance. In 2007/8, a particular coterie of bankers crashed the global economy. Thousands of bankers were involved, but in Europe and the UK only a handful were prosecuted. In the USA, despite the widespread financial devastation caused by the 2008 financial crisis, the number of high-level Wall Street executives arrested and convicted for their roles remains strikingly low.

Why so few prosecutions? Because the elite protect the elite. In America the only arrests were of low-level people fundamentally mis-selling mortgages and other products. Those who created the products and packaged them together into supposed valuable commodities (when the real value was close to zero) paid no price for their cynical misdeeds.

If you look at the amount of harm done to ordinary people, even the significant number of suicides that are attributable to the 2008 crash, you could make a strong case for many bankers to have been incarcerated. In the United Kingdom where there was a limited attempt to control bankers' bonuses, these controls are now being removed at the same time as the mass of the population is suffering further as higher interest rates and inflation erode their earnings.

The financial crisis was a complex event with multiple factors. Assigning criminal liability in such cases would be challenging. But that is no reason to not attempt litigation. Of course, the scenario has been used to make a number of very successful films all of which clearly spell out the wrongdoing. *The Wolf of Wall Street* featured a narrative that helped viewers clearly understand the corruption at the heart of New York's financial centre as far back as the 80s and 90s. (It grossed nearly half a billion dollars). *Margin Call* gave a detailed and complex picture of accounting skulduggery that led to catastrophic failure in 2007/8. *The Big Short* featured Margot Robbie in a bubble bath, drinking champagne and explaining mortgage-backed bonds so that the most ill-informed Joe Public could follow the money trail.

Hollywood understood what had gone on. So why did skilled litigators steer clear of going after the clearly guilty parties at the top of the money tree? It is just a case of the elite protecting the elite. In many cases, civil settlements, fines, and regulatory actions were pursued as a means of addressing misconduct or violations of regulations. If you are poor, you are arrested and harassed for breaking the rule book. If you are rich, that's another story.

However, there were a few notable cases where individuals within the banking industry were prosecuted and convicted, either for their involvement in activities related to the financial crisis, or schemes which unravelled in its wake.

While exact figures are hard to come by, here's what we know:

No major bank CEOs were prosecuted. None of the CEOs of major financial institutions involved has faced criminal charges.

Few high-level executives have been convicted. A handful of executives at lower levels were convicted, mainly for fraud or insider trading. These cases were not directly linked to the systemic failures that led to the crisis.

Kareem Serageldin, a former Credit Suisse Group AG managing director, is one of the few high-ranking Wall Street figures to serve jail time (30 months) after pleading guilty in 2013 to conspiracy to falsify books and records in order to manipulate the valuation of mortgage-backed securities.

Bernie Madoff, while not directly related to the 2007/08 financial crisis, saw his Ponzi scheme unravel in its wake in 2008, leading to his arrest and subsequent conviction. Madoff was an insider, a prominent investment advisor and former chairman of the NASDAQ stock exchange.

Fabrice Tourre, a former Goldman Sachs trader, was convicted of fraud in 2013 for his role in creating and marketing complex mortgage-backed securities leading up to the financial crisis.

These are a small number of examples,[10] because there are so few to choose from. The number of high-level individuals who were prosecuted and sent to prison for actions related to the financial crisis is tiny compared to the enormous damage done. Many other cases involved civil settlements, fines, and regulatory actions rather than criminal prosecutions.

The crash cost the world's economy - you and me, to be precise - an estimated $14T, losing many people their homes, and - according to the International Monetary Fund - having an effect on growth for years to come, suppressing wages to the point that many are earning less comparatively today than they were in 2007. This financial meltdown, triggered by the collapse of the US housing market and the proliferation of toxic mortgage-backed securities, sent shockwaves across the globe. The consequences were devastating: millions lost their homes, unemployment soared, and retirement savings evaporated. The crisis exposed deep flaws in the global financial system, including excessive risk-taking, deregulation, and a lack of transparency. It also highlighted the interconnectedness of global economies, as the crisis spread rapidly from the US to Europe and beyond. The long-term effects of the 2008 crash are still felt today, with stagnant wages, increased debt levels, and lingering economic insecurity for many. It serves as a stark reminder of the dangers of unchecked greed and the urgent need for a more ethical and responsible financial system.

Still, in 2017 the European Banking Authority (EBA) reported that 3,519 UK based bankers collected more than €1 million each.[11] Thirty bankers were paid over €10m each. Banker's salaries will be different from country to country, but it is fair to say that, in general, they are the highest paid professionals as a category. Is it so hard to understand that it is our money that the bankers are playing with? And regulate accordingly? It's not their money, so why do we allow such rewards, not to mention that there is so very little downside when they get it wrong? In the USA in 2023, a number of bankers had earnings over $30 million in total compensation: Jamie Dimon of JPMorgan Chase earned $36 million; James Gorman of Morgan Stanley earned $37 million; and Charlie Scharf of Wells Fargo earned $29 million, for example.

Have financial regulations and enforcement evolved since the 2008 financial crisis? Has there been increased focus on holding individuals and institutions accountable for misconduct in the financial industry? The short answer is an emphatic 'No'.

Yet the misconduct has had far-reaching consequences, way beyond the purely financial and economic. A study published in the British Journal of Psychiatry in 2014, analysed suicide rates in United States, estimating there were approximately 5,000 additional suicides in the United States during and immediately after the 2008, economic crisis. The European Journal of Public Health published a study in 2013 that examined the suicide rates of 24 European countries and found significant increase in suicide rates in several countries - including Greece, Spain, and Italy - most badly affected by the economic crisis. The study concluded that probably 10,000 suicides in the two-year period following could be attributed to the 2008 crash just in the 24 countries studied. So, there were maybe 20,000+ suicides in the immediate aftermath of the 2008 crisis that can be attributed to individuals losing their wealth, investments, pensions and homes as a direct result of the actions of a very small group of international bankers focused/centred in New York.

And it's not like it's an entirely unpredictable consequence. The suicide rate in the United States had also increased previously during the Great Depression, peaking in 1932 at 22.1 per 100,000 people. Given the U.S. population at the time, this translates to roughly 22,000 suicides in the year 1932.[12]

Control of our money is in the possession of a small number of institutions, and it is these we need to influence and encourage to take a more moral attitude.

Who are the few who control the world's money?	
Commercial banks	30% to 37%
Pension funds	15% to 20%
Insurance companies	10% to 15%
Asset managers	15%
Central banks	10%
Sovereign wealth, funds	3%

The above figures are very crude approximations, in 2024, as there is not sufficient data to give a precise set of figures, and the figures in any event will move almost daily. It represents a guide to who controls your money.

This is happening already to a limited extent in environmental investments. Because of customer pressure, institutions are insisting that new Investments are as green as possible, that impact on the environment is considered and that there is an Environmental, Social and Governance (ESG) focus. Who are these institutions in whom we invest so much money and faith?

Commercial Banks hold a significant portion of global wealth - around 30-37% - due to their role in intermediating funds, issuing loans, and managing deposits. Pension funds hold retirement savings for individuals and organisations. They typically invest in diversified assets to meet long-term obligations. Pension funds collectively may control around 15-20% of global wealth. Insurance Companies manage substantial assets through premiums collected from policyholders. They invest these funds in various financial instruments to cover claims and generate returns. Insurance companies may control approximately 10-15% of global wealth. Asset management companies Including Investment Banks, Hedge Funds a further 15%, then central banks with 10%. Sovereign Wealth Funds manage reserves on behalf of governments, often from commodity exports or budget surpluses. They invest these funds globally to generate returns and support long-term economic objectives. Sovereign wealth funds may control around 3% of global wealth.

Except for the sovereign wealth funds (governments control sovereign wealth funds which are mainly managed by the elite) for each of these companies or institutions money comes directly from Individual investors. It comes in the form of pension contributions or direct investment from the likes of you and me - or via a collective investment from a company, trust, fund, association acting on our behalf.

Every one of us can therefore insist on change, and if change is not forthcoming, we can move our money to a more moral Institution. If enough of us protest and ask for change it will have an impact. As pointed out by Nobel Prize-winner Professor Robert Shiller, banks need to change, in more ways than the simplest need for real governance and control of the salaries/bonuses.[13] There needs to be much more flexibility in both the banks' assets and liabilities so that they can respond to varying contingencies. For example, a proportion of bonds any bank issues on its behalf should be hybrid, so they can be turned into equity if the bank gets into trading difficulties. It would then be bondholders who face losses as their bonds are automatically turned into shares, rather than us, the taxpayers.

Below are the leading pension funds, investing millions of your money, almost $10T in the list. Why do they not represent your interests better?

Pensions Fund

Rank	Pension Fund	Country	AUM (T$)	Estimated Number of Investors
1	Government Pension Investment Fund	Japan	1.4	100-150 million
2	Government Pension Fund Global	Norway	1.2	4-6 million
3	National Pension Service	South Korea	0.7	20-25 million
4	Federal Retirement Thrift Investment Board	US	0.7	6-7 million
5	Stichting Pensioenfonds ABP	Netherlands	0.5	3-5 million
6	California Public Employees' Retirement System	US	0.4	1.5-2.5 million
7	Canada Pension Plan Investment Board	Canada	0.4	20-22 million
8	National Social Security Fund	China	0.4	0.9 - 1.1 billion
9	Central Provident Fund Board	Singapore	0.3	3.5-4.5 million
10	Pensioenfonds Zorg en Welzijn	Netherlands	0.3	2-3 million
11	California State Teachers' Retirement System	US	0.3	0.9-1.1 million
12	Employees' Provident Fund	India	0.3	60-70 million
13	Stichting Pensioenfonds Metaal en Techniek	Netherlands	0.2	0.4-0.5 million
14	New York State Common Retirement Fund	US	0.2	1-1.2 million

15	Texas Teacher Retirement System	US	0.2	1.5-1.7 million
16	Employees' Provident Fund	Malaysia	0.2	14-16 million
17	Public School Employees' Retirement System of Pennsylvania	US	0.2	0.5-0.6 million
18	New York City Retirement Systems	US	0.2	0.7-0.8 million
19	National Wealth Fund	Russia	0.2	N/A
20	Stichting Pensioenfonds voor de Gezondheid	Netherlands	0.2	0.25-0.3 million
21	Government Employees Pension Fund	South Africa	0.2	1.7-1.9 million
22	Florida State Board of Administration	US	0.2	1-1.2 million
23	Ontario Teachers' Pension Plan	Canada	0.2	0.3-0.4 million
24	National Pension Reserve Fund	Ireland	0.2	N/A
25	Texas County & District Retirement System	US	0.2	0.25-0.3 million

Chapter 3 - The 10 key points

1. Financial Institutions' Dominance: Financial institutions, central banks, and politicians wield immense power over the global economy, often prioritising their own interests over the well-being of the majority.

2. The US Dollar as a Tool of Control: The US dollar's dominance in the global financial system allows the US to exert significant influence and control over other countries through sanctions and economic pressure.

3. The Illusion of Money's Value: Modern currency, primarily existing in electronic form, has little intrinsic value and is subject to manipulation and devaluation through practices like quantitative easing.

4. The Rise of Electronic Currency: The shift towards electronic and digital currencies is driven by governments seeking greater control over financial transactions and the potential elimination of physical cash, raising concerns about privacy and individual freedoms.

5. Historical Reliance on Banks: Throughout history, rulers and governments have been dependent on financial institutions, highlighting the enduring power of banks in shaping political and economic landscapes.

6. The Financial Sector's Growth and Influence: The financial sector, particularly in the US, has expanded significantly, raising concerns about its disproportionate impact on the economy and its potential for systemic risks.

7. Government Mismanagement and Its Consequences: Governments' reliance on printing money and other monetary policies to address economic challenges can lead to inflation, reduced public spending, and widening inequality.

8. Impact on Essential Workers: Economic mismanagement negatively affects essential workers in healthcare, education, and other social sectors, leading to stagnant wages and decreased quality of life.

9. Lack of Banker Accountability: The lack of accountability for bankers' actions, especially in the aftermath of the 2008 financial crisis, highlights a systemic issue within the financial industry.

10. The Need for Ethical and Responsible Banking: The chapter calls for greater moral responsibility and accountability within the financial sector, advocating for reforms that prioritise the well-being of society and the environment over short-term profits.

Footnotes – Chapter 3

---

[1]https://www.jstor.org/stable/pdf/1819500.pdf

[2] Atlantic Council CBDC Tracker: provides up-to-date information on the development worldwide.https://www.atlanticcouncil.org/blogs/econographics/central-bank-digital-currency-evolution-in-2023-from-investigation-to-preparation/

[3] Based on data from the US Federal Reserve, as of December 2022, there were about $2.3 trillion in notes and coins floating around the globe. This means that only about 8% of the world's currency exists as physical cash. The rest exists only on a computer hard drive, in electronic bank accounts around the world.

[4] King John of England (1199-1216): King John was known for his heavy taxation and his frequent borrowing of money from moneylenders. In 1215, a group of rebellious barons forced King John to sign the Magna Carta, which limited his power to tax and borrow money. King Edward III of England (1327-1377): King Edward III was heavily in debt to Italian moneylenders. In 1339, he repudiated his debts, which led to a war between England and Florence. King Philip IV of France (1285-1314): King Philip IV was also heavily in debt to Italian moneylenders. In 1306, he arrested the Templars, a wealthy order of knights, and confiscated their property. This allowed him to repay some of his debts, but it also led to the downfall of the Templars. Queen Isabella of Castile (1474-1504): Queen Isabella I of Castile and her husband King Ferdinand II of Aragon borrowed money from Genoese moneylenders to finance their voyages of discovery. However, they struggled to repay their debts, and they eventually defaulted on some of their loans. King Henry VIII of England (1509-1547): King Henry VIII was a notorious spender, and he often borrowed money from moneylenders. He also confiscated the property of the Catholic Church in England, which allowed him to repay some of his debts.

[5] Consumer Financial Protection Bureau (CFPB): "Low- and moderate-income borrowers pay more in loan interest as a share of their income than higher-income borrowers. For example, borrowers in the lowest income quintile pay an average of 14.1 percent of their income in loan interest, while borrowers in the highest income quintile pay an average of 3.1 percent of their income in loan interest." A 2023 study by the Centre for American Progress found that "poor people pay more interest on their borrowing than rich people." The study found that the average interest rate on a payday loan is 391%, while the average interest rate on a credit card is 16.4%.

[6] https://www.amazon.co.uk/Adults-Room-Battle-Europes-Establishment/dp/184792445X

[7]The salary of care workers, nurses, teachers, and doctors has not kept up with inflation over the past 25 years. In fact, their real wages have decreased by 8% in real terms over this period. This is due to several factors, including the austerity measures implemented by the government following the financial crisis of 2008, the increasing cost of living, and the fact that these occupations are typically in the public sector, which has seen lower wage growth than the private sector in recent years.

[8] Greed is good, the lifting of the bankers salary cap https://www.theguardian.com/business/2023/oct/31/tories-bankers-bonuses-tuc-rishi-sunak

[9] “I've no remorse about stealing from banks. I've the impression of stealing from someone more of a thief than I am,” wrote Jacques Mesrine - France's ‘public enemy No 1’ - in his book *L'instinct de mort* (*Death Instinct*) published in 1977.

[10] According to a study by the Financial Crisis Inquiry Commission, there were only a handful of convictions of individuals directly related to the crisis. This lack of prosecutions has been attributed to several factors, including the difficulty of proving criminal intent, the complexity of financial instruments involved, and the reluctance of governments to prosecute powerful financial institutions. Here's a breakdown by country: United States: In the United States, Kareem Serageldin, a former Credit

Suisse executive, was sentenced to 30 months in prison in 2013 for mismarking bond prices to hide losses. He is considered the only banker in the US to serve jail time directly related to the financial crisis. Iceland: Iceland, which experienced a severe financial collapse in 2008, had the most notable prosecutions of bankers. Several former executives of Kaupthing Bank, Iceland's largest bank at the time, were convicted of fraud and market manipulation. Sigurd Einarsson, the bank's former chairman, received a five-and-a-half-year prison sentence. United Kingdom: In the UK, several investigations and prosecutions were conducted related to the financial crisis. However, most of these cases focused on regulatory breaches and market manipulation rather than criminal charges. One notable case involved Tom Hayes, a former trader at UBS and Citigroup, who was sentenced to 14 years in prison for manipulating the London Interbank Offered Rate (LIBOR). France: In France, there were no major prosecutions of bankers directly related to the financial crisis. However, several investigations were conducted, and some individuals faced regulatory sanctions. Germany: Germany also saw limited prosecutions of bankers related to the financial crisis. However, the country implemented stricter financial regulations and introduced a new law against market manipulation.

[11]According to the EBA, these numbers mean that the total amount of bonuses paid to bankers in the UK in 2021 was over €3.5 billion.

[12] https://www.researchgate.net/publication/26871254_Life_and_death_during_the_Great_Depression
https://thesocietypages.org/specials/social-fact-suicide/

[13] https://www.weforum.org/agenda/2016/05/robert-j-shillers-message-to-financial-regulators-dont-fight-the-last-financial-crisis/

CHAPTER 4

How Wealth is Distributed

There are currently eight billion+ of us.[1] Let's look at that in cold hard numbers: 8,205,072,800 and ticking upwards at the rate of three per second - watch the Worldometer Population Clock live.[2] At whatever point we clear this book for publication, by the time you read it, the population will have increased by many scores of millions. The Clock includes us all, including everyone under 18. For the purposes of re-adjusting the financial picture in the world we need to discuss the 5.5bn adults who are known to be working for a wage.

In our world, 9% of people live in complete poverty at somewhere between $2 and $3 a day. For simplicity's sake, let's call it $1000 a year. Including this 9%, the bottom 50% of the world's earners average an income of $3,200 per year - just under $9 a day.

At the next level, from 51-90% on the scale, the average salary of workers worldwide Is $1,548 a month or $18,582 per year. It varies from country to country but even if we take a G7 country like France for example, we're talking about $2,568 a month or $30,817 a year for an average worker in 2022.[3]

In the top 10%, earnings average $66,909 a year on the scale from 2%-9%. And then there is a massive jump to $372,727 for the top 1%.

And at the top end of that 1% we have 3,000+ billionaires.[4] It's practically impossible to talk about the annual earnings of billionaires, so we move on to wealth as a measurement. These billionaires, along with the rest of the top 1% - 55m adult individuals - have 46.1% of the wealth of the planet. That's 1% of people who have 25 times the combined wealth of the poorest 50%. Each of the roughly 3,000 billionaires have an average wealth of $4.733 billion, which is 1,629,260 times more wealth than the average individual adult in the world's poorest 50%, who average $2,905 each.

When you combine this top 1% with the next 9% of the world's wealthiest individuals, you are looking at a share of global wealth totalling 85.5%. So how does 85.5% of the planet's wealth end up in the hands of 10% of its population? This distribution cannot be reasonable, moral, or correct. But how do you readjust the distribution of wealth and income? How do you make things more equitable?

There is enough money. The total of wealth in the world, as of 2023, was estimated to be around $434.2 trillion. This figure comes from aggregating data from the IFC and World Bank databases. This is lower than the $463,567 trillion suggested by the UBS Global Wealth Report 2023, a collaboration between Credit Suisse and UBS,[5] but we believe it is a more robust estimate. In any event whatever figure you use, there is enough.

The figure we are relying on refers to net private wealth of $434.2T, which means you consider people's debts and subtract them from the total value of their assets. Despite a decline in 2022, the UBS report predicts global wealth to increase in the next five years, reaching an estimated $629 trillion by 2027. So, there is enough money. It's just that it's distributed and shared extremely unfairly. It has been unfair for thousands of years, but today we have access to much more information, so we can clearly see that it is getting worse by the decade.

We must start by recognizing that we are all part of the same system. Millionaires become millionaires because there are enough people to buy their products and services. In the past 50 years, millionaires became billionaires because the planet's population tripled - from 2.6bn in 1954. Eight billion people are spending money, Investing money in our banks, pension funds, Investment companies, and hedge funds.

The top 1% have reached the position where they can exploit their fellow humans because they have, in most cases, inherited wealth, which automatically places them at the heart of the elite. They have received superior education, access to knowledge, to information, to technology and most importantly of all a network of contacts.[6] The immense wealth accumulated by the top 1% is inextricably linked to the existence and participation of the global population. Whether it's through consumer spending, labour, or investment, the eight billion people on this planet play a crucial role in generating and sustaining the wealth of the few.

The sheer size of the global population creates a massive market for goods and services. This vast consumer base fuels economic activity, driving demand and generating profits for businesses. In turn, these profits contribute to the wealth of individuals, particularly those who own or invest in these companies.

The workforce is currently the backbone of any economy. The labour of billions of people across the globe produces the goods and services that are consumed and traded. This productivity contributes to everyone's wealth and ultimately mostly benefits those who are in control, especially the top 1%.

The combined savings and investments of millions of individuals flow into banks, pension funds, and other financial institutions. Wealth accumulation is influenced by history and structural inequalities. Many wealthy individuals and families have inherited wealth or have benefited from privileged access to education, networks, and opportunities. These advantages have allowed them to capitalise on the economic system and accumulate vast fortunes.

A growing body of evidence suggests that the elite start with a significant advantage in terms of inheritance, better education, and access to bankers and politicians. In terms of inheritance, a study by the Institute for Policy Studies (IPS)[7] found that the top 1% of Americans inherit more than 60% of all wealth passed down each year.[8] In many cases, these people avoided properly paying inheritance tax due to their access to top lawyers, accountants and tax avoidance structures. This means that the wealthy can accumulate and pass on their wealth to their children, giving them a significant head start in life, effectively keeping the dynasty going. In terms of education, the wealthy are also more likely to attend elite schools, giving them access to better resources and networking opportunities. A Pew Research Centre study found that children from high-income families are four times more likely to attend a top-ranked college than children from low-income families.[9] This is all the more remarkable given the disparity in numbers between the relatively few with high income compared to the millions on low income.

Finally, the wealthy have better access to bankers and politicians, who can help them protect their wealth and promote their interests. For example, a study by the Centre for Responsive Politics[10] found that the top 1% of Americans are six times more likely to donate to federal candidates than the bottom 50%. Here are some other specific examples of how the elite start with a significant advantage:

Inheritance - a 2018 study by the Federal Reserve Bank of New York found that the top 1% of Americans inherited an average of $12.7 million over their lifetimes. This is compared to just $11,000 for the bottom 50%.

Education - a 2016 study by the Brookings Institution, found that the top 1% of Americans were six times more likely to attend a top-ranked university than the bottom 50%.

Access to bankers and politicians - A 2015 study by the Centre for Responsive Politics found that the top 1% of Americans were 220 times more likely to have a meeting with a member of Congress than the bottom 50%.

These advantages provide our elite with a significant head start in life,[11] making it much easier for them to accumulate wealth and power, and to access those who can help them in this process. As a result, it is becoming increasingly difficult for those who are not born into wealth to achieve the same level of success. This gap has been increasing, for example, in the United Kingdom lately. The concentration of wealth and power in the hands of the few is a major problem for society. It leads to inequality, injustice, and lack of opportunity. It is also a threat to democracy, because it allows the wealthy to influence government policy in their own interests. We must act to address this problem by reforming our tax system so that the wealthy pay their fair share; by investing in education and job training so that everyone has a similar or equal chance of success; and by strengthening our democracy to ensure that everyone has a voice. Only by taking these actions can we create a more just, equitable and moral society.

I would suggest it is fair and reasonable to share some of the elite's gains and some of their advantages if we do not wish global society to implode. Assuming we agree there should be a redistribution of a small percentage of both wealth and income, one of the questions which needs answering, is: should this be immediate or would it be more reasonable to phase it over several years.

One of the key messages of this book is that we need to agree, as civilised moral individuals, to this redistribution of money over say five, 10, or even 20 years. But it is important that we agree in principle sooner rather than later, because ultimately, we could be faced with a revolution similar to the Russian Revolution when large numbers of those with wealth were killed. In 1917 the Russian Empire had a population estimated at about 175 million. By 1926, nine years after the revolution, the population was recorded as having declined to 93 million. So, it is quite clear that millions of individuals died, were murdered or otherwise disposed of, perhaps moved en masse to different territories.[12] It is suggested that maybe 25% of all the rich individuals, the elite, were murdered.

The Chinese Revolution, 1911, probably killed over 10 million people. The French Revolution saw hundreds of thousands killed, but again mostly elite. King Louis XVI and Marie Antoinette were executed, as were many other nobles and clergy members who were seen as symbols of the old corrupt order.

If we wish to avoid such bloodshed, I suggest we start with some basic targets; then we discuss how long we are going to take to get there; and *how* we are going to get there. These targets will serve as a roadmap for a more equitable and just future, one where the benefits of economic growth are shared more fairly and the basic needs of all are met. In Chapters 18 and 19, we will delve deeper into the specific policies and strategies that can help us achieve these ambitious goals.

The tax system needs to be reformed so that taxation of wealth and income is fairer. We need to start considering universal basic income (UBI). As jobs are taken over by machines, what are we going to do? Are we going to leave the mass of the population without employment, without any income or means of feeding themselves? Or are we going to ensure there is a basic minimum for everyone. Let's look at the poorest, the bottom 9% as described earlier, currently subsisting on $2-3 a day ($60-90 a month).[13] If we set a goal of pushing the UBI of the poorest up to a starting point of $210 a month, $2,520 a year, that would be a good beginning. If we add the next group, 41% of the global population, the combined income of the lowest 50% in 2023 was $8.8 trillion, or $3,200 for each adult. We would suggest that the share of income be increased to $14 trillion, an increase of $5.2 trillion. Again, this would be a significant increase for those who are in the bottom 50% of the world's population. The current income of the bottom 50% represents only 8.5% of total world income, so to move it up to the levels proposed of $14 trillion - 13.5% - would not require a significant reduction of the income of the world's top 1% earners, simply that they pay due tax without exemptions. This feels like a reasonable expectation from the top 1% who currently 'earn' 20% of total global yearly income.

This will be achieved by several measures acting in concert. The priorities are:

That tax avoidance as a concept is abolished, so that the richest 10%, particularly the richest 1%, start to pay tax on the same basis as the rest of us. Because currently they do not; they pay a fraction of the tax that they should pay.

That financial institutions start limiting and suppressing the excessive income paid to the very top executives. These same institutions need to become much more aware of the ratio between the top and the bottom in any business or enterprise.

Proposed World Income Targets

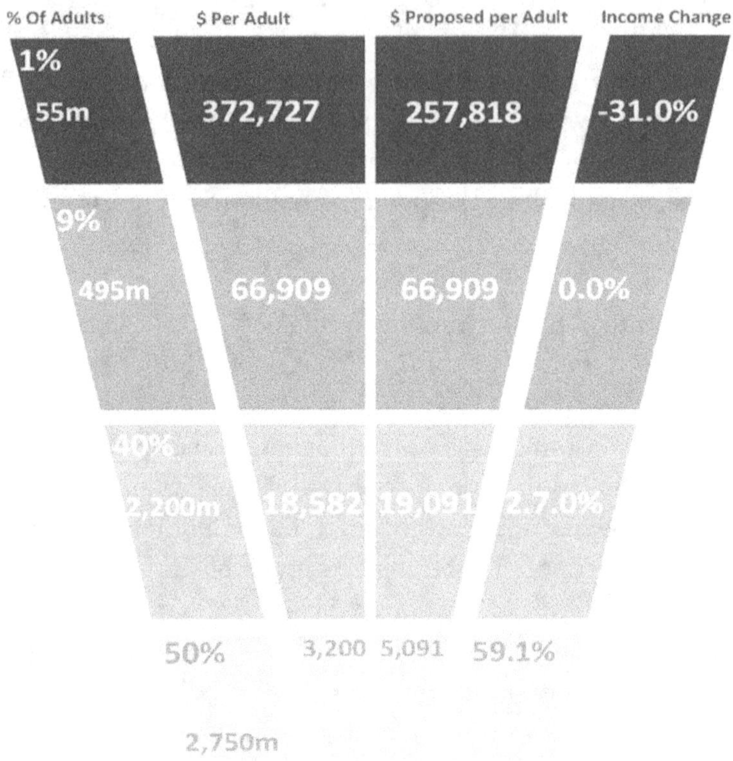

These are proposed targets for raising the income of the poorest four billion+ of global population by reducing the levels of earnings of the richest 1% by 31%.

As we report later on, it cannot be considered moral for a CEO to earn 2,000+ times the average annual salary of their own employees.

That International Law is enacted to make it illegal for accountants and lawyers to help clients evade or avoid tax. Since this does real damage to literally billions of the poorest people, it should be an offence that results in prison sentences. There are some regulations and laws in place, but they certainly are not being imposed or used in any systematic way. They need to be strengthened, added to, and employed a lot more effectively. There needs to be an understanding that helping people avoid tax and sanctions, and to execute money laundering, does as much harm to society as some of the most heinous criminal activities.

In addition, the concept of client confidentiality should be adjusted. Accountants should be bound in law - as they already are in part in the UK, France, America and some other countries - to report attempts at tax evasion or money laundering by their clients. But, again, the ethics are clouded by questionable arguments put forward, such as this proposal[14] that the duty to report a client's fraud 'is an erosion of legal privilege' and also - according to the writer - 'could put solicitors in danger'. All of this points to the need for crystal clear international legislation which advisors cannot wriggle out of, therefore leaving their clients with no choice but to pay up the tax due at the same rate and on the same basis as the rest of us.

Whistleblowers should be protected and potentially rewarded. Accountants and lawyers have codes of ethics that emphasise professional responsibility and acting within the law. They need to start enforcing these codes.[15] If they don't, and an assistant, researcher or secretary blows the whistle, the whistleblower should not live in fear of punishment.

In 2016, what was quite likely the most egregious illustration of the lengths to which the wealthy and their advisors will go to avoid what the rest of us cannot, the leak of millions of financial documents, which became known as The Panama Papers, exposed a global network of offshore tax havens used by wealthy individuals and corporations to avoid taxes. Several law firms and accounting firms were implicated in helping clients set up shell companies and other structures to conceal their assets and income. While prosecutions haven't necessarily happened in every case, investigations and legal actions were triggered based on the information revealed.[16] In 2018, the Swiss arm of accounting giant KPMG was fined millions and lost its banking licence for helping wealthy clients hide assets and evade taxes using offshore accounts.[17]

We give more examples in Appendix 1, Note 15.

We need to be clear: there is always going to be some form of pyramid. But we can make that pyramid more reasonable, equitable, and, yes, moral.

The idea that we can all have the same is never going to happen. Previous experiments in distributing wealth along non-capitalist lines have always seen wealth and resources given to the leaders, the military, and others who are needed to keep the leaders at the top. However much political adherents try to disguise and hide this, communism was never going to work. The idea that everybody can have an equal share of the pie is not simply illogical; it is antithetical to human nature. There must be some difference and a reasonable reward or even good reward for effort, learning and success.

Communism proposed that everyone should have an equal share of the pie, and that the means of production, such as factories and farms, were to be owned and controlled by the community. The wealth produced under this system was to be distributed equally among all members of society. In the event, populations went hungry, found themselves at the mercy of their 'leaders', and saw those same leaders living a life as rich as the aristocrats and tyrants who had come before them. Communism's catastrophic Faultline was its theoretical equality of outcome, which was never, and can never be, achieved.

Communist philosophy proposed, reasonably, that inequality is a root cause of many social problems, such as poverty, crime, and violence. The very concepts of guilt and punishment were seen by dedicated Marxists as 'instruments of bourgeois culture', tools by which the ruling elite had kept the lower orders in their place. By contrast, Joseph Stalin kept the population under control via starvation, torture, exile, banishment to gulags, or simple murder. In 70 years following the Bolshevik Revolution of 1917, experiments with Communism around the world - in the USSR, China, Vietnam, Cuba, Cambodia, and others - resulted in the deaths by starvation or execution of perhaps 70 million people (some estimates put it as high as 110 million).

Communism, wherever and however it has been tried, has failed in its most basic aims. It is unrealistic to expect people to work equally hard if they are not going to be rewarded for their efforts. But communism also stifled innovation and creativity.

These criticisms are hindsight, informed by historical reality. Communism was a powerful idea at its inception, and an inspiration for revolutionaries in the early 20th century. It was a relatively easy sell in many countries where it took hold, because the mass of people wanted a better life and a fair share of the pie combined with, theoretically, a better morality from the top to the bottom of society. Consequently, communist governments held sway over millions of people.

But they failed to deliver any of the dreams and desires of their populations. Rather they have, uniformly, suppressed dissidence, locked away opposition candidates, manipulated the information flow and the media, and destroyed any group that may challenge them. That was at best. At worst, they assassinated those who posed a threat or questioned the regime and then used armed forces and police to control those citizens made restless by critical voices.

So let us abandon the debate about how communism, or socialism for that matter, might be made to work. At the same time, let us acknowledge that the dominant system, capitalism, is also failing the world. *Technofeudalism* by Yanis Varoufakis makes this point very strongly, suggesting that tech giants now govern us.[18]

We don't have to agree with Varoufakis that technofuedalism is yet 'a thing', let alone that techno has already 'killed capitalism' (though personally I think we are almost there, and we should take swift action). But lacking a global moral compass, and driven increasingly by unregulated greed, we have reached a point where the richest 1% of the world's population control 46.1% of global wealth, compared to 14.5% held by the bottom 90% combined.[19]

The world's richest 10 people have a combined wealth of $1.546 trillion. Here's how it breaks down - Bernard Arnault & family: $233 billion, Elon Musk: $195 billion, Jeff Bezos: $194 billion, Mark Zuckerberg: $177 billion, Larry Ellison: $141 billion, Warren Buffet: $133 billion, Bill Gates: $128 billion, Steve Ballmer: $121 billion, Larry Page: $114 billion, Sergey Brin: $110 billion. According to some sources, $1.546 trillion is more wealth than the poorest one billion people combined.[20] To put this into perspective, the combined wealth of these 10 billionaires is equivalent to the GDP of Spain, the 14th largest economy in the world. This stark contrast highlights the extreme concentration of wealth at the top and the urgent need for a more equitable distribution of resources. The average income of someone in the richest 1% is $372,727, which is about 116 times higher than the average income of someone in the poorest 50% group of the world.

The richest 1% are getting richer, while the poorest, especially the 10% at the bottom are getting poorer. Oxfam reports that the richest 1% bagged nearly twice as much wealth as the rest of the world put together over the past two years. They also found that the wealth of the five richest men doubled from 2020, while that of the poorest half of humanity fell. Equality Trust found a 1000% increase in the wealth of UK billionaires between 1990 and 2022. High Pay Centre reported a $2trillion increase in global billionaire wealth in just one year (2023 to 2024). The Institute for Policy Studies reported an 88% increase in the total wealth of U.S. billionaires over four years.

To make matters worse, as the rich get richer and the elite grab more money, the growth of luxury spending is expanding much faster than the general growth of the world economy.[21] Do we really need to spend so much money on status, on showing off?

Notable Luxury Assets

Name	**Notable Luxury Assets**
Sheikh Hamad bin Hamdan Al Nahyan	Owns one of the world's largest car collections, known as the "Rainbow Sheikh," including over 200 custom-painted cars, a Mercedes-Benz covered in diamonds, and a custom-made Dodge Power Wagon replica 64 times the size of the original.
Kim Kardashian	Extensive collection of designer clothing, jewelry, and handbags, multiple luxury homes, private jets, luxury cars like a Lamborghini Aventador, and has rented entire islands for vacations, including a private island in French Polynesia.

Roman Abramovich	Owner of multiple luxury yachts, including the Eclipse (one of the largest and most expensive private yachts in the world), a vast art collection, multiple properties in the UK, US, France, and Russia, and a Boeing 767 private jet.
Sultan of Brunei	Substantial car collection with over 7,000 cars, including custom-made Rolls-Royces, Ferraris, and Bentleys, a palace with 1,788 rooms, multiple private jets, and extensive investments in luxury hotels and properties worldwide.
Paris Hilton	Large collection of designer clothing, accessories, and handbags, multiple luxury homes, custom-made luxury cars, and frequent luxury vacations to exclusive destinations.
Vijay Mallya	Owned a collection of luxury cars, including vintage models, a 95-metre superyacht, multiple lavish properties in India and abroad, and hosted extravagant parties and events, including the Kingfisher Calendar and the Force India F1 team.
Jeff Bezos	Multiple properties, including a $165 million mansion in Beverly Hills, a $23 million townhouse in Washington D.C., a $96 million apartment in New York City, a vast ranch in Texas, private jets, and investments in space exploration (Blue Origin).
Kylie Jenner	Collection of luxury cars, including a Bugatti Chiron, multiple Rolls-Royces, Lamborghinis, and Ferraris, a private jet, several multi-million-dollar homes, and a designer handbag collection worth millions of dollars.
Sheikh Mohammed bin Rashid Al Maktoum	Owns an impressive stable of racehorses, including the Godolphin Racing operation, multiple luxury properties in Dubai and around the world, a private yacht, and significant investments in real estate and luxury resorts.
Celine Dion	Extensive collection of high-end designer clothing and accessories, multiple luxury homes including a $28 million estate in Florida, a private island in Quebec, and a $10 million mansion in Las Vegas.

Floyd Mayweather Jr.	Collection of luxury cars, including multiple Bugattis, Ferraris, Lamborghinis, and Rolls-Royces, private jets, extensive jewelry collection worth millions, and multiple lavish properties, including a $25 million mansion in Beverly Hills.
Tamara Ecclestone	Owns a lavish mansion in London's "Billionaire's Row," extensive collection of designer clothing and accessories, luxury cars, and frequently hosts extravagant parties and events.
Silvio Berlusconi	Collection of extravagant properties, including villas and mansions in Italy and abroad, a private island, luxury yachts, and has been associated with hosting lavish parties and events.
Daphne Guinness	Known for her avant-garde fashion choices and extravagant wardrobe, including custom-made designer outfits, owns multiple luxury properties, and has an extensive art and jewelry collection.
Richard Branson	Owns Necker Island in the British Virgin Islands, multiple luxury homes, private jets, a fleet of luxury cars, and participates in extreme sports and adventures, including space travel with Virgin Galactic.
Elon Musk	Collection of luxury cars, including rare and unique models like the Lotus Esprit submarine car, multiple high-end real estate properties, including a $50 million mansion in Bel-Air, and significant investments in space exploration (SpaceX).
Oprah Winfrey	Owns multiple properties, including a lavish estate in Montecito, California, a home in Maui, Hawaii, and a ski chalet in Colorado, extensive collection of high-end designer clothing and accessories, and a private jet.
Jay-Z and Beyoncé	Multiple luxurious properties, including an $88 million mansion in Bel-Air, a $26 million East Hampton estate, and a $2.6 million New Orleans church mansion, luxury cars, private jets, and high-end fashion and jewelry collections.
Sheikh Khalifa bin Zayed Al Nahyan	Owns numerous palaces, including the Emirates Palace in Abu Dhabi, extensive investments in

	luxury ventures, including art collections, hotels, and a fleet of private jets.
Tamim bin Hamad Al Thani	Collection of luxury cars, private planes, multiple properties around the world, including a $300 million mansion in London, and significant investments in high-profile sports events and projects.
Mariah Carey	Extensive collection of rare and expensive jewelry, high-end fashion and accessories, multiple luxury properties, including a $5.5 million mansion in Beverly Hills, and has been seen with luxury cars and private jets.
Bernard Arnault	Owns an impressive art collection, rare and expensive wines, multiple luxurious properties, including a mansion in Paris, a château in Bordeaux, and significant investments in the world's leading luxury brands (LVMH).
Vladimir Putin	Reported to own multiple palaces, luxury watches worth millions, expensive vehicles, including a custom-made limousine, and has been seen with high-end fashion and accessories.
Kim Jong-un	Reportedly owns luxury vehicles, including a fleet of Mercedes-Benz cars, expensive watches, enjoys fine dining, and imported luxury goods despite North Korea's economic conditions.

This chart shows some of the more egregious examples of conspicuous consumption of essentially meaningless items while 9% of the population survives on $2-3 a day.

Does anyone really need a pair of trainers costing $5,800? Does anyone need a $510,000 watch? Or even a Patek Phillippe at $7.7m? After marketing, branding and the cost of business, the purchase price of a luxury handbag - costing less than $200 to make - has now reached astronomical levels. The top five bags without any significant amounts of decorative jewellery range in price from $100,000 to $300,000. Once you start adding a significant amount of jewellery to handbags you are talking a range of $3.8 million to $1.4 million.[22]

The cost of physically producing a top-end luxury handbag bears no relation to its purchase price. According to a 2021 report by the New York Times, the cost of materials and labour for a luxury handbag is typically around $200. And yet a Hermès Birkin bag can cost anywhere from $10,000 to $300,000, depending on the size, materials, and craftsmanship involved. In some ways this flagrant waste of money on fripperies shows us how far we've diverted from a moral path; how greatly those whose earnings deliver unimagined wealth find themselves disconnected from ordinary people, let alone the bottom 50% of the global population.

Which brings us back to the question of what a fair distribution of money and income is. We need to look at what is earned at the top. Surely for any business there should be a ratio between what the management are earning and what the workers are earning? What is a reasonable multiple of an average worker's salary to the salary of the directors and the senior managers who lead a business? If $1,267 a month or $15,206 pa is the global average for 99%, how does 50 times that sound to you for a top manager? That would be $63,350 a month, $760,200 a year. Too much, too little, or somewhere in the ballpark?

Finally, near the very top of the pyramid, those running businesses with hundreds of thousands of employees or massive investments? Would a salary of $1m a month, $12m a year, be sufficient? What is the actual justification for a director being paid 5,414 times the average salary of their own workers? Looking at Standard & Poor's (S&P) top 500 companies - in which nearly every pension fund invests - the top 200 companies operate on a ratio where top management are paid a minimum of 200 times the average employee. At Coca Cola, according to an AFL report,[23] the CEO James Quincey earns 1,799 times the average employee's pay of $13,752.

It is also significant that there are very few top companies where the founder is still the CEO. At least founders could make an argument that massive remuneration is fair compensation for developing an idea and continuing to operate a successful business based around that idea. In the USA only about 4% of CEOs are founders. This is where the directors of pension funds and financial institutions are seriously letting us all down, by not questioning the remuneration of those 96% who are not founders but are paid employees. Also, in recent years there has been much talk in the media about Environmental, Social & Governance Policy (ESG) as guiding principles for running any business. But there are very few examples of shareholders being represented forcefully, of their representatives pushing back against management and board directors to ensure their salaries, bonuses, perks, and other non-tangible benefits are reasonable, and linked to performance and achievement, particularly in the arena of ESG.

What is the justification, then, for hired executives earning, say, 200 times the average they pay their workforce? Or 2,000 times? Or 5,000 times? There is none. The people controlling the votes are all part of the same elite, the same club. I admit to being on the fringe of this group, so open to accusations of hypocrisy. But having seen this from within, I believe my points are rational. Either we start distributing income, wealth, education, resources, and opportunities more equally or we suffer the consequences. I realise that these changes are not going to be easy and many of the points I'm raising are going to be very difficult to resolve.

We have already acknowledged the need for there to be a pyramid. The top of the pyramid is never going to make everyone happy. But if it has some form of logic and morality it will be an improvement on what we have now. Those who see a reduction of their currently massive earnings might be discontent to put it mildly. Those looking up from the bottom will still see a massive gap between their earnings and those at the very top. But the gap will have narrowed, and opportunities will have opened up for the less well off.

This new moral proposal imagines a significantly fairer model of wealth sharing compared to the current global income distribution. Capitalism is still the best model. But it has discredited itself by running out of control, with the elite and the winners sweeping away any limitations. By allocating a larger share of income to the lower and middle-income groups, this proposal aims to address the substantial inequality that exists in the world today. This would also stimulate the growth of all economies.

The case for a more moral and equitable distribution of earnings at the top, is clear to see. Let's look a little closer at the list of top earners in the world. In September 2023, looking at the top hundred Chief Executives worldwide, the AFL-CIO (the website of American Unions) reported that the top individual salary was $253,122,146 for the year 2022, which, as you will see from our chart further on, is more than 1,000 times the salary of that CEO's, average employee wage. Number 10 on the list is still earning more than $100m a year. Number 50 in the table is $46 million a year - almost four times my proposed limit of $12 million.

We must ask investors - the owners of these businesses: the pension funds and insurance companies, who have a responsibility for corporate governance - why they have not done something about this. The President of the American Finance Association, Luigi Zingales, said in his 2015 presidential address: "There is no theoretical reason or empirical evidence to support the notion that all the growth of the financial sector in the last forty years has been beneficial to society." This was a view repeated by Lord Adair Turner, ex-chair of the Financial Conduct Authority, who famously described much of the financial sector activity as 'socially useless'. This is why we need a new morality. Why do those who are tasked with the governance of investment, of ESG and of protecting shareholders' rights, perform so poorly and yet continue to earn vast sums of money? One possible reason is they are all from the same club, the same group. They have no wish to rock the boat, or alter the status quo (and, again, I acknowledge that I am on the fringe of the club).

The argument is always about the CEO and senior management being irreplaceable, or what the market demands in terms of remuneration. The myth is that business will suffer if you disrupt it. This is not correct. For example, in 2009, Sam Palmisano resigned as CEO of IBM. The company was facing several challenges at the time, including the decline of its core mainframe business. Palmisano's successor, Ginni Rometty, has overseen a transformation of IBM into a cloud computing company and IBM's stock price has more than doubled.[24] More examples in Appendix 1, Note 17.[25] So the idea that business will suffer if you disrupt it is a poor argument, looking through the wrong end of the telescope. The problem is more about lack of governance, lack of control and oversight. Policymakers and gatekeepers have been allowed to be the friends of those who benefit. In recent years there has been a lot of focus on whether a business has a policy on ESG, before even looking to see if there is a supplier policy, a whistle blower policy, an equal opportunities policy or an anti-slavery policy. (And let's not pretend that, in the modern world, slavery is not more widespread than ever before. It still exists but hidden from view). Are you taking the governance part of ESG seriously? Proper oversight on the disparity of salaries, between the top and the bottom is one of the biggest single problems facing the world as we go forward. Because it highlights very clearly to everyone below the top one percent that there is no justice in the world.

How does a S&P 500 Company CEO's pay break down? Aside from the base salary and the bonus schemes you also have to look at the other perks - the cars, the planes, the homes, the holidays, the opera tickets etc, all at company expense, or bonuses of questionable merit.

In 2019, Rite Aid, a pharmacy chain struggling financially, revealed that their CEO, John Standley, had spent a whopping $11 million on a corporate jet in a single year. This exorbitant expense on a non-essential luxury item during a time of hardship for the company drew heavy criticism.

In 2017, Equifax, a credit reporting agency, suffered a massive data breach which compromised 143m customer records.[26] While the company faced public scrutiny and regulatory fines, CEO Richard Smith received a bonus of over $8 million, leading to accusations of misplaced priorities. Whatever is a benefit should be included fully in the salary and fully taxed. But using the data we can access; the reported salaries are only the start of the total cost for many companies in the USA.

Why does this happen? To quote the USA's labour federation, AFL-CIO: "Too many working people across the country are struggling to afford the basics, much less save for college or retirement." Here are 20 examples of the incredible gap between CEOs and the hardworking people who make their companies profitable. We have shown the salary per year of the CEO and then the average salary of their employees, finally giving a ratio of CEO to median worker.

CEO Employee Ratio

Company	CEO	CEO Salary $	Median Salary $	CEO: Employee
Blackstone Inc.	Stephen Schwarzman	253m	237k	1068
Alphabet Inc.	Sundar Pichai	225m	279k	808
Hertz Global Holdings, Inc.	Stephen Scherr	182m	36k	4983
Peloton Interactive, Inc.	Barry McCarthy	168m	73k	2299
Palo Alto Networks Inc.	Nikesh Arora	151m	206k	735
Live Nation Entertainment, Inc.	Michael Rapino	139m	25k	5414
Sarepta Therapeutics, Inc.	Douglas Ingram	124m	249k	494
Pinterest, Inc.	Bill Ready	122m	239k	999
Workday, Inc.	Aneel Bhusri	102m	233k	439
Apple Inc.	Tim Cook	99m	84k	1177
Luminar Technologies, Inc.	Austin Russell	93m	211k	443
Docusign, Inc.	Allan Thygesen	85m	196k	433

KKR & Co. Inc.	Joseph Bae	79m	225k	352
Zoom Video Communication, Inc.	Eric Yuan	75m	217k	350

The chart shows the ratio of CEO pay to that of their average employee. Source: https://aflcio.org/paywatch/company-pay-ratios m=millions, k = thousands

The worst example in 2023 is CEO Michael Rapino from Live Nation Entertainment. With a salary of $139 million, he was earning 5,414 times the average salary of his company's employees. Rapino is followed by Stephen Scherr of Hertz Global Holdings Inc, whose salary of $182 million is almost 5,000 times the average Hertz worker's salary of $36,683. There are 54 other examples on the S&P 500 list where the ratio of CEO salary to employee wage is 500+ times the average. There is no justification for this. So, what is a reasonable top ratio? Is it 200, 100, 50? We need to find a way of answering this question without consulting the people making the decisions regarding CEO remuneration, because they are all members of the same club. By setting the mark so high for the Chief, they knowingly set a standard for their own salaries and fees. If the world is going to be a more equitable and a more moral place, we need to aggressively adjust the earnings and undeserved wealth of the super-rich and claw back some of that which has been built up and hidden away over generations.

According to the World Wealth Report 2022, there are an estimated 226,450 individuals in the world - 0.003% of global population – each with a net worth of more than $100 million. Of those, about 3,000 have net assets of over $1 billion. It's hard to get an accurate report on this top group but in all probability, you are talking about 250,000 people who have a salary above $12 million per year once you include stock options and other intangible bonuses.

Global millionaires and billionaires 2021

Wealth Group ($)	Number of Adults	Total Wealth ($bn)	Average Wealth (m$)
Over 100b	9	1,321	146,778
10b-100b	157	4,128	26,293
1b-100b	2,470	7,051	2,855
100m-1b	73,800	17,070	231
10m-100m	1,769,200	33,588	19
1m-10m	60,319,500	111,059	1.8
All Above 1m	62,165,200	174,216	2.8

The group of 62.2m individuals represent all adults with wealth over $1m. Their average wealth was 2.8 million$, representing a total of 174 trillion$. Source: wir2022.wid.world/methydology

The problem for change is that this is also the group with the most power, political influence, and access to the legal and communication infrastructures. They will not easily accept a cut in their remuneration. (As the joke says, 'Turkeys never voted for Christmas').

To remind ourselves: almost half of the world's net wealth (46.1%) is held by 1% of global population. The top 10% of adults hold 85.5% of global wealth. The remaining 14.5% of the world's total wealth is shared by the remaining 90% of global population.

To start making the world a more moral, a more just place, we need to recalibrate our levels of earning, inheritance and profits from shares and investments, adding in equal education for all just as a beginning. Then we need those of us who have more to give more, because it will take some time to hopefully implement some of the suggestions in this book and we need to start making it better immediately. So, I suggest we give 1% of our wealth each year from the age of 50.

The same message has been given over and over by religion, all religions across the world. It's simply that, in the increasingly secular societies where wealth is largely held, we've stopped listening. Every religion and faith are quite clear that we should all be giving:

> 'And they give food, in spite of their love for it, to the needy, the orphan, and the prisoner.' - Quran 76:8 (Islam)

> 'One who is kind to the poor lends to the Lord, and he will reward him for what he has done.' - Proverbs 19:17 (Christianity)

> 'He who has surplus wealth should give it to him who does not have enough, so that he may live a life of comfort.' - Baba Tahir (Sufism)

> 'A man's wealth is not in the abundance of his possessions.' - Luke 12:15 (Christianity)

> 'The rich should give to the poor out of compassion, not from a sense of duty.' - Confucius (Confucianism)

> 'The gift of wealth is not given to benefit ourselves, but to benefit others.' - The Sutras of the Wise (Buddhism)

> 'Wealth which is not used for helping others is like a poisonous snake.' - Mahatma Gandhi (Hinduism)

> 'The rich have a duty to give to the poor.' - Tao Te Ching (Taoism)

> 'The path of the wealthy is to give generously to the poor.' - The Baha'i Faith

> 'The rich have a moral obligation to use their wealth to help the poor and disadvantaged.' – Sikhism

> 'The rich should use their wealth to benefit others, especially the poor and needy.' – Zoroastrianism
>
> 'The rich should share their wealth with those in need, for it is a blessing to give to others.' – Rastafarianism
>
> 'The rich should use their wealth to benefit society, not just themselves.' - Unitarian Universalism
>
> 'Wealth is a blessing, and it is our duty to use it to help others.' – Hinduism
>
> 'The greatest act of charity is to help someone become self-sufficient.' – Jainism

That last quote, from Jainism, is at the very root of what I am trying to convey in this book. It should be clear from the above that every religion and every faith is saying the same. I have tried to find as many quotes as I can to show that all the religions and all faiths say that the rich should give to the poor, that the wealthy should distribute part of their money to help the disadvantaged. Let's repeat that: all religions, and all faiths carry the same message of giving. We should give money to those less well-off. We should share what we have achieved.

There is a complex discussion required about how to do this and to make sure that the wealth shared is used effectively. Many individuals have already donated significant amounts, their pledges are often intended to be fulfilled over their lifetimes or through their estate after death. Bill Gates, co-founder of Microsoft, and his ex-wife Melinda French Gates, have pledged to give away between 50% and 100% of their wealth, as have Warren Buffett, CEO of Berkshire Hathaway; Mark Zuckerberg, CEO of Meta (formerly Facebook), and his wife Priscilla Chan; Chuck Feeney, co-founder of Duty-Free Shoppers; Paul Allen, co-founder of Microsoft; Sir Tom Hunter, Scottish entrepreneur; Michael Bloomberg, founder of Bloomberg

L.P.; and George Soros, investor and philanthropist. In Paul Allen's case, his Atlantic Philanthropies closed in 2020 having disbursed all its funds. There is more detail of these and other philanthropic donations in Appendix 1.[27]

Along with billionaire Bill Gates, Warren Buffett co-founded The Giving Pledge,[28] and made a public call for other billionaires to give away more than half their wealth. However, we need to see how much of this will be real positive action which will filter down and make life better for some of the poor and how much of it is simply a PR and communication initiative. Here are a few examples of the money being transferred, and questions arising.

In 2019, Laurene Powell Jobs - widow of Steve Jobs, and inheritor of most of his wealth - donated $11.5 million to the Emerson Collective, a philanthropic organisation that she founded.[29]

In 2017, Melinda Gates - co-founder with her ex-husband of the Bill & Melinda Gates Foundation - donated $100 million to the Centre for Global Development, a think tank that focuses on global poverty and development.

In 2022, MacKenzie Scott - ex-wife of Amazon boss Jeff Bezos - donated $4.36 billion to 465 organisations working on a variety of causes, including education, economic opportunity, and climate change.

In 2021, Sean Parker - co-founder of Napster, first President of Facebook - donated $1 billion to the Parker Foundation to support efforts in global health, education, and climate change.

In 2020, Ray Dalio - investor, hedge fund manager, founder of Bridgewater Associates - donated $100 million to the Long Now Foundation to support long-term thinking and planning.

In 2019, John and Laura Arnold - John Arnold founded Arnold Ventures LLC, and was formerly at Enron; Laura Arnold was a mergers and acquisition lawyer - donated $400 million to Arnold Ventures to support evidence-based policy reforms in the areas of criminal justice, education, and health care.

In 2018, Ted Turner - founder of CNN - donated $1 billion to the United Nations Foundation to support sustainable development and global health.

As of August 2024, there are 240 signatories, from 30 countries to the Giving Pledge, who have pledged over $500 billion in total. It would be good to see a lot more of the actual promises taking place, before the donors are no longer with us. My suggestion as outlined above is that the top 1% at least start giving 1% of their wealth away each year for a minimum of 10 years. The world's richest five individuals each have significantly more than $100 billion.[30] So $500 billion is not as large as it sounds.

Name	Commitment (%)	Achievements
Bill Gates	50	Bill & Melinda Gates Foundation has given $60+ billion, focusing on global health (e.g., malaria eradication, polio), poverty, and education. They have also supported initiatives for COVID-19 vaccine distribution and climate change mitigation.
Warren Buffett	99	Has given away over $46 billion, mostly to the Gates Foundation. His contributions support health initiatives, education, and tackling global poverty. Buffett has also supported reproductive health and nuclear threat reduction.
Mark Zuckerberg	99	Through the Chan Zuckerberg Initiative, committed $3 billion to cure diseases by the end of the century. They also support education reform and personalized learning, criminal justice reform, and affordable housing.
Laurene Powell Jobs	50	Focuses on education and immigration reform through

(Steve Jobs)		Emerson Collective. Key initiatives include funding for Dreamers (undocumented students) and investments in media and journalism to promote social justice.
Chuck Feeney	100	Gave away $8 billion, primarily through Atlantic Philanthropies, focusing on education (e.g., Cornell University, Limerick University), health (e.g., Vietnam Assistance for the Handicapped), and human rights.
Paul Allen	50	Through Vulcan Inc., contributed $2 billion to various causes including science (e.g., Allen Institute for Brain Science), education (e.g., Upstream Music Fest + Summit), and wildlife conservation (e.g., elephant protection).
Sir Tom Hunter	70	Sir Tom Hunter has pledged to donate a substantial portion of his wealth to philanthropy throughout his lifetime, potentially reaching £1 billion. However, this is a pledge, current donations $63m .
Michael Bloomberg	100	Given $12+ billion, focusing on public health (e.g., anti- smoking campaigns, COVID-19 response), the arts (e.g., Bloomberg Philanthropies' arts program), and the environment (e.g., Beyond Carbon initiative).
Oprah Winfrey	50	Donated over $2.9 billion, focusing on education (e.g., Oprah Winfrey Leadership Academy for Girls), disaster relief (e.g., Hurricane Katrina, COVID-19 relief), and supporting women and children through various grants.

George Soros	50	Given $18 billion to Open Society Foundations, supporting democracy (e.g., anti-corruption initiatives, legal reform), human rights (e.g., Roma rights, LGBTQ+ rights), and education (e.g., scholarships for marginalized groups).
Melinda French Gates	Not specified	Continues significant contributions through the Gates Foundation. Focus areas include global health, development, education, and climate change.
Elon Musk	50	Focuses on science and technology advancement, including renewable energy projects, space exploration (SpaceX), and artificial intelligence (OpenAI). Musk has also contributed to COVID-19 relief efforts.
Richard Branson	Not specified	Contributions through Virgin Unite, focusing on social and environmental issues, such as climate change, conservation, and supporting entrepreneurs. Branson also supports global health initiatives and conflict resolution.
David Sainsbury	Not specified	Focuses on scientific research and education through the Gatsby Charitable Foundation, which funds neuroscience research, plant science, and technology in education. Sainsbury also supports social mobility and public policy.
Azim Premji	50	Through the Azim Premji Foundation, focuses on education (e.g., teacher training, school infrastructure), healthcare (e.g., supporting public health systems), and rural development. Premji has donated billions to these causes.

George Lucas	Not specified	Contributions through the George Lucas Educational Foundation, which promotes innovative educational practices. Lucas has also donated to arts and cultural institutions, and has funded the preservation of historic sites.
MacKenzie Scott	Not specified	Donated over $12 billion to various causes including racial equality, LGBTQ+ rights, public health, and climate change. Scott's unrestricted donations have empowered many nonprofits to address urgent needs.
Ted Turner	Not specified	Contributions through the Turner Foundation focusing on environmental conservation, including wildlife protection, sustainable energy, and water resource management. Turner also supports UN causes and public health.
Jeff Skoll	Not specified	Focuses on social impact through Participant Media, which produces socially relevant films and documentaries, and the Skoll Foundation, which invests in social entrepreneurs addressing critical global issues.
Reed Hastings	Not specified	Contributions to education through the Hastings Fund, including support for charter schools, education technology, and policy reform. Hastings also supports initiatives for criminal justice reform and rural broadband access.

In fact, once you investigate the details, in some cases the pledges are not very meaningful. For instance, we should try to donate money while we are still alive to make sure it is adequately distributed, using efficient charities and causes that see the money goes to the poorest and that it is not spent on offices and admin.

Here are some thoughts on the rich giving to the poor:

> 'The rich must live more simply, so that the poor may simply live.' - Mahatma Gandhi
>
> 'The rich man is not one who is in possession of much, but one who gives much.' - St. Augustine
>
> 'The only true wealth is the good we do in the world.' - Muhammad Ali
>
> 'It is not the rich man's wealth that makes him rich, but rather his compassion and kindness.' – Confucius
>
> 'We are all wealthy in proportion to the things we can do without.' - Henry David Thoreau
>
> 'The greatest wealth is to live content with little.' – Plato
>
> 'The best way to find yourself is to lose yourself in the service of others.' - Mahatma Gandhi
>
> 'The rich should be asking themselves not how little they can get away with giving, but how much they can afford to give.' - Bill Gates
>
> 'The rich should give more, because they can.' - Warren Buffet

> 'The richest among us have a responsibility to use their wealth to make a positive impact on the world.' - Oprah Winfrey
>
> 'The wealthy have a responsibility to give back to society and to use their wealth for the greater good.' - Mark Zuckerberg
>
> 'Those who have been blessed with wealth have a responsibility to use it to make the world a better place.' - Paul Tudor Jones
>
> 'The wealthy have a moral obligation to use their wealth to make a positive impact on society.' - Howard Schultz
>
> 'Businesses owned by responsible and organised merchants shall eventually surpass those owned by wealthy rulers.' - Ibn Khaldun[31]

All these statements are valid, and - if nothing else - we need to look at all the completely unnecessary things that we are spending on. People starve, children are dying but we find plenty of money to buy handbags, jewellery, super yachts, and bejewelled watches that still only function to tell the time. One could make a very long list of items that are not essential for a healthy life, but rather are expressions of vanity. In this context, how crass to say: "I have money. I can afford to spend it on this." Or "I have succeeded, and this is one of the badges of my success." Is it really a badge of success? Or does it, rather, signal a lack of morality and compassion? When taken to excess, we can surely all agree this kind of excessive consumption is wrong? At least it shows a lack of humanity and morality.

What is the most effective way to donate?

The most effective way to donate depends on an individual's goals and priorities. Some people may prioritise donating to organisations that provide immediate relief to those in need, while others may prefer to donate to organisations that work on long-term solutions to social issues. When determining the most effective way to donate, there are some very important considerations.

For instance, thoroughly research any organisation you are considering donating to, including their mission, their goals, and how they use their funds. You may find a cause that's attractive to you, but discover that 10% or more of income goes on admin.

Consider the impact that the organisation has on the issue or community it is working with. Can the organisation conclusively demonstrate a significant difference in the lives of those they serve?

An emotive response to an emerging or existing crisis can draw millions into donating, hooked in the moment. You may prefer to look for organisations that have a long-term approach to addressing social issues, rather than just providing temporary relief. This, for me, is one of the most important areas to give, where it will have long-term benefit. Empowering the disenfranchised and helping them improve their situation must surely be the goal of any giving, rather than temporary relief?

It is important to donate to organisations that are transparent about their finances and how they use donations. I'm in the process of setting up my own charity which I will fund, and which will distribute 100% of the money received. I will fund the administration and other costs. The percentage of money of any charity that is spent on administration and office space should be very low. There is a very useful book by Alexandre Mars titled *Giving: Purpose Is The New Currency*,[32] which explains in detail the charity that Mars has set up, in which he states, "We can now change the world one small donation at a time". A percentage of the money generated by sales of this book will be given to Epic. "Epic is a global foundation that curates and supports game-changing nonprofits to accelerate social change and build a more just, equitable and sustainable world. Epic applies a thorough and cutting-edge sourcing, vetting and monitoring process. Epic builds and manages two portfolios of groundbreaking social organizations: Children & Youth and Environment & future generations. Epic embodies and encourages innovative and strategic giving. The foundation bridges the gap between donors and charities through transparency, trust and accountability to its community of donors. Epic pools the resources of diverse donors - individuals and families, entrepreneurs, corporates, funds and financial institutions etc.- who want to invest strategically in social impact, carefully monitors the organizations of its portfolios and reports back. Epic acts as an innovative philanthropic one-stop shop, and tailor giving solutions that are adapted to its donors and what they do. Epic's Advisory Board covers 100% of operational expenses to ensure that 100% of the donations received go to the nonprofits in their portfolio." By donating a portion of the proceeds from this book to Epic, we hope to contribute to their impactful work and inspire others to join the movement for a more just and equitable world.

Consider also your personal values and what causes you are most passionate about. Donating to organisations that align with your values will likely be more fulfilling and meaningful.

Chapter 4 - The 10 key points

1. Extreme Wealth Inequality: The global distribution of wealth is highly unequal, with the top 1% owning a disproportionate share while the bottom 50% struggle with poverty.

2. The Elite's Dependence on the Masses: The wealth of the elite is generated and sustained by the labour, consumption, and investments of the global population.

3. Inherited Advantages of the Elite: The elite benefit from inherited wealth, superior education, and access to powerful networks, perpetuating inequality and limiting social mobility.

4. The Need for Tax Reform: The tax system needs to be reformed to ensure a fairer distribution of wealth and income, including addressing tax avoidance and evasion by the wealthy.

5. Universal Basic Income (UBI): UBI should be considered as a potential solution to address job losses due to automation and provide a safety net for all citizens.

6. Curbing Excessive Executive Pay: The excessive earnings of top executives need to be addressed to promote a more equitable society and reduce the gap between the rich and the poor.

7. International Cooperation on Tax: International laws and agreements are needed to prevent tax evasion,

money laundering, and the exploitation of loopholes by corporations and wealthy individuals.

8. Whistleblower Protection: Protecting and rewarding whistleblowers who expose tax evasion and other financial misconduct is crucial for ensuring accountability and transparency.

9. A More Equitable Wealth Distribution: The author proposes a fairer model of wealth distribution, with specific income targets for different segments of the population and limits on extreme wealth accumulation.

10. The Role of Philanthropy: Encouraging the wealthy to donate a portion of their wealth to address social issues and promote a more just world is emphasised as part of the solution to inequality.

Footnotes – Chapter 4

[1] According to the Worldometer elaboration of the latest United Nations estimates, the current world population as of January 10, 2025, was 8,205,080,000. The world population is growing at a rate of around 0.88% per year, adding around 70 million people per year to the total. The population is expected to reach 9 billion in 2037 and 10 billion in 2058. However, the growth rate is expected to decline in the coming years, reaching below 0.50% by 2048, reaching 0 in 2086, and declining by -0.11% in 2100.

[2] https://www.worldometers.info/world-population/

[3] https://www.insee.fr/en/outil-interactif/5543645/tableau/50_MTS/53_SRA

[4]As of November 5, 2023, there were reportedly 2,668 billionaires in the world, according to Forbes' Real-Time Billionaires list. This number has fluctuated in recent years, reaching a high of 2,755 in 2021 and a low of 2,640 in 2023. The United States has the most billionaires of any country, with 735, followed by China (including Hong Kong and Macau) with 562. India has the third-highest number of billionaires, with 169. Most billionaires have made their fortunes in technology, finance, and retail. The top 10 richest people in the world are all multi billionaires, with a combined net worth of over $1 trillion. Other sources place the number of billionaires at just over 3,000.

[5] https://www.ubs.com/global/en/wealthmanagement/family-office-uhnw/reports/global-wealth-report-2023/exploring.html

[6] True rags-to-riches stories: These are uncommon. The Forbes 400 list assigns a "self-made score," with 10 indicating starting from poverty. In 2023, only 29 out of 279 self-made billionaires on the list received a perfect 10 [source: Forbes].

[7] https://ips-dc.org/inequality-org/

[8] Institute for Policy Studies (IPS) that found the top 1% of Americans inherit more than 60% of all wealth passed down each year was published on October 30, 2018.

[9]2014 report titled "College enrolment among low-income students still trails richer groups" discusses the challenges low-income students face in attending college, even high-achieving ones https://www.pewresearch.org/short-reads/2014/01/15/college-enrollment-among-low-income-students-still-trails-richer-groups/.

[10] https://www.opensecrets.org/elections-overview/donor-demographics

[11] Reduced Social Mobility: Studies by the Institute for Fiscal Studies (https://ifs.org.uk/) show that social mobility in the UK is low compared to other developed countries. This means someone's background has a strong influence on their future success. Inherited wealth and attending elite schools solidify this pattern, limiting opportunities for those without such advantages. Inequality: The gap between the UK's rich and poor has been widening for decades. This can lead to social unrest, decreased trust in institutions, and a decline in overall well-being. Reports by the Joseph Rowntree Foundation (https://www.jrf.org.uk/) document the extent of UK poverty.

[12] Note 14, Appendix 1 for more information on movement of Russian people

[13]There are five income groups that the World Bank uses to classify countries: Low-income countries (LICs): These are the poorest countries in the world, with a gross national income (GNI) per capita of $1,135 or less in 2022. Some examples of LICs are Burundi, Ethiopia, and Haiti. chartsbin.com Lower-middle-income countries (LMICs): These countries have a GNI per capita of between $1,136 and $4,465 in 2022. Some examples of LMICs are Bangladesh, India, and Nigeria. www.researchgate.net Upper-middle-income countries (UMICs): These countries have a GNI per capita of between $4,466 and $13,845 in 2022. Some examples of UMICs are China, Brazil, and Mexico. www.oecd-ilibrary.org High-income countries (HICs): These are the richest countries in the world, with a GNI per capita of $13,846

or more in 2022. Some examples of HICs are the United States, Canada, and Japan. en. wikipedia.org Non-classifiable countries: These are countries that do not have sufficient data to be classified into one of the four income groups. There are currently only a few non-classifiable countries, such as Liechtenstein and Monaco.

[14]https://www.lawgazette.co.uk/news/lawyers-under-fire-the-duty-to-report-clients-fraud-is-an-erosion-of-legal-privilege-and-could-put-solicitors-in-danger-/21256.article

[15] Note 15, Appendix 1, tax avoidance by advisors

[16] https://www.theguardian.com/news/2016/apr/03/what-you-need-to-know-about-the-panama-papers

[17] https://www.bbc.com/news/topics/cxw7q5e7ldet

[18] https://www.amazon.com/Technofeudalism-Killed-Capitalism-Yanis-Varoufakis/dp/1685891241

[19] Note 16, Appendix 1, Rich people

[20] https://www.oxfam.org/en/tags/inequality

[21] sales of luxury goods have been increasing out of proportion to the general growth of the economy over the last 20 years.

According to a report by Bain & Company, the global luxury goods market grew by 15% in 2022, reaching a total value of

€305 billion. This is significantly faster than the global economy, which grew by just 3.6% in 2022.

[22] 1. Debbie Wingham (Handbag) – $6.7 Million
2. Mouawad 1001 Nights Diamond Purse – $3.8 Million
3. Hermes Kelly Rose Gold – $2 Million
4. Hermes Birkin Bag by Ginza Tanaka – $1.4 Million
5. Hermes Chaine'd Ancre Bag – $1.4 Million
6. Hermès Himalaya Birkin (Price: Upwards of $300,000)
7. Chanel Diamond Quilted Purse with 18K Gold Hardware (Price: Upwards of $250,000)
8. Hermès Matte Black Birkin with Palladium Hardware (Price: Upwards of $200,000)
9. Louis Vuitton Petite Malle Monogram Shadow Box
10.Fendi Selleria Cuff Bag in Mink (Price: Upwards of $100,000)

[23] https://aflcio.org/paywatch/company-pay-ratios

[24] https://chiefexecutive.net/romettys-legacy-leading-to-ibms-promised-land/

[25] Note 17, Appendix 1, Excessive bonuses

[26]https://www.ftc.gov/enforcement/refunds/equifax-data-breach-settlement#:~:text=In%20September%20of%202017%2C%20Equifax,50%20U.S.%20states%20and%20territories

[27] Note 18, for A. more philanthropy and B. efficient charities

[28] a 2022 report by Oxfam, the world's 10 richest men own more wealth than the bottom 40% of the world's population combined. This level of inequality is simply unsustainable, and more needs to be done to redistribute wealth and create a more equitable society. There are several ways to achieve this, including: Progressive taxation: This means the rich should pay a higher percentage of their income in taxes than the poor. This would generate more revenue that could be used to fund social programs, such as education, healthcare, and housing. Living wages: All workers should be paid a living wage, which is enough to afford necessities such as food, housing, and healthcare. Investment in education and infrastructure: Investing in education and infrastructure can help create jobs and opportunities for the poor. Breaking up monopolies: Monopolies can drive up prices and stifle competition, which can harm the poor. Breaking up monopolies can help create a more competitive market and lower prices. Achieving economic equality will require a concerted effort from governments, businesses, and individuals. However, it is a goal that is worth striving for, as it can lead to a more just and equitable society for all.

[29]pledged to spend $3.5bn through Waverley by 2035. (The best information I can uncover is behind a paywall).

https://www.insidephilanthropy.com/home/2024/3/7/what-happened-to-laurene-powell-jobs-and-leonardo-dicaprios-once-ambitious-green-group#:~:text=Laurene%20Powell%20Jobs%2C%20for%20instance,spend%20%243.5%20billion%20by%202035

[30]Estimate based on recent reports (as of April 1, 2024): Bernard Arnault & family: $235.6 billion (source: Forbes India) Jeff Bezos: $192.8 billion (source: Forbes India) Elon Musk: $188.5 billion (source: Forbes India) Mark Zuckerberg: $169.8 billion (source: Forbes India) Bill Gates: $154 billion (source: AP News)

[31] Ibn Khaldun is an interesting 14th/15th century Islamic philosopher and one of the first acknowledged economists - he was the first to notice (800 years ago!) that civilians don't mind being taxed for the benefit of all, but that there's a tipping point in the amount of tax levied where they begin to feel ripped off.

[32] https://www.amazon.com/Giving-Purpose-Currency-Alexandre-Mars/dp/0062912402

CHAPTER 5

How Wealth Was Created

It is a fair observation to make that the origin of most inherited wealth is clouded in violence, exploitation, and even downright criminality by today's laws and standards. So, since the wealth itself was frequently undeserved, it follows that the fruits of that wealth - the advantages that fall to successive generations - is therefore also undeserved.

Let's agree for our purposes that wealth can be, among other things, the accumulation of money, letters of credit, shares, farms, land, forests, rivers, companies, production facilities, and precious items such as gold, silver, diamonds, rubies, emeralds or works of art.

The accumulation of wealth and power has traditionally been based on strength, violence, the sword, and later the gun. The strong took from the weak, and promoted themselves to chief, leader, lords, kings and queens. Is there any doubt that, historically, wealth has come from subjugating people, amassing slaves and servants to work at their master's behest, thereby growing their master's wealth?

Slavery, it is worth noting here, has existed throughout human history. In the Middle Ages, for instance, the slave trade centred on Russia was probably as big as the transatlantic slave trade, which is now the focus of all attention, as if it were the only slave trading ever to happen. Two points of interest:

Britain was the first country in history to legislate to criminalise slave trading; and, there are very likely more slaves in the world in 2024 than at any time in history,[1] somewhere between three and five times that of the transatlantic slave trade.[2]

The use of subjugated people makes further wealth possible. There were/are mines to be exploited; mineral resources to be realised; a mill to be built on the river or water you controlled. If your neighbour had more wealth than you, you could combine your families through marriage, or you might take their assets through violence. If another country had more than yours and you wished to keep your team happy and under control, you invaded and took what you wanted.[3]

Advances in population and income over the past millennium have been sustained by three interactive processes: conquest or settlement of relatively empty areas which had fertile land; new biological resources, which would include new crops and livestock; or a potential to accommodate transfers of population, crops, and livestock. Nomadic tribes, explorers and travelling merchants opened up international trade and capital movements. Technological and institutional innovation have added to the potential for even greater wealth.

Most wealth, though, has its origin in violence. Access to an advantage granted via status, political nous or negotiating skills have been mostly consequential to acts of violence.

And since wars, invasions, power struggles, coup d'états and slavery have all created wealth, our basic proposition is that much wealth has been created immorally, using advantages not open to everyone, or through access and patronage consequent to those immoral acts. We will call this *undeserved wealth*. Inheritance from undeserved wealth is largely *unwarranted. Unwarranted inheritance* should be limited in consequence of its dubious source.

Let us look at examples of potentially unwarranted inheritance: -

The descendants of the Clive family: Robert Clive was a British military officer and politician who played a key role in the East India Company's conquest of India. His descendants include the Duke of Wellington, the Marquess of Anglesey, and the Earl of Powis.

The descendants of the Van der Hoop family: The Van der Hoop family was a Dutch merchant family involved in the Dutch West India Company. The family's fortune was built on the slave trade and the exploitation of resources in the Americas and Africa. The

Van der Hoop family is still one of the wealthiest families in the Netherlands today.

The descendants of Leopold II of Belgium: Leopold II of Belgium was the personal owner of the Congo Free State from 1885 to 1908, where he exploited the resources of the Congo and forced the Congolese people to work as slaves. His descendants include King Philippe of Belgium and Princess Astrid of Belgium.

The descendants of the Rockefeller family: John D. Rockefeller was an American businessman who co-founded Standard Oil, which became one of the largest and most powerful companies in the world. Rockefeller's fortune was built on the ruthless exploitation of oil workers and brutal elimination of his competitors. His descendants include David Rockefeller Jr. and John D. Rockefeller IV.

The descendants of the Carnegie family: Andrew Carnegie[4] was a Scottish American businessman who founded Carnegie Steel Company, which became one of the world's largest steel companies. Carnegie's fortune was built on the exploitation of steel workers and the use of child labour. His descendants include Andrew Carnegie III and Margaret Carnegie Miller.

The descendants of the Vanderbilt family: Cornelius Vanderbilt was an American businessman who founded the New York Central Railroad, which became one of the largest railroad companies in the world. Vanderbilt's fortune was built on the exploitation of railroad workers and the use of government subsidies. His descendants include Alfred Vanderbilt III and George Vanderbilt III.

The descendants of the Astor family: John Jacob Astor was a German American businessman who made his fortune in the fur trade and real estate. Astor's fortune was built on the exploitation of Native Americans and the displacement of poor people. His descendants include Vincent Astor and John Jacob Astor IV.

The descendants of the Gould family: Jay Gould was an American businessman who made his fortune in railroads and finance. Gould's fortune was built on corruption and manipulation. His descendants include Edwin Gould I and George Gould I.

The descendants of the Mellon family: Andrew W. Mellon was an American businessman and politician who served as Secretary of the Treasury under Presidents Warren G. Harding, Calvin Coolidge, and Herbert Hoover. Mellon's fortune was built on banking and oil. His descendants include Paul Mellon and Andrew W. Mellon II.

The descendants of the Walton family: Sam Walton was an American businessman who founded Walmart, the world's largest retailer. Walton's fortune was built on exploiting workers and suppliers. His descendants include Jim Walton and Rob Walton.

The descendants of the Rothschild family: The Rothschild family is a banking dynasty that originated in Frankfurt, Germany. The family played a key role in financing the Napoleonic and other European wars. The Rothschild family is still one of the world's richest families today.

The descendants of the Koch family:[5] Fred Koch was an American businessman who founded Koch Industries, one of the world's largest private companies. Koch's fortune was built on oil and gas. His descendants include Charles Koch and David Koch.

The descendants of the Mars family: Frank C. Mars was an American businessman who founded Mars, Incorporated, one of the world's largest confectionery companies. Mars' fortune was built on the exploitation of child labour and the use of unethical marketing practices. His descendants include Jacqueline Mars and Forrest Mars, Jr.

Let's look at a *fictional* family history to understand how wealth has been created.

The Blackthorn-Ashcroft Family Saga:
A Six-Century Legacy of Power, Exploitation, and Moral Reckoning

15th Century: Foundations Forged in Blood and Steel

The Blackthorn-Ashcroft family's ascent begins with Elias Blackthorn, a ruthless soldier who thrives amidst the bloodshed of the Wars of the Roses. His prowess in battle garners him not only a modest fortune in plundered riches but also a substantial grant of land from the victorious Yorkist king. This initial acquisition, while tainted by violence, forms the cornerstone of the family's burgeoning wealth. Elias, a shrewd manager, expands the estate through ruthless land consolidation, often displacing tenant farmers and exploiting vulnerable communities. This marks the beginning of a pattern of wealth accumulation built upon the suffering of others.

16th Century: Mercantilism, Piracy, and Royal Favour

Elias' son, William Blackthorn, inherits his father's ambition and ruthlessness. He expands the family's wealth through a combination of legitimate trade and covert piracy, capitalising on the burgeoning era of exploration. William's cunning and ruthlessness, coupled with well-placed bribes to court officials, secures him royal favour, further solidifying the family's position and paving the way for greater expansion.

17th Century: The Slave Trade and Imperial Ascendancy

By the 17th century, the Blackthorns had woven themselves into the fabric of the British aristocracy, securing marriage with the influential Ashcrofts, and currying favour with the monarchy. This privileged position enables them to exploit the burgeoning transatlantic slave trade. Their ships, flying the British flag and protected by royal patronage, became notorious for their brutal efficiency in transporting enslaved Africans to plantations in the Americas. The immense profits from this abhorrent trade fuels the family's rise to prominence, funding opulent lifestyles and lavish estates. In the West Indies, the family establishes vast sugar plantations, where enslaved Africans are subjected to brutal conditions, with many dying from overwork, disease, and malnutrition. Back in England, the family's relentless pursuit of profit leads to the enclosing of common lands, dispossessing countless peasants and forcing them into poverty and destitution. Many die of starvation or are imprisoned for petty crimes like stealing bread, with some being transported to the penal colony of Australia.

18th Century: Industrial Dominance and the Plantation Economy

The Industrial Revolution presents new opportunities for the Blackthorn-Ashcroft family to expand its wealth and influence. They invest heavily in manufacturing, exploiting cheap labour and new technologies to dominate industries ranging from textiles to steel. In parallel, they acquire vast plantations in the Caribbean, where enslaved Africans are forced to cultivate sugar, tobacco, and other cash crops, further enriching the family's coffers. Their children, educated at prestigious institutions like Eton, Harrow, Oxford and Cambridge, form alliances with the financial elite, ensuring the family's access to capital and political power.

19th Century: Colonial Expansion and the Guise of Philanthropy

The 19th century sees the Blackthorn-Ashcroft family extend its reach into the heart of the British Empire's colonial expansion. They invest in mining operations in Africa and plantations in Asia, exploiting both natural resources and indigenous populations. To mask their exploitative practices, the family engages in performative philanthropy, funding hospitals, schools, and cultural institutions, while simultaneously perpetuating systemic inequality and oppression.

20th & 21st Centuries: Global Conglomerate, Corporate Power, and Land Exploitation

In the 20th and 21st centuries, the Blackthorn-Ashcroft family's wealth and influence continues to grow exponentially. They consolidate their holdings of prime real estate in London and the Home Counties, exploiting antiquated property laws to retain freehold ownership of land while leasing it to tenants for generations. This enables them to extract substantial ground rents, further fuelling their wealth accumulation. Their deep-rooted connections with the banking sector grant them privileged access to new investment opportunities and government schemes, ensuring their continued financial dominance.

As the family diversifies into various industries, including finance, technology, media, and natural resources, their corporate empire expands *globally. They wield significant political influence, shaping policies and regulations to their advantage. However, their legacy of exploitation and injustice has not gone unnoticed. With the rise of social justice movements and increased scrutiny of corporate power, the family faces a reckoning with their past. Demands for reparations and greater social responsibility are forcing them to confront the dark origins of their wealth and to consider how to use their vast resources for genuine social good.* *

* The fictional Blackthorn-Ashcroft family saga is a cautionary tale of ambition, power, and the enduring consequences of exploitation. While their rise to prominence was fuelled by innovation and entrepreneurial spirit, it was also built on the backs of countless victims of war, slavery, colonialism, and land exploitation. Their legacy is stained with the blood and suffering of those they exploited for profit.

****

The accumulation of wealth throughout history is a narrative - like our fictional example - replete with instances of exploitation, conquest, and the subjugation of marginalised groups. While some families rose to prominence through legitimate means such as trade and innovation, many others amassed fortunes through morally reprehensible practices.[6] These practices included slavery, piracy, land theft, and the exploitation of the poor. Examining the histories of various powerful families across different regions and eras reveals a common thread of wealth built upon the backs of others.

In ancient Rome, families like Massimo, Colonna, and Orsini solidified their positions through a combination of political power, military dominance, and economic exploitation. They claimed lineage to ancient Roman families, possibly as a means to legitimise their wealth and power, even though their true origins are shrouded in myth and uncertainty.

The Byzantine Empire's Palaiologos family-maintained power during a period rife with slavery and other forms of servitude. Their wealth and influence likely stemmed from a complex interplay of factors, including control over trade routes, taxation, and military might. These practices often came at the expense of the common people and those living in conquered territories.

European colonialism stands out as a particularly egregious example of wealth accumulation through exploitation. In the United Kingdom, families like Drax and Lascelles profited immensely from the transatlantic slave trade and sugar plantations in the Caribbean. Even the Gladstone family, known for its political contributions, benefited from plantation wealth. This pattern of exploitation extended to other European powers, with various families amassing fortunes through colonialism, mercantilism, and the exploitation of resources and labour in their colonies.

The United States, despite its ideals of freedom and equality, is far from exempt from this history. The Astor family, for instance, made its fortune in fur trading and real estate, often acquiring land through exploitative practices with Indigenous groups. Families like the Washingtons, Jeffersons, Madisons, Lees, and Carringtons all held extensive plantations that relied heavily on the forced labour of enslaved Africans. The Brown family, on the other hand, amassed wealth directly through their involvement in the transatlantic slave trade.

In more recent history, industrialization and the dominance of capitalism have provided new avenues for wealth creation, but they haven't eradicated exploitation. In the United States, as we have mentioned above, families like the Rockefellers and Carnegies built vast fortunes in the oil and steel industries respectively. While their contributions to philanthropy are notable, it's essential to acknowledge that their wealth was amassed during a time of widespread labour exploitation and environmental degradation. Consequently, no-one should feel guilt at the prospect of some of their inherited wealth being diverted to raise up the poorest and most unfortunate on the planet.

Even in modern times, the issue of exploitation persists. The fashion industry, for example, often relies on cheap labour in developing countries, where workers may face unsafe conditions and low wages making clothes for people infinitely better off. Similarly, the technology industry has been criticised for its reliance on conflict minerals, those mined in regions plagued by violence and human rights abuses.

The following table provides a comprehensive overview of families whose wealth can be traced back to exploitative practices.

Family	Country	Primary Source of Wealth/ Exploitation
Astor	USA	Fur trading, land acquired from Indigenous groups
Beckford	Jamaica	Sugar plantations (slave labour)
Brown	USA	Slave trade
Butler	USA	Rice plantations (slave labour)
Carrington	USA	Tobacco plantations (slave labour)
Codrington	Barbados	Sugar plantations (slave labour)
Drax	UK, Barbados	Sugar plantations (slave labour)
Gladstone	UK	Sugar plantations (among other sources)
Lascelles	UK	Sugar plantations
Lee	USA	Tobacco plantations (slave labour)
Madison	USA	Tobacco plantations (slave labour)
Manigault	USA	Rice and cotton plantations (slave labour)
Massimo	Italy	Feudal system, land ownership
Orsini	Italy	Feudal system, land ownership
Palaiologos	Byzantium	Feudal system, taxation
Van Rensselaer	USA	Land grants, tenant farming
Washington	USA	Tobacco plantations (slave labour)
Jefferson	USA	Tobacco plantations (slave labour)

I am expecting to get a lot of criticism for some of the content of this book. But I find it reassuring that some of what I am saying is only repeating what key people from our past, including US Presidents, have said before me.

Comments on inheritance.

'I am in favour of a graduated income tax on big fortunes, and in favour of a graduated inheritance tax.' - Theodore Roosevelt

'The idea of unlimited inheritance is preposterous. We do not wish to leave children the burden of wealth we have accumulated.' - Andrew Carnegie

'Unlimited inheritance is a crime against society, a sin against humanity.' - Louis D. Brandeis

'The principle of inheritance tax is sound. It is not only fair, but it helps to preserve a greater balance in the distribution of wealth.' - Franklin D. Roosevelt

'It is essential that inheritance be limited, for unlimited inheritance is a violation of the principle of equality.' - John Kenneth Galbraith

'Inheritance fundamentally violates the meritocratic justice principle of society. The top of inheritance is not only about wealth, but about values.' - Pirmin Fessler and Martin Schürz[7]

'Unlimited inheritance is a recipe for social and economic inequality, and it is vital that we have limits in place to prevent the concentration of wealth in the hands of a few.'

'The principle of limited inheritance is essential for promoting social justice and ensuring that wealth is distributed more fairly throughout society.' -John Rawls

There is also the scenario that quite soon all money will be electronic, and we will be able to see in aggregate the total cash wealth of the richest. We need to prepare for this time, because one option could be for governments to instigate a negative interest rate where unutilised cash (cash simply sitting there, for the purpose of earning interest) is held in excess of $10 million in a single account or across multiple banks. Implementing this policy would see the bank holding the money charging a fee (the negative interest) on accounts with balances above the threshold. Those holding excessive cash would see their balances gradually decrease over time. This would discourage them from keeping large sums idle and encourage them to find more productive uses for their wealth. With the use of artificial intelligence, governments are also going to be able to inquire where money has come from, what its likely source was, and whether tax has been paid on it or avoided.

Extreme wealth becomes a driver of many debilitating aspects of wider society. Those with wealth cling viciously to the associated privileges, reluctant to share in any meaningful way.

I include myself in that group. Giving my proportion away will still be a struggle, because for our whole lives we are trained to believe that success is measured by money and material possessions. But I know that what I'm suggesting is correct and good for the **We** at the cost of **I**. All money and wealth come from being part of society. Wealth is not created in a vacuum. But it ends up existing in what might as well be a vacuum, for all the access the millions of workers who made it possible have to it.

Meanwhile, the advantages consequent to wealth come from family, status, inheritance, education, and one's position in the pyramid. if you are already 9/10 of the way to the top, it's a lot easier to achieve the final leap. So, I'm proposing that we need to flatten the pyramid and not only make it more moral, but also easier for those at the bottom to move upwards.

If you allow people the opportunities of improvement and advancement you have an alternative to Revolution, because wider availability of opportunities is, in itself, a Revolution.

Chapter 5 - The 10 key points

1. Historical Origins of Wealth: Much of inherited wealth is rooted in morally questionable practices like violence, exploitation, and colonialism.

2. Undeserved Wealth and Inheritance: Wealth acquired through unjust means is considered undeserved, and its inheritance perpetuates inequality and privilege.

3. Examples of Exploitative Wealth Accumulation: The chapter provides historical and contemporary examples of families and individuals who amassed fortunes through slavery, colonialism, and unethical business practices.

4. The Blackthorn-Ashcroft Saga: A fictional narrative illustrates how wealth can be accumulated and passed down through generations, highlighting the enduring consequences of exploitation and the need for a moral reckoning.

5. Persistent Exploitation: Exploitation continues in various forms today, such as the use of cheap labour and conflict minerals in global supply chains.

6. The Need for Reparations: The chapter calls for acknowledging and addressing the historical injustices of colonialism and exploitation, potentially through reparations and greater social responsibility from those who benefited from these practices.

7. Tax Reforms and Wealth Redistribution: The chapter proposes tax reforms, including a wealth tax and

stricter inheritance tax policies, to achieve a fairer distribution of wealth and address historical injustices.

8. Challenging the Elite's Dominance: The power and influence of the elite, who often perpetuate inequality through their control of resources and political systems, need to be challenged and reformed.

9. Promoting Social Mobility: Creating a more equitable society requires providing opportunities for upward mobility, including access to quality education and economic opportunities for all.

10. A Moral Imperative: Addressing the unjust origins of wealth and promoting a fairer distribution of resources is not only an economic necessity but also a moral imperative for creating a more just and sustainable world.

Footnotes – Chapter 5

[1]https://www.lexisnexis.com/blogs/gb/b/compliance-risk-due-diligence/posts/there-are-more-slaves-today-than-ever-before-in-the-history-of-the-world

[2]There were an estimated 50 million people living in modern slavery in 2023 https://www.statista.com/chart/30666/estimated-number-of-people-in-modern-slavery-per-1000/#:~:text=An%20estimated%2050 %20million%20people,report%20Global%20Slavery%20Index%202023 .

[3] Note 19, Appendix 1, examples of territorial grabs

[4] Carnegie might, paradoxically, also be used as a model for giving. He gave most of his fortune to educational and social causes after he retired. 2,500 Carnegie libraries, mostly in America, but also around the world, for instance.

He also said: "A man who dies rich dies disgraced", and wrote an essay titled The Gospel of Wealth, which can be downloaded https://www.carnegie.org/publications/?q=gospel+of+wealth&per_page=25&per_page=25%23!%2Fpublications%2Fthe-gospel-of-wealth%2F

[5] https://www.amazon.co.uk/Dark-Money-History-Billionaires-Radical/dp/0385535597

[6] Note 20, Appendix 1, examples of morally unjustifiable wealth

[7]http://www.pse-journal.hr/en/archive/inheritance-and-equal-opportunity-it-is-the-family-that-matters_6302/#:~:text=Inheritance%20fundamentally%20violates%20the%20meritocratic,about%20wealth%20but%20about%20values.

CHAPTER 6

Politicians and the System

The 2019–24 UK Parliament will enter the record books not only for the extraordinary turnover of prime ministers, chancellors, and cabinet ministers, but also for the record number of 97 MPs from all parties who resigned, were suspended, or apologised to Parliament over sexual misconduct, ethical lapses or bullying and harassment charges. Fifty-eight of them were Conservative. No business organisation could survive nearly 15% of its members falling below acceptable standards of behaviour without major questions over whether it remained fit for purpose, and without putting forward significant proposals for reform.

This is happening in other countries worldwide. There is a need for a major reset of how each country manages itself, and how we all elect our representatives. The first very difficult question is: how long should one person oversee the running of any country?

There is no ideal length of rule for leaders. Different political systems and circumstances may require different approaches to leadership. But while it may be argued that long-term leadership can bring stability and continuity, experience shows us that power - and especially long-term power - does, indeed, corrupt, as the following examples from just the past 50 years demonstrate.

Ferdinand Marcos (Philippines) - Elected in 1965, Marcos initially brought economic growth and stability to the Philippines. However, he became increasingly authoritarian, cracked down on dissent, and enriched himself and his cronies through corruption.

Mobutu Sese Seko (Zaire, now the Democratic Republic of the Congo) - Mobutu took power in a 1965 coup and initially promised to restore order and prosperity. He renamed the country Zaire and ruled as a dictator for over 30 years. During his rule, he became notorious for his corruption and brutality. Estimates vary as to his net worth when he died, but one source put it at $5bn.[1]

Saddam Hussein (Iraq) - Saddam Hussein rose to power in Iraq in the 1970s and implemented several social and economic reforms that initially improved the lives of many Iraqis. However, he became increasingly repressive and used chemical weapons against his own people. He also became a billionaire, and enabled his sons access to his wealth, making them, effectively, billionaires also.

Muammar Gaddafi (Libya) - Muammar Gaddafi came to power in a coup in 1969 and initially implemented several socialist policies. Over time, though, he became increasingly authoritarian, using violence to suppress dissent, and enriched himself to such an extent that there was wide speculation that he had died 'the richest man in the world' (disputed elsewhere).[2]

Jean-Claude Duvalier (Haiti) - Jean-Claude Duvalier inherited power from his father, François Duvalier, in 1971. He initially promised to reform his father's brutal regime, but he soon became just as repressive. He was eventually overthrown in a popular uprising in 1986.

One political construct that has been adopted around the world is the idea of limits to time in office (called a term) before an election must be held; and limits to the number of terms leaders are allowed to serve, after which they must step down. This helps ensure there is regular turnover of leadership and prevents leaders from becoming too entrenched in power.

The ideal length of rule for leaders will depend on the specific needs and circumstances of the country and its people. It is important for leaders to be responsive to the needs of their citizens and to be held accountable for their actions, regardless of how long they have been in office.

But it is true that political systems, having evolved from the past, designed around the needs of the past, have not evolved to face the future. Systems which were probably ok pre-WW2 are now creaking under the challenges posed by a fast-moving technological age. If we think in terms of countries as corporations - Margaret Thatcher's notorious UK PLC, for instance - future governments will be running vastly bigger and more complex businesses than was the case up until, say, the beginning of the 21st century. As home computers, the internet, mobile phones, and other smart devices began to take hold, governments have struggled to keep up with, let alone get ahead of, the steep technological curve.

And having failed to keep up with these developments, governments must now face a future where Artificial Intelligence will dominate. No government in the developed West is remotely ready for such challenges. If we were to start from scratch, as if we were a team of consultants coming in to improve or review a failed company, we would ask, what do we really need? How are we going to run this massive business effectively? To deliver results we would want to ensure there is proper governance and implementation of ESG policies. We would be looking for the best managers, clear agendas, and accountability. Most of all, we would want to know from candidates for leadership of this company, what is their vision for the business: where could it improve, what it needs to ditch, how it might expand.

Politicians rarely have vision. It would be hard to come up with a dozen examples from the last century whereby a President or Prime Minister had guided their country to new and sunny uplands. Perhaps Roosevelt's New Deal? Attlee's NHS? Kennedy's promise to put a man on the moon. Gandhi. Much easier to find leaders who led their people to the gates of hell - Stalin, Hitler, Mussolini, Pol Pot, Idi Amin, Saddam Hussein, Muammar Gaddafi. That particular list is depressingly long.

Apparently, politicians, including leadership candidates, are largely devoid of inspiration. All the more important, then, to limit their time in office to maybe nine years, in increments of three-year terms - one as a representative, one perhaps as a minister, one as First Minister/PM if they reach that pinnacle.

More important is to decide who qualifies to be a representative of the people, as President or Prime Minister, or at the different levels of administration that come below these top positions. Current systems in the West allow people straight out of university with - in the UK, for example - a degree in Philosophy, Politics and Economics. The career path is straight to Head Office of a political party; become an advisor to a representative; be promoted to advisor to a Cabinet Minister (in the UK); then sent to some outback constituency, nominated to be their Party representative. These same people will then be making key decisions that affect the lives of all of us, including how much tax we will pay, having had no experience of the workplace the rest of us toil in.

France stands out as an exception to these low expectations, having an established system - the Grandes Ecoles - dedicated to educating, among other specialisations, future Civil Servants. The standard of public servants this system turns out may be superior to those in other countries. But the ultimate result is the same. Les Grandes Ecoles have been an elite institution feeding an elite into government.[3] Emanuel Macron attended one such, as did all other Presidents of France since Charles de Gaulle created the system, and many of its Prime Ministers.

It's possible that a system like the Grandes Ecoles is a good way of turning out Civil Servants. But we must question whether it, and the private school systems elsewhere in the West that provide so many of our leaders, is filling the pool with suitable candidates to make decisions at democratic government level.

Perhaps a better system would start with disqualifying anyone under 25 from putting themselves forward to be a representative of the people. This would allow us to choose from a pool of people who have worked and paid taxes for a minimum five years. We should also encourage the very best academics, engineers, scientists and business managers to put themselves forward if they are able to carve a limited period out of their career life. Society would benefit from the real-life experience of representatives who have been the cream of their particular crop in a wide range of disciplines.

The case for choosing representatives who have real life experience in managing people and resources is possibly most eloquently made if you look at the percentage of GDP that is controlled by governments in the developed world. It really is quite frightening. The percentage of GDP controlled by the government comes to it in the form of taxes, which are supposed to pay for those services assumed by all governments to be essential - public sector jobs from the armed forces, to policing, to education, social care and, possibly, health.

In France, for instance, the government has 58.0% of GDP, Italy has 56.74%, Germany 49.48%, UK 44.3% and Japan 44.1%, with which to fund public services and the social net. But the departments with oversight for managing individual services are run by people who have no experience, very little appropriate training, and in most cases have come straight from university with no previous work experience. They are also subject to limited accountability. This applies to politicians and officials. Civil servants may be skilled in policy analysis, implementation, and bureaucracy. But they lack the business acumen and entrepreneurial mindset that comes from working in the private sector. This is a challenge when managing large-scale projects or departments that require financial and operational expertise.

And to add to the problems this creates at a bureaucratic level, our elected representatives are still amateurs, people with no training for the job, individuals you would certainly not allow to run a major business if you were the owner. The UK, for example, would also benefit from stopping the 'reshuffle' culture that moves people from one discipline to another within government - head of education one day, minister for finance the next, trained for neither. Since 2010, the Ministry of Justice in the United Kingdom had the following individuals as Secretary of State for Justice (also known as Lord Chancellor) leading up to the 2024 general election:

1. Kenneth Clarke (2010-2012)
2. Chris Grayling (2012-2015)

3. Michael Gove (2015-2016)
4. Elizabeth Truss (2016-2017)
5. David Lidington (2017-2018)
6. David Gauke (2018-2019)
7. Robert Buckland (2019-2021)
8. Dominic Raab (2021-2022)
9. Brandon Lewis (2022)
10. Dominic Raab (2022-2023)
11. Alex Chalk (2023-2024 election)

The Department for Business, Energy, and Industrial Strategy (BEIS) Is another example. How can you develop a strategy if you are only in post for a few months? Even for the cleverest of administrators it must take three to six months to get to grips with the basics of a department that is responsible for 3,640 staff.

Secretaries of State who led the BEIS department during the period from 2016:

1. Greg Clark (July 2016 - July 2019)
2. Andrea Leadsom (July 2019 - February 2020)
3. Alok Sharma (February 2020 - January 2021)
4. Kwasi Kwarteng (January 2021 - September 2022)
5. Jacob Rees-Mogg (September 2022 - October 2022)
6. Grant Shapps (October 2022 - February 2023) Department abolished
7. Kemi Badenoch - Dept for Business and Trade (February 2023-2024 election)

But first we must decide how we elect these people in the first place. Proportional representation is the best way of electing people because it results in the best possible representation of all citizens, instead of a left versus right battle and the focus on gaining media coverage rather than running the country effectively, to make life better for everyone. Proportional representation ensures that there is a discussion: the consensus or compromise tends to the middle ground rather than a continual swing from extreme left to extreme right. The Conservative Party in the UK has been an electoral minority for almost all the 139 years since the 1885 Reform Act and has exploited the first past-the-post voting system and the divisions in the progressive vote to be in government for nearly two-thirds of that time. There has been no concern for what is best for the country and best for the people living in the country. It's all been about winning and retaining power. Very much an elite thought process.

We need to replace the first past-the-post voting system with an electronic proportional voting system. Parties should receive state funding, with a cap on contributions by donors and an overall cap on party income. The current system in America allows interested parties to make massive contributions to political parties and candidates, to buy influence, for their own benefit, rather than for the good of their fellow citizens. Did Elon Musk's PAC give-away of $1 million a day for about 18 days during the 2024 US election, qualify as an attempt to purchase influence? Did this raise ethical and legal questions about Musk's ultimate influence on the election?

Length of all key appointments should be limited to three years maximum with strong limitations on repeat or follow on appointments. If we agree there are four levels at the top: 1. President; 2. Prime Minister/CEO/First minister; 3. Cabinet of 20 +/- members; 4. Junior Ministers, probably between 30 to 40 individuals, depending on the size of the country.

So, let us say, a junior minister having served a three-year term could be promoted to a cabinet minister for a further three years and then ultimately may rise to become Prime Minister for three years only. A Prime Minister, having served those three years, should not be put forward as a candidate for President until at least 10 years has passed. And then would also be restricted to a single three-year term.

But more importantly every Cabinet Minister (head of a department) should, at the beginning of their appointment, have an agreed agenda of key points/KPIs that they plan to achieve, agreed with the PM, and published for all to see. There should be very severe restrictions on the ability to move a minister to a different department once the politician has been appointed to a post to manage that segment of the country's government machine.

Position	Years in office	Length of office	Conditions
President	3	1 term only	Presidents can stand for election again after a significant period out of office
Prime Minister, First Minister	3	1 term only	Can become president after 6-year gap
Cabinet Member 20	3	1 term only	Can move to PM for 1 term
Junior Cabinet Member 20-40	3	1 term only	Can move to full cabinet for 1 term
Elected Representatives 100-300	6	2 terms only	Can move up to full or junior cabinet

There should also be a serious attempt to fill these positions with people who have some experience or relevant knowledge. The wrong person in the wrong job can be catastrophic. It's worth reading at least the introduction to *How Westminster Works...and Why It Doesn't* by Ian Dunt. One case reviewed in the book, if it is correct, gives a very clear example of a minister[4] who it is suggested contributed to a number of deaths, arguably through his probable incompetence and allegedly complete rejection of advice presented. The result of this catastrophe was not the possibility of prison or serious censure, but promotion to cause further harm elsewhere over the next few years.[5] The most remarkable thing about what happened was the promotion and how *un*remarkable it is. There is nothing remotely special about it. The same process takes place in department after department, policy area after policy area, in the

UK. This systemic failure highlights the urgent need for greater accountability and transparency in government. We need to implement mechanisms to ensure that policies are based on evidence, that decision-makers are held responsible for their actions, and that the public interest is prioritised over political expediency.

Ministers need to focus on getting the job right as you would in any business and be marked against success or failure. This applies the world over.[6]

We view the President as the head of state but that is, in most parliamentary republics, a merely ceremonial role. However, at the very least the President should have clear powers to limit the First Minister's ability to shuffle ministers and junior ministers. The President is, effectively, the Chairman, and should also be tasked with ensuring that the police and security forces and military are working to the benefit of the citizens, not to the benefit of any elite or individual group.

There should be no removal of individual ministers unless there is a clear failure to deliver the agenda. A minister who has failed in one department should not be moved to another. Six-monthly reports should be required to compare KPIs against actual progress. 'This is what we have achieved; these are the problems we came across; so, we have not been able to move these forward as we hoped to; here is our revised list of targets for the next six months.'

Salaries need to be at a level where outside income or outside appointments are unnecessary, and disallowed. The ability to obtain jobs after politics, where the role is to lobby the government, communicating with politicians and civil servants, should be banned or severely limited.

Civil servants and advisors should also have real responsibility and have a similar agenda and KPIs that they can be held accountable for against performance. It should be possible to remove civil servants from office for consistently failing to deliver as you would in any normal business. While theoretically it is possible for civil servants to be dismissed it is very much a rarity and an exception. The system takes care of its own. However, they must also be paid a proper salary. Here are examples of approximate salaries for senior civil servants in some countries but note that the majority are at the lower end of the range and the top salary is enjoyed by very few individuals, usually the very top person.[7]

In G7 Countries (USD):

- United States: $150,000 - $250,000+ (Senior Executive Service)
- Canada: $150,000 - $250,000+ (Deputy Minister level)
- United Kingdom: $120,000 - $200,000+ (Permanent Secretary level)
- France: $100,000 - $180,000+ (Directeur d'administration centrale)
- Germany: $100,000 - $180,000+ (Ministerial direktor)
- Italy: $80,000 - $150,000+ (Dirigente Generale)
- Japan: $90,000 - $160,000+ (Administrative Vice-Minister)

When you are running between 45-55% of an entire country these salaries are simply not high enough.

But let's revisit the past. There is no clear date when we moved from a world ruled by Monarchs, Dictators, Emperors and Empresses to rule by the new elite. The 'modern aristocracy' of politicians and Civil Servants in France, for example, were all processed through the Grand Ecoles system (established in 1945), preparing them for a life of public service. In the UK they still seem disproportionately to come from a background of private education and to have graduated from a limited number of universities.

There was a gradual transition from monarchical to parliamentary government, which took place in Europe over centuries. But there are a few key milestones that accelerated the process:

The English Civil War (1642-1651) and the Glorious Revolution (1688) both limited the power of the English monarchy and established the principle of parliamentary sovereignty. The French Revolution (1789-1799) overthrew the French monarchy and established a republic, which served as an inspiration to revolutionaries throughout Europe. The Revolutions of 1848 were a series of uprisings against monarchical rule that led to the establishment of constitutional monarchies or republics in many European countries. These events are also known as the Springtime of Nations or the Spring of Peoples, referring to a series of revolutionary events that occurred across Europe in 1848.

1848 was very much a starting point, when the power of the monarchies began to reduce, and some forms of democracy were introduced. It's important to recognize that this was less than 200 years ago. In France, the February Revolution of 1848 led to the eventual establishment of the French Second Republic, replacing the July Monarchy under King Louis-Philippe. In Germany, the March Revolution of 1848 resulted in widespread uprisings across German states, leading to the Frankfurt Parliament and the adoption of a liberal constitution for a unified Germany. However, these efforts ultimately failed to establish a lasting unified German state. Austria's March Revolution also affected the Austrian Empire, leading to widespread unrest and demands for constitutional reforms. Emperor Ferdinand I was forced to abdicate, and a series of liberal reforms were introduced, although they were later rolled back under Franz Joseph I. The Hungarian Revolution of 1848 resulted in the declaration of Hungarian independence from the Austrian Empire and the establishment of a constitutional monarchy under the Habsburg dynasty, with the Hungarian Diet (parliament) gaining significant power.

As though all this change was infectious, the Revolutions of 1848 played a significant role in changes occurring in many other countries. They led to the beginning of the Italian unification process known as the Risorgimento. Several Italian states experienced uprisings against Austrian and local rulers, leading to the establishment of provisional governments and the push for unification under a constitutional monarchy.

1848 also saw uprisings in various parts of Poland, then divided between the Russian Empire, the Kingdom of Prussia, and the Austrian Empire. These uprisings aimed at achieving Polish independence and constitutional reforms, though they were ultimately suppressed by the occupying powers.

Meanwhile, Belgium had already gained independence from the Netherlands in 1830, and the Revolution of 1848 influenced political developments in the country, leading to constitutional reforms and the strengthening of parliamentary democracy. The impact was also felt in Switzerland, leading to the establishment of the Swiss Federal State through the adoption of a new federal constitution, marking a significant shift towards a more unified and democratic Switzerland; in Denmark, the Revolutions of 1848 led to the adoption of a new constitution, known as the June Constitution, which established a constitutional monarchy with a bicameral (two chamber) parliament and expanded civil liberties; and in Portugal where events began that led to the adoption of a new constitution in 1851, establishment of a constitutional monarchy, and expanded political rights for citizens.

By the late 19th century, most European countries had become constitutional (rather than absolute) monarchies, or republics. There were still a few absolute monarchies left, such as Russia and the Ottoman Empire. These monarchies were overthrown in the early 20th century, during the Russian Revolution and the First World War, respectively. However, despite this flood of radical changes, it took until after the Second World War for many of these countries to move towards full democracy, with women allowed to vote, as we can see from the following chart.

Right To Vote

Country	Right to Vote Women	Right to Vote Men
Norway	1913	1898
Denmark	1918	1915
Germany	1919	1918
Netherlands	1919	1917
United Kingdom	1928	1918
France	1944	1848
Hungary	1945	1920
Italy	1946	1912
Romania	1946	1918
Greece	1952	1864
Switzerland	1971 (federal level)	1848

Thus, the democracy we are currently focused on has only been a reality in most of the developed world for the last 175 years, with suffrage limited initially to the wealthy and property owners.

Women and working men achieved the vote a lot later. More than half of our list above only granted suffrage to women post-WW2. The most recent was Switzerland, granting the right just 54 years ago, in 1971.

So, you could argue that our ideal of democracies enshrining rights for all has only been achieved in the last 75 years.

And while it can be argued that the aristocracies' power has declined in Europe, it is still a significant source of influence in some countries, possibly most notably Great Britain. The British aristocracy, including the nobility and landed gentry, has historically held considerable power and influence in politics, society, and the economy.

Aristocracy throughout Europe has historically exercised similar influence and power. Spain, Italy, France and Germany, for instance, have a long history of noble families with significant land holdings and influence. While Italy's political landscape has undergone significant changes, particularly after the unification of the country in the 19th century, some aristocratic families still hold influence in certain regions. In France the aristocracy historically held immense power and privilege before the French Revolution, which drastically altered the country's social and political landscape. The dynamics in Germany also shifted dramatically in the 20th century, particularly since the abolition of the monarchy after World War I. But some German noble families still have significant land holdings and cultural influence.

Many noble families wherever they exist still hold vast estates and play roles in various sectors. Many have diversified their wealth into investments, businesses, and other assets, so the loss of political and societal influence would not adversely affect their standard of living.

The UK's House of Lords, though, is a standout anachronism, wielding unelected power in plain sight, despite having undergone significant reforms to reduce the influence of hereditary peers, those who inherit the title and property of their forefathers.

Nevertheless, even if we succeed in removing these historically influential families from conduct of our politics, the old aristocracy may be seen to have been replaced by a new aristocracy - the new elite - in many countries, made up of people who have achieved their wealth and power through a variety of means, including business, politics, and the media. The new elite comprises mainly those who are highly educated with degrees from prestigious universities; and with access to financial resources most people do not have. They are also well-connected. They have networks of government, business, and media contacts. They are influential. They can shape public opinion and policy.

Like the old aristocracy, this new elite is often criticised for being out of touch with the concerns and conditions of ordinary people. They are also accused of being more interested in promoting their own interests, wealth, and ilk than they are in the entirety of humanity. We may talk of a meritocracy rather than an aristocracy, but we have seen in recent decades how sheltered the rich and powerful become, how alienated from the interests of the majority.

People who are often considered to be part of the new elite are:

Founders of tech companies; CEOs of large corporations; media moguls; high-level politicians; academics; aristocrats; and sports stars, online influencers, and celebrities.

Tech Billionaires and Entrepreneurs: Individuals who founded or lead massively successful tech companies are now among the world's wealthiest and most influential. Examples: Elon Musk (Tesla, SpaceX), Jeff Bezos (Amazon), Bill Gates (Microsoft), Mark Zuckerberg (Meta/Facebook) Their power comes from enormous wealth; control over technologies that shape our lives; and the ability to shape public discourse through social media ownership.

Global Financiers: CEOs and top executives of major banks, investment firms, and hedge funds. Examples: Jamie Dimon (JPMorgan Chase), Warren Buffett (Berkshire Hathaway), Larry Fink (BlackRock). Their influence stems from control over vast amounts of capital; ability to influence markets and economies; and access to politicians and policymakers.

Media Moguls: Owners and top executives of large media conglomerates and news outlets. Examples: Rupert Murdoch (News Corp), Michael Bloomberg (Bloomberg), the Sulzberger family (The New York Times). Their power derives from control of information flow; ability to shape public opinion and set the agenda; and influence over political narratives.

Top Academics and Think Tank Leaders: Renowned professors at elite universities, particularly those specialising in fields like economics, policy, or technology. Heads of influential think tanks that shape policy debates and provide intellectual backing for political agendas. Their power lies in expertise and intellectual authority; ability to influence policy makers; and shaping the next generation of leaders

Celebrities and Social Media Influencers: stars in film, music, and sports who command large audiences and cultural capital. Social media personalities who have built massive online followings. Their power lies in the ability to command attention and influence public opinion; increasingly used to promote political agendas or endorse products.

Others who might be part of the new elite: Heads of transnational corporations with huge footprints around the globe; top-tier lawyers and lobbyists able to shape and influence legislation; and leaders of international organisations (IMF, World Bank, UN etc.) whose decisions affect millions of lives.

The new elite is not a monolithic group. There is some diversity in terms of their backgrounds, values, and beliefs. However, they all share several common characteristics. The new elite has been forged by several factors, including globalisation of the economy, which has led to the concentration of wealth and power in the hands of a few; the decline of unions and other worker organisations, which has made it more difficult for ordinary people/poor people to have a voice in the workplace and in society; and the rise of social media, which has given a platform to a small number of people to shape public opinion and influence policy.

Throughout history, politicians have played a significant role in shaping the course of human events. While some have undoubtedly made the world a better place, others have left a trail of destruction and despair in their wake.

A list of successful politicians/leaders would include Nelson Mandela, a towering figure in the fight against apartheid. Mandela's unwavering commitment to equality and reconciliation transformed South Africa into a democratic nation.[8] Franklin D. Roosevelt, 32nd President of the United States, guided his nation through the Great Depression and World War II. His leadership, social programs and economic policies helped to lift the country out of its deepest economic crisis and played a crucial role in defeating the Axis powers. Mahatma Gandhi was a symbol of non-violent resistance and led India's struggle for independence from British rule. His philosophy of Satyagraha, emphasising truth and non-violence, inspired countless individuals and movements around the world. As Prime Minister of the United Kingdom during World War II, Winston Churchill's leadership and unwavering determination played a pivotal role in the Allied victory. His speeches and resilience

- which demonstrated an understanding of the attitudes of ordinary people - rallied the British and inspired resistance against Nazi Germany. Eleanor Roosevelt was a champion of human rights and social justice. She was instrumental in shaping the United Nations and the Universal Declaration of Human Rights. Her advocacy for women's rights, racial equality, and the protection of children made a lasting impact on the world. Martin Luther King campaigned for Civil Rights for black people in America, but unlike his counterparts - the Black Panthers, The Nation of Islam, for instance - he adopted Gandhi's nonviolent approach to protest.

Unfortunately, this list is not as long as we would all like, whereas examples of corrupt politicians are part of a predictably much longer list. Saddam Hussein was the brutal dictator of Iraq for over two decades. His reign was marred by human rights abuses, political repression, and wars that caused immense suffering. His invasion of Kuwait in 1990 led to the Gulf War and further destabilised the region. He used nerve gas to inflict attempted genocide on the Kurdish people.

Idi Amin was President of Uganda from 1971 to 1979. Amin's regime was characterised by a brutal ruthlessness, corruption, violence, and economic mismanagement. His reign is estimated to have resulted in the deaths of hundreds of thousands of Ugandans.

Jean-Claude Duvalier, the notorious 'Baby Doc' Duvalier, who ruled Haiti from 1971 to 1986, used his position to enrich himself and his cronies while the Haitian people suffered in extreme poverty and deprivation. His reign was marked by human rights abuses and political repression.

Mobutu Sese Seko was the long-time dictator of Zaire (now the Democratic Republic of the Congo). Mobutu's rule was characterised by corruption, mismanagement, and political violence. His kleptocratic regime plundered the country's resources, leaving the population in poverty and neglect.

Ferdinand Marcos was the authoritarian President of the Philippines for over two decades. Marcos's regime was marked by corruption, human rights abuses, and economic stagnation. His family amassed vast wealth while the country's economy suffered. His wife's shoe collection alone could have cost as much as $3m.

Some of these, as we have noted earlier, may have started off quite well, achieving some good things for their population. But there is no doubt that they ended up corrupt, and that the list of the corrupt is much, much longer than the list of those who achieved good outcomes for their constituents. Why?

Beyond a certain period - and it gets demonstrably worse the longer they are in power - leaders find themselves increasingly surrounded by sycophants, hangers on, flatterers, yes-men and yes-women, court jesters, lackeys and freeloaders, people who are at the table to feed off the crumbs and to be gifted wealth, power, advantage, or position.

The solution is to limit the length of time any one person can be leader of any country. This should be as short as possible. My view is that this should be three years, with a maximum of nine years in government covering all roles - representative, minister, or leader - because the longer leaders cling to power, the more they start to lose contact with reality. The team, advisers, consultants, those they have appointed to ministerial and other posts, the security naturally surrounding them, ensure that they become more and more remote. The team surrounding them are further culpable in this process because no individual wants to be replaced or moved sideways. They want to keep their particular portion of power in their own hands, so they fight against newcomers, new ideas and initiatives that they have not created themselves.

Part of the solution, where 'first past the post' (FPTP) is still operating, is to replace it with proportional representation (PR), a much more democratic electoral system. One of the key benefits is that PR tends to encourage a more diverse range of voices and perspectives within the political landscape. This diversity often leads to greater representation of minority viewpoints and increased political participation from various segments of society.

One of the main reasons for this is that PR systems typically allocate seats in proportion to the overall share of votes each party receives. This means that smaller parties have a better chance of gaining representation, which can help prevent the marginalisation of certain ideas or constituencies. It also means that voters have more options to choose from, as they are not limited to just two major parties, punching each other in the head most of the time, playing a point-scoring game.

Additionally, PR can promote consensus-building and co-operation among political parties. Since no single party usually wins an outright majority of seats, parties often need to form coalitions to govern effectively. This can foster a more collaborative approach to policy making, as parties must negotiate and compromise to advance their agendas.

Furthermore, PR can help mitigate the 'us vs them' mentality that can sometimes arise in winner-takes-all systems like FPTP. By promoting a more inclusive and diverse political landscape, PR encourages dialogue and debate across a wider spectrum of ideas. This can lead to more thoughtful and nuanced policymaking, as different perspectives are considered and debated.

Still, it has to be acknowledged that PR systems - there are several[9] - also have their challenges and drawbacks. They can sometimes lead to more fragmented political landscapes, making it harder to form stable governments. They can also cause the proliferation of smaller parties, which may struggle to effectively represent their constituents or implement their agendas. But overall, while PR is not without its complexities, its proponents argue that its benefits in terms of representation, inclusivity, and deliberation make it a more democratic and effective electoral system in many contexts. But we need to try the new, experiment and develop. What we have in many countries is not fit for purpose, so try the new. But if it's not working move on, try again.

If you can add to PR a proper and efficient way of appointing the rest of the governing team you will really improve the way we are managed. Effectively running a country is the same in many ways as running a major company. What we must do is move away from the short-term seeking of public approval and rating points. One of the ways of doing this as said before is to come up with a new way of appointing the team, just as you would within any business. Every member of the team should have a clear job brief of what they are expected to achieve over the two years of appointment. This brief - KPI's or agenda - should be in writing and should be made public. There should be an assessment every six months, and at the end of the period, as to whether the minister responsible had achieved, at least in part, the agenda. It should be transparent whether they had over-performed or under-performed on any item they had agreed to. Any mitigating circumstances for failure to hit a target, such as a change in the world economy or unexpected disasters, should be taken into account.

If we can follow through in getting rid of monarchies and dictatorships, the normal system going forward should be led by a President who has the role of ensuring the written constitution is followed and monitoring that the actions of the administration are moral and just. The leader of the majority political party, which will lead any coalition, is usually termed Prime Minister or First Minister. This position is effectively as CEO for the country. A team of ministers, 20 or 30, who run the various departments, will be directly responsible to the Prime/First Minister. By having clear written agendas, you can also introduce rules about ministers not being shuffled, and not being removed unless they are significantly failing to deliver.

It is crazy to move ministers from departments with only a short period in each. It must take at least six months to get to grips with any new government department. The measurement of success or doing well should be performing to the brief, to the agenda. Which of course should be adjusted as the world/country changes. The prime minister should not be able to move or fire members of the team, unless they are clearly underperforming.

Part of the President's role should be to monitor this. It's all about checks and balances - to ensure that decisions are made rationally, and that all patronage and favouritism is removed and that proposed limits on politicians' tenure are enforced. Power corrupts, and individuals get used to the trappings and levers of power. By limiting the term, they can serve and by making sure that those who govern the country have clear written agendas that they must perform to, you will arrive at a much more balanced system. The President should have reasonable powers to ensure they can act as gamekeepers and limit the prime minister's ability to play politics.

What we all want is a better outcome, better managed countries, and thus a better life for their citizens.

There are several countries where there are already some limitations on the tenure of president or chief executive. However, there is also an unfortunate trend to enact new laws to overcome this. A number of dictators have extended their terms in office by having the law changed. As a public relations sop to democracy, they proceed with 'elections', but no-one is in any doubt who will be returned to power when the 'votes' are counted.

1. **United States:** The President is limited to serving two terms, each consisting of four years. This restriction was established by the 22nd Amendment to the United States Constitution, ratified in 1951, after President Roosevelt had won a fourth term without disclosing to anyone, let alone the electorate, that he was seriously ill. He died just four months into that fourth term, leaving Vice-President Harry Truman to pick up the pieces.

2. **Mexico:** The President is limited to a single six-year term. This was established in 2014, after a constitutional amendment.

3. **China:** While there is no formal limit on the number of terms a President can serve, the unofficial norm has been two five-year terms. However, in 2018, China removed presidential term limits, allowing President Xi Jinping to potentially serve indefinitely. A good example of the point above.

4. **France:** The President is limited to serving two consecutive five-year terms, as per the 2008 constitutional amendment.

5. **South Korea:** The President is limited to one five-year term.

6. **Brazil:** The President is limited to two consecutive four-year terms.

7. **Argentina:** The President is limited to two consecutive four-year terms.

8. **Indonesia:** The President is limited to two five-year terms.

9. **Philippines:** The President is limited to a single six-year term, as per the 1987 Constitution.

10. **South Africa:** The President is limited to two five-year terms, as per the South African Constitution.

11. **Turkey:** The President is limited to two five-year terms, as per the constitutional amendments adopted in 2017.

As far as possible the government of any territory/country should be as devolved as possible. Efficiency does not come from having large central organisations stuffed with bureaucrats. It comes from having a clear agenda, clear priorities and a good understanding of responsibilities and authority to act. Helping run the 'business' that is controlling 50% of our expenditure and life should be seen as a good and responsible role.

But term limits should apply at all levels. Local governments have a deeper understanding of their communities' unique needs and challenges. Devolution allows them to craft policies and allocate resources that directly address local priorities. Imagine a coastal region needing to invest in seawall defences due to rising sea levels. A devolved government could prioritise this issue more effectively than a central government with broader national concerns. Central bureaucracies are slow and cumbersome. Devolution streamlines decision-making by placing it closer to the point of implementation. Local governments can react faster to emerging issues and experiment with innovative solutions without waiting for central approval.

Switzerland is a perfect example. It is 132nd on a list of countries by size (the UK is 78th), and 101st by size of population (the UK is eight times larger). So, it is a small country, with a small population. This small country is, nevertheless, divided into Cantons, each a semi-autonomous state. The Cantons are then divided into municipalities which govern themselves. There are 26 Cantons, divided into 2,131 municipalities, each with their own power to allow the bigger cities to have their own city parliament. Federal and local tax is raised at Canton level. In a country of 8.7million people, government devolved to 2,131 areas means local government is answerable to an average of 4,000 citizens.

We must, surely, take some lessons from the fact that Switzerland has the sixth richest population in the world by GDP per capita,[10] and places ninth on the list of happiest citizens.[11]

When citizens can hold their local representatives directly accountable for their decisions, it fosters a sense of ownership and civic engagement. Devolution makes it easier for citizens to track how their tax dollars are being spent and express their concerns directly to those in power. Local government meetings are typically more accessible to citizens than national assemblies. Devolution creates opportunities for greater public participation in the decision-making process. This can lead to more inclusive policies that reflect diverse community needs. Devolution also empowers local regions to leverage their unique strengths and resources to spur economic growth. Local governments can tailor economic development strategies to attract businesses and create jobs specific to their region's needs.

However Local governments may lack the expertise or resources to effectively manage devolved powers. Switzerland has 600 years' experience of refining its system and readying its people to represent themselves. Elsewhere, such radical change would require investment in training and infrastructure to achieve success. Devolution can exacerbate existing inequalities, but it is the role of the central government to identify the areas that are under-resourced, making sure the money to uplift is available. Some regions may have stronger administrative capabilities or resource bases than others. Measures to ensure equitable distribution of resources are necessary. When multiple levels of government are involved, ensuring coordinated and accountable decision-making can be complex. Clear lines of responsibility, written and agreed agendas or KPIs and communication channels are essential.

However, if you are arriving from outer space with the daunting task of redesigning Earth's global administration, here are some thoughts, focusing on efficiency and effectiveness:

Observation and Understanding: I'd begin with intensive unbiased research on existing systems of administration – their strengths, weaknesses, and the historical/cultural reasons behind them. Understanding the motivations and needs of diverse populations would be crucial. Look for the core desires of humanity beyond borders: safety, health, opportunity, development, and some form of shared purpose. Analyse where the current systems cause friction, waste, unnecessary conflict, and hinder progress towards common goals.

Data-Driven Decision Making: Prioritise a global infrastructure for collecting and analysing data on everything from resource distribution, environmental impact, public health, to social indicators. Unbiased data would inform every aspect of the new administration.

Roles should be assigned based on skill, experience, and demonstrable management and problem-solving abilities. The days of inherited power and political favours should be over.

Local communities should retain a high degree of autonomy in day-to-day matters that directly affect them. However, a central body with limited authority coordinates on issues that transcend borders (pollution, resource management, etc.) Every decision has a clear rationale available for public scrutiny with rigorous mechanisms to hold those in power accountable.

Accountability is currently a very sore point. Few politicians have ended up in prison or even been prosecuted via the courts, however much their citizens or their country as a whole have suffered due to their actions. So, let's have a proper system going forward. Acknowledge that no system is perfect at inception. Built-in mechanisms for regular review and adaptation, guided by data, are critical.

Implementation – A Phased Approach, Pilot Programs: Test potential administrative models in small, diverse regions. These would prove or disprove concepts quickly and with minimal disruption. Focus initial efforts on universally beneficial solutions easily understood by the public. Successes with issues like clean water access or pandemic response build trust for larger-scale changes. Emphasise that the new system is an evolving toolkit for better self-governance, not a rigid structure imposed by force.

Resistance from Existing Powers: Those enjoying power under old systems will understandably resist change. Managing this involves a mix of diplomacy, demonstration of tangible benefits, and possibly phases of coexistence with legacy systems. Imposing a 'one-size-fits-all' approach would be a disaster. Adapting the framework to varying cultures while maintaining core principles is paramount. Effective administration may call for tech not yet widely accessible. A global infrastructure investment is needed here.

Then you have the thorny question of a second chamber. Do you need the Senate (in America) or the House of Lords (UK)? What are the arguments for having a second chamber? Surely these must be to ensure that the administration does not overstretch itself and take unconstitutional action against the interest of the population. It's about balance and being able to make the legislature reconsider particular aspects of a new law they are looking to enact. This is a critical function in designing a balanced and effective legislature. The second chamber can provide a crucial 'cooling off' period for legislation. The first chamber, necessarily the more proactive house, can be swayed by the passions of the moment. The second chamber allows for a more deliberate review, proposing amendments or even rejecting flawed bills. This fosters better-crafted legislation. First chambers typically focus on geographic representation, with each district electing a representative. Second chambers can offer a different lens, perhaps representing professional bodies, regional interests, or even appointed members with specific expertise. To me there's a very real logic that in a second chamber you would appoint people from the roles in life that contribute to society as opposed to those associated with simply making a profit. So, no need for financiers, insurance brokers or investment bankers. But doctors, dentists, surgeons, nurses, teachers, farmers, people from the caring industry, and also police, prison staff, and artists, should all be present. As should engineers, scientists, mathematicians and historians.

This expands the range of voices considered in law-making. But again, the appointment should be term limited and have no connection to hereditary right. And absolutely the appointment should not be from the political party in power or the leader, First Minister or Prime Minister. And maybe people should be older, 25 or 30 and have had some valuable time in the industry/group they are representing?

Safeguarding against the tyranny of the majority: Even the most democratic elections can cause a situation where a single party holds overwhelming power in the first chamber. A second chamber, potentially with different electoral rules or composition, can act as a check against one party imposing its will on the entire population. Most of all, we have to reach a point of agreement that those to whom we hand the power to legislate and to govern can be held to account for their actions, specifically that they can expect criminal prosecution if their actions, or neglect, lead to public or individual harm or even death.

As mentioned earlier, governments and civil servants are currently managing 40% to 55% of all expenditures of each country, running to hundreds of billions of dollars in bigger countries, trillions in the biggest. Companies that fail in a significant way sometimes see senior managers punished and occasionally sacked (although, as we have said elsewhere, not nearly enough). In politics, even that never seems to happen. In civilian life we seem to prosecute smaller offenders and the weak and underprivileged, whose harm caused to society is a fraction of that caused by corporate and political malfeasance. We need a new approach. Our system and government, our system of administration and civil service has been built up over the last 150 years and essentially it was built on the old imperial model. We need to completely reform governments and civil services, so they are fit for duty, fit for purpose. Fit for our sped-up future.

The contaminated blood scandal in the UK is a tragic example of systemic failure within a government and its healthcare system. Thousands of people were infected with HIV and hepatitis C through contaminated blood products, exemplifying the devastating consequences that can occur when governments prioritise cost-cutting and bureaucratic inertia over the safety and well-being of their citizens. It underscores the urgent need for greater accountability and transparency in government decision-making, especially when it comes to matters of public health. Sadly, it's not an isolated incident. There have been other major catastrophes around the world where administrative failures led to significant harm and suffering, usually to the weakest in society, the least able to litigate or fight back.

Bhopal Gas Tragedy (India, 1984): A leak of toxic gas from a Union Carbide pesticide plant in Bhopal killed thousands and injured hundreds of thousands. Government oversight and safety regulations were lax, contributing significantly to the disaster. The Bhopal Gas Tragedy is a complex case where the question of accountability and criminal liability remains a contentious issue to this day. While there were arrests and legal proceedings, the ultimate outcome has been widely criticised for failing to hold top-level officials and executives accountable. The chairman of Union Carbide, Warren Anderson was arrested but never faced trial in India. He left the country after being briefly detained and died in the US 40 years later, in 2014.

In 2010, 36 years after the disaster, a court in Bhopal convicted seven Indian executives of Union Carbide India Limited (UCIL) of causing death by negligence. They were sentenced to two years in prison but immediately released on bail. This is not accountability.

Despite allegations of corruption and negligence, no Indian politicians or high-ranking government officials were held criminally liable for the disaster. The focus of legal action was primarily on UCIL executives, with allegations that the Indian government shielded Union Carbide officials and prioritised protecting foreign investment. Union Carbide agreed to a settlement with the Indian government, paying $470 million in compensation to victims. This amount was widely criticised as inadequate.

A catastrophic nuclear accident at the Chernobyl Nuclear Power Plant in 1986, caused by design flaws and human error, resulted in a massive release of radiation, forcing the evacuation of hundreds of thousands of people and causing long-term health effects. Following the Chernobyl disaster, there were legal consequences for some officials. Viktor Bryukhanov, Director of the Chernobyl Nuclear Power Plant, was sentenced to 10 years in a labour camp for gross violation of safety regulations and creating conditions that led to the explosion. However, he only served five years. Anatoly Dyatlov, Deputy Chief Engineer, was also sentenced to 10 years for his role in overseeing the failed safety test that triggered the disaster. He served only three years. Another 10-year sentence was given to Nikolai Fomin, Chief Engineer, for his participation in safety violations. Other plant employees were sentenced to prison terms of two to five years. Several other high-ranking officials were dismissed or demoted due to their involvement or perceived mishandling of the disaster response.

An explosion on the Deepwater Horizon oil rig operated by BP led to the largest marine oil spill in history, causing extensive environmental damage and economic losses. Regulatory failures and lax oversight contributed to the disaster. There were 11 deaths as a direct result of the explosion and subsequent sinking of the oil rig on April 20, 2010. The dead were crew members who were unable to escape the rig before it exploded and sank. Their bodies were never recovered despite a three-day search by the U.S. Coast Guard. In addition, there were 17 other crew members who were injured.

While not directly caused by the explosion, the oil spill that resulted from the Deepwater Horizon disaster had significant environmental and economic impacts, affecting wildlife, fisheries, and coastal communities. The long-term health effects on humans exposed to the oil and dispersants used in the clean-up are still being studied. The focus of legal accountability primarily fell on BP as a corporation and some lower-level employees directly involved in the rig's operation. BP pleaded guilty to 11 felony counts of misconduct or neglect of ship officers (criminal charges), resulting in the deaths of 11 workers. This resulted in BP agreeing to pay $20.8 billion in a civil settlement, the largest environmental damage settlement in U.S. history.

But no senior management was arrested or charged. Two BP site managers were charged with manslaughter. One was convicted and sentenced to 10 years' probation. While no high-level government officials were charged, the disaster led to investigations and criticism of regulatory agencies like the Minerals Management Service (MMS) for lax oversight and cosy relationships with the oil industry. The MMS was eventually reorganised and renamed the Bureau of Safety and Environmental Enforcement (BSEE) to strengthen oversight and prevent future disasters.

Flint Water Crisis (US, 2014-present): The city of Flint, Michigan, switched its water source to the Flint River, whose water was highly contaminated with lead and highly corrosive. Government officials failed to properly treat the water, leading to a public health crisis with widespread lead poisoning. Several politicians were indicted on felony charges, including former Michigan Governor Rick Snyder. However, as of May 2024, 10 years later, none have been convicted or sentenced to prison. The legal proceedings are ongoing. Fifteen officials, including state and local civil servants, were charged with various crimes, including involuntary manslaughter, misconduct in office, and obstruction of justice. Some have been convicted on lesser charges.

COVID-19 Pandemic (Global, 2020-present): While the pandemic was a global event, its impact varied significantly due to differences in government preparedness, response, and healthcare infrastructure. Some countries were criticised for their slow response, lack of transparency, and inadequate support for healthcare workers. The pandemic is still ongoing, and its full impact and potential legal ramifications are yet to be determined. While there have been criticisms of government responses in various countries, no major prosecutions of politicians or senior civil servants for their handling of the pandemic have occurred. The 14.9 million excess deaths estimated by the WHO serve as a stark reminder of the potential consequences of inadequate public health measures and the importance of holding leaders accountable for their decisions, or lack of decisions, during crises. For instance, in the UK, If Boris Johnson had been the chief executive of a major company, overseeing a disaster in which people were killed, we might reasonably expect prosecution and a possible jail term. All this was exacerbated by photographs of celebrations at the centre of government while people were dying of Covid in hospitals, their nearest and dearest excluded from visiting. Worse, due to his inaction and the poor response of his team, further loss of life occurred. Accountability for this has been severely lacking, as it has been for other disasters.

Morandi Bridge Collapse (Italy, 2018): The collapse of a major bridge in Genoa, Italy, killed 43 people and highlighted the neglect of infrastructure maintenance and safety standards. No politicians have been directly implicated or charged in relation to the bridge collapse. Several officials from Autostrada per l'Italia (the company responsible for maintaining the bridge) and government agencies were indicted on charges of manslaughter and negligence. The trial was ongoing as of May 2024.

Surfside Condominium Collapse (US, 2021): The collapse of a residential building in Surfside, Florida, killed 98 people. Investigations revealed structural deficiencies and delayed maintenance as contributing factors. As of May 20, 2024, no politicians or civil servants had been criminally charged or sent to prison directly due to the Surfside Condominium collapse. However, investigations are still ongoing, and several lawsuits have been filed against various parties, including the Champlain Towers South Condominium Association, accused of neglecting maintenance and repairs that contributed to the building's structural deterioration. Several firms involved in the building's design, construction, and inspection are facing lawsuits for alleged negligence and professional malpractice. While not criminally charged, Surfside city officials are facing lawsuits for allegedly failing to enforce building codes and address safety concerns raised by residents.

Grenfell Tower Fire (UK, 2017): A fire in a residential tower block in London killed 72 people due to flammable cladding and inadequate fire safety regulations. The tragedy exposed failures in building regulations and oversight. As of May 2024, no prosecutions have been forthcoming, and no politicians have been indicted or sent to prison, despite the block being local government run. A public inquiry has reported and while no criminal charges have been filed yet, the actions and decisions of various civil servants involved in the building's refurbishment and fire safety inspections are under scrutiny. Police following up the findings of the public inquiry estimate no prosecutions will be forthcoming until late in 2026, nearly 10 years after the event itself.

These examples demonstrate the devastating consequences that can occur when governments fail to fulfil their responsibilities to protect their citizens. They highlight the importance of strong institutions, effective governance, transparency, accountability, and a commitment to public safety and well-being. Hurricane Katrina, the opioid crisis, Veterans Affairs (VA) Scandal (2014), Lac-Mégantic Rail Disaster (2013), Fukushima Daiichi Nuclear Disaster (2011), and the Italian Earthquake (2009) are all examples of governments singularly failing to protect their populus.

Why are high-level officials and decision-makers so frequently able to evade criminal liability? Certainly, it is partly due to the difficulty of proving direct causation and intent. But is this reasonable? One of the fundamental expectations of a new social contract between citizens and government ought to be that a politically appointed minister responsible for a department should be held responsible when things go wrong. If you are to run a department that impacts on public health, you should be duty bound to ask yourself and your department: What can go wrong? Has my department sufficiently reviewed the possibilities? Do we have the best contingency plans? As the person in charge, you must take a level of responsibility for success or failure. If failure results in harm or deaths, there ought to be consequences.

It is almost an unwritten rule that once a disaster has happened, judgement day should be kicked down the road. As above, there are multiple examples of inquiries taking decades. A cynic might say that this enables the responsible party - whether they be corporate or government - to build a war chest of money for the day they are finally forced to pay up. Cases involving large corporations and complex systems are handled similarly, and civil settlements, rather than criminal prosecutions, are more commonly the result.

So, the pursuit of accountability for disasters is a complex process, often hindered by political pressure, legal challenges, and the difficulty of establishing individual responsibility within complex systems. Nonetheless, the examples below demonstrate that it is sometimes possible to hold those in power accountable for their negligence, lack of action, or downright criminality.

Oliver North (Iran-Contra Affair): North, a military officer working at the National Security Council, was convicted of several felony charges for his role in the illegal sale of arms to Iran to fund Nicaraguan Contras. However, his convictions were later overturned on appeal.

Lois Lerner (IRS Targeting Scandal): Lerner, a senior official at the Internal Revenue Service (IRS), was held in contempt of

Congress for refusing to testify about the agency's targeting of conservative groups.

France: The Elf Aquitaine scandal in the 1990s saw several executives and officials, including a former foreign minister, convicted of corruption and embezzlement related to the state-owned oil company.

Italy: The 'Clean Hands' investigations in the 1990s led to the prosecution of numerous politicians and officials for corruption, including several former prime ministers.

South Korea: Choi Soon-sil, a close confidante of former President Park Geun-hye, was sentenced to prison for her role in a corruption scandal that led to Park's impeachment and removal from office.[12]

Chapter 6 - The 10 key points

1. Erosion of Trust in Politicians: The chapter highlights the declining public trust in politicians, citing examples of misconduct and ethical lapses, and calls for a major reset in how countries are governed, and leaders are elected.

2. The Corrupting Influence of Power: The chapter argues that prolonged periods in power can lead to corruption and detachment from the needs of the people, emphasising the need for term limits for leaders.

3. Outdated Political Systems: Current political systems are often ill-equipped to handle the challenges of the 21st century, particularly the rapid pace of technological change and the rise of AI.

4. The Need for Qualified Professionals in Government: The chapter advocates for attracting and empowering experienced professionals from various fields to enter government and contribute their expertise to policymaking and administration.

5. Term Limits and Accountability: Strict term limits for all key positions, coupled with clear agendas and performance evaluations, are essential for ensuring accountability and preventing power consolidation.

6. Proportional Representation: Replacing first-past-the-post voting systems with proportional representation can lead to a more diverse and inclusive political landscape, fostering collaboration and mitigating polarisation.

7. Addressing Financial Influence in Politics: Stricter campaign finance regulations and transparency in lobbying activities are necessary to curb the undue influence of the financial sector on political decision-making.

8. Empowering Independent Regulatory Bodies: Independent regulatory bodies are crucial for overseeing financial institutions, ensuring fair competition, and protecting consumers from predatory practices.

9. Promoting Financial Literacy: Enhancing public understanding of financial matters through education is essential for informed decision-making and civic engagement.

10. Reforming the Civil Service: The civil service needs to be reformed to attract and retain qualified professionals, improve efficiency and accountability, and ensure that it serves the public interest effectively.

Footnotes – Chapter 6

[1] https://www.latimes.com/archives/la-xpm-1997-05-17-mn-59626-story.html

[2] https://www.forbes.com/sites/edwindurgy/2011/10/25/did-moammar-gadhafi-die-the-richest-man-in-the-world/

[3] Emanuel Macron has abolished the curriculum for public servants, launching its replacement, the Ecole nationale d'administration (ENA), in 2022

[4] Note 21, Appendix 1 for an excerpt re Government incompetence

[5]https://www.amazon.co.uk/s?k=ian+dunt+how+westminster+works&i=digital-text&crid=3V2TIMEIIM2BF&sprefix=ian+d%2Cdigital-text%2C92&ref=nb_sb_ss_ts-doa-p_2_5

[6] Note 22, Appendix 1, Government accountability, and lack of.

[7] Canada employs a meritocratic system with a strong emphasis on performance management. Regular performance reviews are conducted, and consequences for poor performance can range from additional training to dismissal in extreme cases. In 2018, a senior public servant at the Canadian Food Inspection Agency (CFIA) was fired for neglecting their duties related to food safety inspections at meat processing facilities. This case highlighted the importance of accountability in protecting public health. France has a more bureaucratic system, with a strong emphasis on following established procedures.

[8]https://www.ashgrove.cheshire.sch.uk/_site/data/files/year%206/week%2011/9EE2E2604144166BC109F181D49BBD07.pdf

[9] https://www.electoral-reform.org.uk/voting-systems/types-of-voting-system/

[10] https://www.worldatlas.com/gdp/the-richest-countries-in-the-world.html

[11] https://www.afar.com/magazine/the-worlds-happiest-country-is-all-about-reading-coffee-and-saunas

[12]Note 23, for details on unethical behaviour.

CHAPTER 7

The Failing Dream of Democracy

Examples of current successfully run countries are, in the main, Anglo Saxon and are wealthier, better educated and frequently more liberal. The top 30 in terms of democracy as we understand it are (in order): Norway, New Zealand, Finland, Sweden, Iceland, Denmark, Ireland, Taiwan, Australia, Switzerland, Netherlands, Luxembourg, Germany, Canada, Uruguay, Austria, Costa Rica, Mauritius, Spain, South Korea, United Kingdom, Japan, United States, Chile, Portugal, Slovenia, Czech Republic, Estonia, France, Belgium.

That list includes only 18 from Europe. Given there are 50 countries on the continent, including 27 that are members of the European Union, 18 is a quite shockingly low number.

While these countries have achieved relative success in terms of economic development and social progress, it is important to recognize that their governance models are not without flaws. They continue to grapple with issues like income inequality, environmental degradation, and social divisions. It is worth noting that the USA, UK and Japan are low on the list. All three countries have experienced a decline in their democratic scores over the past few years according to various democracy indices. This downward trend is attributed to various factors. Concerns have been raised about restrictions on freedom of expression, privacy issues, and the treatment of minorities and immigrants. Deep divisions within society and political gridlock have hampered effective governance and led to public disillusionment. Concerns about the independence of the judiciary and media, and instances of corruption and undue influence, have undermined public trust.

In the United States, issues such as gerrymandering, voter suppression, and the influence of money in politics have raised questions about the fairness and inclusivity of the electoral process. Additionally, the January 6th insurrection (2021) in the USA highlighted the fragility of democratic norms.

With Trump now President again for a second four-year term, it will be interesting to see if he tries to change the constitution to give himself a further term in office.

In the United Kingdom Brexit has exacerbated political divisions and led to concerns about the stability of the political system. Again, with yet another new leader for the Conservative party in the United Kingdom, we need to ask ourselves would any of these candidates be able to manage and properly run a major company? I find it very doubtful that they would even get past the first interview. So why would we allow them to run 50% of the entire function of the UK, if they are elected in the future?

Additionally, there are concerns about the erosion of media freedom and the centralization of power, despite devolution of certain powers to Scotland, Wales and Northern Ireland, and some local authorities. Japan, meanwhile, enjoys high levels of political stability and civil liberties. But its political system is dominated by one party, limiting competition and plurality. Furthermore, issues such as gender inequality and limited opportunities for political participation remain challenges.

It is also crucial to acknowledge that successful governance models can emerge from diverse cultural and political contexts, and we should not limit our exploration to Western examples. For example, we could be looking at The Abbasid Caliphate (750–1258), The Maurya Empire (322–185 BCE), The Song Dynasty (960–1279).

If we are to develop and expand on the democratic and socially liberal systems which have developed only in reality over the past 75 years, where we have strived for more equality in society, it is very important that we start thinking much more deeply about the morality of the systems currently in place. We also need to be able to show that these are/can be much better systems than the competition has to offer. Given that the competition is communism, totalitarianism, or just plain despotic rule, the argument for social moral democracy wouldn't appear too difficult to make.

Those who believe that capitalism and democracy, working together, have been shown to work best for the greater number of people, need to be confident enough to argue that we can adapt these systems and structures to better deliver equality of opportunity on a global scale; confident enough to acknowledge that wealth can be distributed on a much fairer basis without the need to adopt the 19th century theories of Marx, Engels and others, which have proved so disastrous wherever and whenever they've been put into practice; and confident enough to argue that capitalism does not have to be a winner takes all system, but can be regulated so as to be more beneficial for more people.

First of all, though, we need to acknowledge that society always hangs on the thinnest of threads. Even the most successful of governments have the seeds of failure sewn into their fabric. American President Richard Nixon liked to make the comparison between the hippie philosophy of peace and drugs and the decline of the Roman Empire, which eventually failed after descending into a culture of hedonism and immorality. On July 6, 1971, he gave a speech in which he said: "I think about what happened to Greece and Rome, and you see (all that) is left - only the pillars. What has happened, of course, is that the great civilisations of the past, as they have become wealthy, lost their will to live, to improve. They then have become subject to the decadence which eventually destroys a civilisation." He warned that "the United States is now reaching that period".[1]

The Roman Republic, which was in power from 509 to 27 BCE - almost 500 years, is considered one of the most successful governments in history.[2] But as the Republic succumbed to the ambitions of those who would be Emperor, the Roman Empire replaced it. The Empire itself also lasted 500 years, eventually failing through an elite enjoying the fruits of conquest while ignoring the masses. This is exactly what Nixon was saying: two hugely successful governments, one, "having become wealthy, lost its will to survive"; the other "became subject to the decadence which eventually destroys a civilisation".

We see this pattern repeated throughout history, in Ancient Greece, in the Dynasties of China, the Ottoman Empire, the British Empire, Imperial Japan - a rise, and then a fall, seemingly inexorable but exhausting for the general populace who always come off worst.

So how much bearing does 'successful in the past' have on the present, and - even more to the point - the future? Having a strong army available to conquer and control other territories which then supplied resources and wealth to your own country and elite is not a working model for the future. The ideal model for the future is one where everyone is guaranteed a minimum standard of living and the opportunities to improve it; access to a decent education and medical care; where the military is for defence, not attack. Change in the world is accelerating at an alarming rate. Institutions must be modernised, and we must move on from the past.

And the fact is that the difference between developed countries, those that have adopted some form of liberal and social democracy, and the rest of the world is currently not that great. Hungary and Poland, for instance, full members of the EU and of NATO, both disdain the more liberal policies of colleague countries. Populist candidates are popping up around the world, unafraid to argue that liberalism has gone too far, that national selfishness has its place, that charity, in effect, begins at home.

In 2024, even the uber-liberal European Union saw its constituent parts voting for illiberal representatives in enough numbers to change the makeup of the European Parliament. France, in its own 2024 general election - called, some said, in panic - faced the prospect of the far right grabbing power. Only the Two Round system of voting, which brought out voters shocked by the first-round win for Marine LePen's RN Party and its allies, brought the social liberals back into contention. But that was a prelude to a long-drawn-out negotiation between the left, the social liberals, and the right about who would govern, and how. As 2024 drew to a close, those negotiations had clearly failed, and the Prime Minister of just three months, couldn't pass his budget, and lost a 'no confidence' vote in Parliament.

There is tension throughout the developed world: tension caused by the massive gap that has opened up in the past 20 years between rich and not rich (let alone the abjectly poor); between governments that empathise with the plight of refugees and economic migrants, and their citizens who see their cultural and societal identity changing; and again between those governments and their citizens who see housing, schools, and healthcare in particular under strain because the influx of migrants has not been planned for.

These concerns are fodder for the populists, who exaggerate and offer solutions which, frequently, they know are unworkable. President Donald Trump and his wall across Mexico, and his promise of bringing back jobs for coal mining communities, are prime examples.

In the UK, the population has increased by 12%, eight million people, since 2010. That's the equivalent of almost doubling Greater London's population. And it happened without the building of new schools, new hospitals, new houses, or new prisons. The law of averages says that eight million new people are likely to require 10,845 prison places. The net increase in prison places between 2010 and 2024 in the UK was 300. This is easy pickings for a new populist party like Reform UK, which took 14% of the popular vote, against the Lib Dems 12%. The first past the post system, though, meant the Lib Dems won 71 seats, while Reform won only five - another weapon with which populists can berate the establishment. Just because I do not agree with their message, does not stop me from believing that, in a truly representative system, Reform should have more seats. Everyone should be represented.

By contrast, in the same period since 2010, Germany's population has increased by less than three million - 3.3% compared to the UK's 12%. And yet that small increase in Germany has also caused unrest, and led to an uplift in support for AfD, a party some think harks back to the worst of Germany's past. In 2015, Germany took in one million refugees, mostly fleeing Syria, but also from Afghanistan and Iraq. Within five years, half of those asylum seekers had found a job, but half hadn't. AfD was able to foment unrest regarding the cost to the country, but in addition, around the resultant lack of integration from such a one-off influx.

Governments in history, and governments in the present, that are, or have been considered to be successful, are in no way bound to continue to be successful. Modern democracy, in particular, requires the acquiescence of its citizens. When those same citizens feel they are not being looked after on a number of key societal and cultural levels, they are - as we can clearly see - likely to rebel against the status quo. Bring a reduction in standards of living into the mix, and trouble feels inevitable.

Liberals have long held Scandinavian countries as a beacon of hope for social democracy. But even Sweden, Norway and Denmark are now showing the cracks of societal breakdown. Abuse of women is a major problem, as are racism against incomers, and alcoholism. Homophobia is on the rise, as is antisemitism.

The problems America faces have been clear for some time. At one point, easily the most successful country of modern times, it is now split between the rich (a distinct minority), the haves (possibly 40% of the population) and the have nots (50%).[3] A country which built itself, postwar, via the American Dream - where all was possible for all the people - now finds itself with maybe 160 million disaffected citizens, ready to believe the promises of a Donald Trump, even in the face of reality.

In the 2020 Presidential Election, more people voted for Trump than had ever voted for a President in history. Unfortunately for Trump, seven million more people voted for Joe Biden. But the nearly 75 million votes for Trump (12 million more than when he won in 2016) sounded a stark warning of divisions in the country. Most of the states across the middle of the country - what the political class and the bi-coastal media dismiss as 'flyover states' - voted in Trump's favour, as did the 'rust belt' states, where coalmining and car-manufacturing communities have been decimated without any apparent thought given to their future.

The 'flyover states', meanwhile, are custodians of some of the world's most precious ecology and are still home to traditional hunting and fishing customs - all now limited by green policies coming from 'that distant Washington' whose far-removed legislators have no understanding of the way these people live, and want to live, their lives.

The voters have now spoken again and re-elected Trump. It seems however flawed a person he is, he resonates with the 50% of the electorate who have seen their income, wealth and opportunities decline rapidly over the past 20 years. They have voted for the simple message: let's make the USA great again. The have nots want to see action, they want to see tariffs on Chinese goods and other's. Trade wars could damage the country even further, but that's a problem for tomorrow. The electorate want action now.

Similar problems beset the entirety of Europe, home to 740m people. Nearly half a billion of those live in the European Union, whose voters gave clear signals to their legislators in 2024 that they were fed up with the governance they are subject to.

And these are not the only challenges to our government systems. The historical free-for-all approach to war, conquest, and elevation to supreme leader (emperor, monarch, religious or other) was codified for centuries into a developing concept of international law which is no longer recognised in the 21st century. A 'right of conquest' existed to satisfy the power lust of monarchies and the elite around the globe, and to ensure other leaders did not find themselves in diplomatic opposition to those with whom they had no wish to engage in war.

This all began to change in the 20th century, after the First World War with the formation of The League of Nations, the first international body to be tasked with maintaining world peace. The 'right of conquest' increasingly diminished, and was finally dismissed under the Nuremberg Principles, which introduced the concept of 'crimes against peace' after World War 2. By this time, The League of Nations - deemed to have failed, some might say spectacularly - had been replaced by The United Nations. The Nuremberg Principles were - are - a set of guidelines as to what constitutes a war crime, a direct response to the behaviour of German politicians and military who claimed to be 'just following orders'.

Sixty-three countries had been members of The League of Nations at various times during its brief tenure. At its inception in 1945, The United Nations had 51 founder-member States. Today it has 193. There are a further 11 nations which, for one reason or another, do not qualify for United Nations membership. Among them are Kosovo - recognised by some UN members, but still debated because of the nature of Kosovo's declared 'independence'[4] from Serbia after the 1998/99 Kosovo War; and Cyprus - an apparent attempt to annex the island by a Greek military junta in 1974 was rebuffed by a Turkish invasion. Cyprus is now split in two, between Greece and Turkey, and the lack of resolution disbars it from UN membership. Other non-members include The Republic of China (the disputed territory of Taiwan); Palestine; and Western Sahara, territory whose status is disputed by the Sahrawi Arab Democratic Republic.

But a more revealing omission from UN membership - because it reveals important qualifications for being recognised as a State - is The Holy See, the world's smallest city-state, often wrongly referred to as The Vatican. The Holy See disqualifies itself from membership of The United Nations because it fails on a supremely important aspect of formal UN recognition: it does not exist to govern and serve its citizens, but only to provide governance to the Catholic Church and The Vatican.

In that singular example, we can see that the very least that is required for formal recognition under international law as a nation state, and therefore membership of the United Nations, is to look after the citizens of that State. (So, one might ask, what is the process for removing membership, if you fail to look after the citizens of your state?). To establish a new country under existing custom, that country must first satisfy the international rules that all UN members acknowledge and follow, as set forth by the Montevideo Convention on the Rights and Duties of States, adopted in 1933. These are:

- A permanent population
- A defined territory
- A government
- The capacity to conduct international relations.

So, nothing about the type of government. No agreement under international law that the country must be a democracy, or even vaguely democratic. Thus, a despotic and repressive regime like North Korea is not excluded from the United Nations. More significant, though, is the reversal of democracy, with fewer countries qualifying as such today compared to 20 years ago.[5]

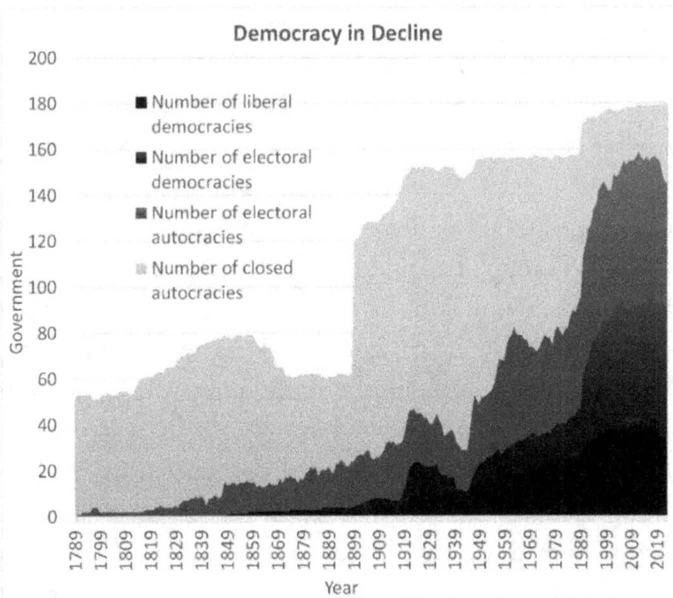

The world has seen a decline in democracy since the early 2010s, with 42 countries becoming autocracies by 2023-close to an all-time high. Fewer people are living in democracies, with democratic rights eroding. However, similar declines in the past were reversed, offering hope for a future democratic resurgence. Source: https://ourworldindata.org/democracy

Whether democracy is effective on a long-term basis is therefore a complex subject, argued and debated about among scholars and political theorists. While it is true that not all countries are currently under democratic regimes, it is important to consider a few points when evaluating the effectiveness of democracy.

Democracy has evolved over centuries and has been shaped by various political, social, and cultural contexts. Many countries have seen progress in terms of democratic governance, with, until this century, a measurably increasing number of nations adopting democratic systems over time. Democracy was apparently an unstoppable force. This can no longer be taken for granted.

One argument in favour of democracy is the 'democratic peace theory', which suggests that democracies tend to have fewer conflicts and are less likely to go to war with each other. Empirical studies have shown a correlation between democratic governance and a lower incidence of international conflict. Democracy has often been associated with economic growth and development. While it is not a guaranteed outcome, democratic systems with strong institutions, rule of law, and accountability mechanisms can provide a conducive environment for economic progress and human development.

Democracy can safeguard civil liberties, protect human rights, and provide a platform for citizen participation and freedom of expression. Democratic societies often value basic rights and strive for social progress. One of democracy's strengths is its accountability mechanisms. Through free and fair elections, citizens can hold their leaders accountable, making it possible for power to be peacefully transferred and for public policies to reflect the will of the people.

Democracy, then, has shown itself to be the best model for running a country when compared to any other system, whether that be despotism, dictatorship, fascism or socialism/communism. However, it is also important to acknowledge the challenges and limitations that democracy faces today, as evidenced in both established and emerging democracies. Issues such as corruption, political polarisation, voter apathy, and institutional weaknesses undermine the functioning of democratic systems.

Additionally, the spread of democracy may be influenced by a range of factors, including historical circumstances, geopolitical considerations, cultural norms, and economic conditions. The path to democracy can vary across countries and regions and is certainly not guaranteed purely by what we in the developed world might consider to be rational logic.

Clearly, democracy is not a panacea and has its own set of challenges. But there is evidence to suggest that it can be effective on a long-term basis, promoting stability, peace, economic development, and protection of rights. However, the success of democracy relies on the continuous engagement of citizens, the presence of robust institutions, and national and international commitments to democratic principles and values. Democracy needs the inbuilt ability to improve its own morality in order to be seen as far superior to anything else.

The classification of countries as 'democratic' or 'non-democratic' can vary depending on different indices and methodologies used by organisations that assess the state of democracy worldwide. Some commonly referenced indices include the Democracy Index by The Economist Intelligence Unit (EIU), Freedom House's Freedom in the World report, and the Varieties of Democracy (V-Dem) project.

Based on these indices, it is estimated that a significant portion of the world's countries can be considered democratic. However, the specific percentage can vary depending on the criteria and thresholds used to define democracy.

For instance, according to the Democracy Index 2020 by The Economist Intelligence Unit, which assesses the state of democracy in 167 countries, around 49.3% of the global population lives in democracies. The report categorises countries into four broad categories: full democracies, flawed democracies, hybrid regimes, and authoritarian regimes. Full democracies accounted for approximately 8.4% of the global population, while flawed democracies accounted for around 40.9%.

Freedom House's Freedom in the World report for 2021 assessed the state of political rights and civil liberties in 195 countries and 15 territories. According to their report, approximately 43% of the global population lived in countries deemed 'free', characterised by high levels of political rights and civil liberties.

Chapter 7 - The 10 key points

1. Democracy's Fragility: The chapter highlights that the success of democracies, even those considered successful, is not guaranteed and faces challenges such as inequality and social divisions.

2. The Need for Moral and Societal Progress: The future of democracy depends on addressing moral and societal issues and demonstrating its superiority over alternative systems.

3. Learning from History: The text emphasises the importance of learning from the historical rise and fall of governments to ensure the long-term success of democracies.

4. A Vision for the Future: The ideal model for the future is one that guarantees a minimum standard of living, opportunities for improvement, access to education and healthcare, and a military focused on defence rather than aggression.

5. The Rise of Populism: The text points out the rise of populism and illiberal sentiments globally, challenging the notion of an unstoppable force towards democracy.

6. Addressing Citizen Concerns: The text emphasises the importance of addressing the concerns and anxieties of citizens to prevent societal breakdown and rebellion against the status quo.

7. Challenging the Scandinavian Model: The text questions the notion of Scandinavian countries as

perfect models of social democracy, highlighting their own societal challenges.

8. Deep Divisions in the US: The text discusses the deep divisions in the United States, exemplified by the stark contrast between the rich and the poor, and the susceptibility of a significant portion of the population to populist promises.

9. Similar Challenges in Europe: The text points out similar challenges and divisions across Europe, reflected in the rise of populist movements and voter dissatisfaction.

10. The Importance of International Law: The text emphasises the importance of international law and cooperation in maintaining peace and stability in the 21st century.

Footnotes – Chapter 7

[1]https://www.presidency.ucsb.edu/documents/remarks-midwestern-news-media-executives-attending-briefing-domestic-policy-kansas-city

[2] Note 24, Appendix 1, for other examples of successful governments

[3]https://www.statista.com/statistics/203961/wealth-distribution-for-the-us/#:~:text=In%20the%20third%20quarter%20of,percent%20of%20the%20total%20wealth.

[4]https://www.forbes.com/sites/katharinabuchholz/2023/02/17/kosovo--beyond-where-the-un-disagrees-on-recognition-infographic/

[5] https://ourworldindata.org/less-democratic

CHAPTER 8

Could Monarchy Lead the Change?

We may, of course, ask ourselves how individuals became 'Royal'. Here we find a history of violence that elevates a mere human from tribal leader to Monarch. There are many examples throughout history of ordinary mortals using violence to raise themselves above the rest of humanity, claiming divine right, or actual descendancy from the Gods.

Genghis Khan in China (The Yuan Dynasty), Ismail 1 in Persia (The Safavid Dynasty), Babur in India (The Mughal Empire) and Ivan The Terrible in Russia (The Romanov Dynasty) all used violence to establish their rule and plundered their enemies' belongings. Violence was also used to keep dissenters in check. There are many examples in Gt Britain, as one ruling family superseded another - the Tudors, for instance, defeating and killing the last of the Plantagenet Kings at the Battle of Bosworth in 1485, and embarking on a turbulent period that included Henry Vlll killing not only several wives, but also attempting to wipe out all Catholics as he established the Church of England.

Past successful governments are tainted by their own history. Absolute monarchs, or those of similar status, were intent on accumulating more power, more wealth, and - above all - hanging on to it by whatever means necessary. We cannot escape the fact that the majority of wars, the destruction of life and the increase of suffering for the poor has been caused by whatever ruling class held sway in any specific territory at any specific time. When we get to our chapter on Solutions, we will see that a major focus will be to disabuse ourselves, once and for all, of romantic notions about the purpose of monarchy. But monarchies could somewhat redeem themselves in the meantime by leading the change we need. As the elite of the elite, they can not only set a positive example, they could also, through their position in society, use their powerful networks to help to bring about change from the top.

Still, we must always remember that the winners write history, and monarchy has been, historically, inherently ruthless at winning. While we accept that there have been a few examples of rulers who have put their people first and have done all they can to make their life better, this is very much a minority. It has been, and continues to be, an oppressive system of governance, predicated on violence and the systematic marginalisation of people. Monarchies have frequently maintained their power through acts of exemplary violence. So, we shouldn't be surprised at the vicious and nasty warfare modern governments can be seen to wage against their own populations (Syria, for example). They are, in a way, copying lessons from history.

Throughout history, monarchs have shown little regard for their own populations. The Hundred Years' War (1337-1453) between England and France was largely fuelled by the ambitions of the English King Edward III and the French King Philip VI; the War of the Spanish Succession (1701-1714) involved several European powers, including France, Great Britain and Austria, sparked by the desire of Louis XIV of France to secure the throne for his grandson, Philip of Anjou; the Napoleonic Wars (1803-1815) were sparked by the ambitions of Napoleon Bonaparte, who rose to power as the First Consul of France and eventually declared himself Emperor.

How were Royal families created?

Royal families, also known as monarchies, are systems of government in which a single family holds the right to rule a country or territory which passes down through the generations. In many cases, the right to rule is inherited through a system of primogeniture, in which the oldest son or daughter of the reigning monarch is next in line to the throne.

In many cases, the history of a royal family is closely tied to the history of the country or territory they rule. The British monarchy traces its roots back to the 9th century, when the first king of England, Alfred the Great, consolidated his power, overcoming Viking, Mercian, Kent, and other territories and establishing the first English monarchy. Japan's monarchy traces its origins back to the 4th century, when the first Japanese emperor, Emperor Jammu, is said to have ascended to the throne.

Essentially this is a group at the top of the elite, that has sucked the wealth out of their countries for hundreds of years. Modern monarchies continue in their elitist position with no real detailed acknowledgement of the damage their ancestors wreaked on ordinary citizens. To this day there are countries where you can be put into prison for saying anything negative about their royal families. Consequently, it is very hard for an intelligent mind to reconcile much of the popular support for monarchs and royal families in the 21st century.

Historically we were all ruled by royal families, emperors and empresses or warlords. So, let's call them the old elite, which is now being replaced by the new elite. But what we need is real democracy where every person has a better life and there is a real effort to minimise inequality. Wealth and power in the past have mostly been created by wars and violence, the control of land and resources, and exploitation of the weakest people. Monarchies are a real impediment to democracy. They are anachronisms whose time has passed.

The argument is often made that royals are good for business and good for tourism. But since the elite control the media, and they support their own, there is no substantive evidence that a ruling royal family is essential for tourism. If you took the English Royal family and demoted them to ordinary citizens; stopped paying them $108m a year and taxed them on their income and their inheritance, tourism would not be affected. There was a good start made by John Major in February 1993,[1] but it needs to go further. Royalty anywhere should be taxed on the same basis as everyone else, especially regarding inheritance tax.

People would still come and visit the United Kingdom's castles and landmarks if the monarchy was discontinued or faded into history. Of course, it would be to view where the royal family used to live, not where they might be currently living.

For confirmation of this, we only have to look to France. According to Euromonitor, Paris is not only the most popular tourist destination in Europe but was the most popular world tourist destination in 2023.[2] Many of the sites visited are former homes to French royalty and nobility, like The Louvre - a sprawling former palace of the French royal family, that now houses one of the world's largest and most prestigious museums. Or the Palace of Versailles - A UNESCO World Heritage Site and a former royal residence located southwest of Paris.

Another argument is that the UK's royal family creates trade and business. This is a specious argument when we can clearly see that other countries create trade and business by having their Presidents visit one another. The future can be clearly shown from the current visit of King Charles to Australia, October 2024 where many politicians, including leaders of all six states, refused to greet him, and are asking for the end of the monarchy in their country.[3]

Then there is the question of all the accumulated wealth: paintings, works of art, gold crowns, jewellery, much of which has been looted from other countries, all of which should come back to the Treasury of each country it was taken from.

The UK's royal family has wealth estimated at $28 billion (£21.3 billion) according to Forbes, although Nathan Reiff on Investopedia (January 2024) says this is "largely guesswork - assessing the royal family's wealth is extremely difficult because of the vast array of its holdings, the historical value of these holdings, and a tradition of secrecy about financial particulars".[4] How does this 'guesswork' stack up, particularly given that provenance is challenging to prove?

The late Queen Elizabeth II's personal fortune: $500 million (£380.7 million). [Investopedia - British Royal Family Net Worth].

The Crown Estate: This vast property portfolio, valued at around $20.5 billion (£15.6 billion), belongs to the Crown, not the royal family. Under terms of an agreement made with George lll in 1760, income from The Crown Estate is surrendered to the Treasury each year 'for the benefit of the nation's finances'. In exchange, the reigning monarch receives 'the sovereign grant', a proportion of the profits assessed by the Treasury.[5] But this income is essentially from land stolen with force over the years or centuries from the poor and weak. There is no logic to continuing to pay the British royal family, and every logic to taxing the family on the same basis as everyone else.

Artworks and Jewellery: Valuing these is subjective and depends on market fluctuations.

Royal Collection Trust: Manages the Royal Collection, a vast collection of art, artefacts, and jewels. While not explicitly stating the origin of each piece, some of the most famous paintings in the collection include works by Rembrandt, da Vinci, Michelangelo, and Vermeer. While individual values are subjective, a single masterpiece by any of these artists can easily fetch hundreds of millions at auction. Considering the vast number of significant artworks, the total value could easily be in the tens of billions of pounds but has variously been estimated at least £10bn.[6]

Crown Jewels: These priceless jewels, including the crown worn by the monarch at coronations, are irreplaceable. Estimating their worth is difficult, but their historical and symbolic significance is immeasurable. A conservative estimate could be in the billions of dollars ($4-6bn, according to The Natural Sapphire Company).[7]

Other Objects: The collection includes furniture, historical artefacts, etc. Attributing a value is even harder here, but considering their historical and artistic importance, it could also be in the billions of pounds range.[8]

Putting it all together: Given these considerations, a very rough estimate for the entire Royal Collection Trust's value could be in the range of hundreds of billions of pounds.

Wealth of royal families.

Family	Country	Estimated Wealth (USD)
House of Saud	Saudi Arabia	100 billion (Oil)
House of Khalifa	Abu Dhabi (UAE)	150 billion (Oil)
Al Thani Family	Qatar	300 billion (Oil)
House of Sabah	Kuwait	360 billion (Oil)
Brunei Royal Family	Brunei	28 billion (Oil)
Moroccan Royal Family	Morocco	50 billion (Investments and resource control)
Thai Royal Family	Thailand	60 billion (Crown Property)
Luxembourg Royal Family	Luxembourg	4 billion (Investments and holdings)
Liechtenstein Royal Family	Liechtenstein	7.2 billion (Family-owned businesses)
Norwegian Royal Family	Norway	500 million (Sovereign wealth fund)
Swedish Royal Family	Sweden	400 million (Land ownership)
British Royal Family	United Kingdom	28 billion (The Crown Estate)
Dutch Royal Family	Netherlands	10 billion (Royal estates)
Belgian Royal Family	Belgium	300 million (Land ownership)
Jordanian Royal Family	Jordan	3.5 billion (Investments and phosphate)
Qatari Royal Family	Qatar	10 billion (Separate from the Al Thani family)

Malaysian Royal Family	Malaysia	1 billion (Investments and state holdings)
Omani Royal Family	Oman	8 billion (Oil)
Monegasque Royal Family	Monaco	1 billion (Real estate and Tourism)
House of Bhutto	Pakistan	1 trillion

The wealth of most royal families has been accumulated in ways that 21st century ethical considerations would not find tolerable. A democratic world where everyone is supposedly valued has no place for royal families, emperors, and the historical elite. Let us not envision a French-style revolution, but rather legislate for their constitutional role to simply fade away over an agreed period of time. In the meantime, existing monarchies, with their natural position as heads of the elites in their own countries and their ability to network with each other, and therefore wield influence worldwide, could undo centuries of harm by persuading others at the top that the time has come for radical change.

Chapter 8 - The 10 key points

1. Violent Origins of Monarchies: The chapter highlights the historical violence and exploitation associated with the establishment and maintenance of monarchies.

2. Monarchs' Disregard for their People: The text argues that monarchs throughout history have often prioritised their own ambitions and power over the well-being of their subjects.

3. Oppressive Systems of Governance: Monarchies are portrayed as inherently oppressive, relying on violence and marginalisation to maintain control.

4. Modern Governments and Historical Violence: The chapter draws parallels between the violent tactics of past monarchs and the actions of some modern governments, suggesting a continuation of oppressive practices.

5. The Questionable Value of Monarchy: The text challenges the notion that monarchies are essential for tourism or trade, questioning their relevance in the 21st century.

6. Monarchs as Impediments to Democracy: Monarchies are seen as outdated systems of governance that hinder progress towards a more equitable and democratic society.

7. The Need for Monarchies to Reform: The chapter calls for monarchies to adapt to modern values by

relinquishing power and returning wealth to the nations they rule.

8. The End of an Era: The text suggests that current monarchs should pave the way for a peaceful transition from monarchies to republics. At the same time, they could use their considerable influence to help usher in a more ethical and moral democratic world.

9. The Rise of New Elites: The chapter acknowledges the emergence of new elites who may perpetuate inequality and calls for a focus on establishing true democracy.

10. Accumulated Wealth and its Origins: The vast wealth accumulated by royal families through historical exploitation is questioned, and the text suggests that some of this wealth should be returned to the countries it was taken from.

Footnotes – Chapter 8

[1] https://johnmajorarchive.org.uk/1993/02/11/mr-majors-commons-statement-on-royal-taxation-11-february-1993/

[2]https://www.euromonitor.com/press/press-releases/dec-2023/euromonitor-internationals-report-reveals-worlds-top-100-city-destinations-for-2023

[3] https://apnews.com/article/australia-king-charles-visit-sydney-dcb4baf655f28fc20068c5991f09f28f

[4] https://www.investopedia.com/british-royal-family-wealth-6741349

[5]https://www.theguardian.com/uk-news/2023/jan/19/cash-and-the-crown-estate-a-look-at-the-british-monarchys-funding-deal

[6] https://www.thecollector.com/what-art-is-in-the-british-royal-collection/

[7]https://www.thenaturalsapphirecompany.com/education/famous-sapphires/the-british-crown-jewels/#:~:text=The%20term%20“crown%20jewels”%20refers,between%20%244%20to%20%246%20billion.

[8] Note 25, Appendix 1, items to return to country of origin

CHAPTER 9

Controls of the Top Companies

It was simpler in the 19th and early 20th centuries, when most of the world's biggest companies were American. Despite being a steadfastly capitalist economy, America also had a collective dread of corporate power and, in particular, of monopolies. Various laws, especially the Sherman Antitrust Act of 1890 put the national government firmly in control of limiting corporate power.

In the 21st century the trend is for the larger companies to become larger, because they are global, meaning no single national government can limit their growth. Nor can they, as American law was framed to deal with American companies, break up the bigger corporations into smaller entities.

Today, the top 10 companies in the world arguably have more power and more resources than most countries. Apple, at $3.48 trillion, Microsoft at $3.1 trillion, and Nvidia at $2.94 trillion (on 16th Sep 2024) are currently the top three companies by market capitalization in the world, though day by day they often interchange depending on their share price. However, their capital value is much bigger than the GDP of nearly all the countries in the world. Only five countries currently remain larger: USA, $25.4 trillion; China, $18.5 trillion; Japan, $4.1 trillion; Germany, $4.6 trillion; and India: $3.9 trillion. The United Kingdom at $3.5T and France at $3.1T have essentially the same value as Apple, Microsoft and Nvidia.

The Big Tech - or FAANG (Facebook, Amazon, Apple, Netflix, and Google) - companies, have massive resources. As of September 2024, the FAANG companies have a joint combined market capitalization of over $8.82 trillion, which is larger than the GDP of all but the top two economies in the world, United States and China.

As the world speeds up, the rate at which companies can develop and grow is increasing. The things that make money these days do not need the building of massive factories and the mining of Natural Resources to the level that was required a hundred, or even 50 years ago. That new flexibility, aided by incoming AI technologies, means that companies with no legal limitations on their growth will continue to outstrip all but the most powerful countries.

The 10 biggest companies in the world now, by market capitalization, are:

Company	Market Cap Trillion $	Comments
Apple	3.452	The tech giant behind iPhone, iPad and Mac remains a leader in innovation and consumer loyalty.
Microsoft	3.229	A dominant force in software, cloud computing, and gaming.
NVIDIA	2.831	Leading producer of graphics processing units (GPUs), essential for gaming, AI, and data centres.
Amazon	2.025	The e-commerce titan also leads in cloud services and streaming entertainment.
Alphabet	2.015	Google's parent company, with diverse businesses including search, advertising, and cloud services.

Saudi Aramco	1.769	The Saudi Arabian oil company is one of the world's largest crude oil producers.
Meta	1.429	Formerly Facebook, still a giant in social media, virtual reality, and advertising.
Berkshire Hathaway	0.983	Warren Buffett's conglomerate with diverse holdings across various industries.
TSMC	0.906	The leading super advanced semiconductor manufacturer.
Eli Lilly	0.824	A major pharmaceutical company based in the USA.

These figures are based on the latest available data (23/09/2024 source: companiesmarketcap.com) and may fluctuate slightly depending on the source. It is important to note that market cap is just one metric to assess a company's value, and other factors like revenue, profitability, and growth potential should also be considered.

As you can see, six of the world's top 10 companies are based around technology, the internet, and microcomputers/chips. A seventh company, Tesla, manufactures electric cars whose batteries rely on evolving technology. Coupled with the extent of tech involved in the cars themselves - hardware and software - we would suggest qualifies the company as a seventh tech giant. Even Berkshire Hathaway, an investment business, chooses mostly to invest in tech, two oil majors being the only exception in this top 10 portfolio.

Who controls these companies? Theoretically it's the shareholders. But we see very little evidence that this is so. If you look at the top companies, except for Tesla - where Elon Musk owns approximately 13.5% of the stock - the boards of most of the top companies in the world often control less than 1% of the shares.

Company	Estimated Board/ Insider Ownership	Notes
Apple	0.1%	Very low direct ownership, significant institutional ownership
Microsoft	1.6%	Includes Bill Gates' stake; significant institutional ownership
NVIDIA	4.2%	Includes Jensen Huang's stake; significant institutional ownership
Alphabet	12.7%	Includes Page & Brin's stakes; high for a tech giant
Amazon	9.8%	Includes Jeff Bezos' stake; significant institutional ownership
Berkshire Hathaway	32.0%	Unique structure, high insider ownership due to Buffett's stake
Meta Platforms	13.4%	Includes Mark Zuckerberg's stake; high for a tech giant
Tesla	13.5%	Includes Elon Musk's stake; relatively high for a tech company
TSMC	0.5%	Low direct ownership, high government-linked entity ownership
UnitedHealt h Group	1.0%	Relatively low direct ownership, high institutional ownership
Johnson & Johnson	0.1%	Very low direct ownership
JPMorgan Chase	0.3%	Very low direct ownership
Visa	0.2%	Very low direct ownership
Walmart	28.2%	Includes Walton family holdings

And yet it seems to be the boards, not the owners, that really call the shots. They increase their own salaries, dividends, and bonuses with very little visible accountability. Business as usual, and jobs for the boys (except for the 10% of the Fortune 500 companies which are now female-led).[1] In fact, as of 2022, another sea-change had happened: 30% of Fortune 500 Board members were women.[2] How much of a change in culture that might cause remains to be seen. Or is this just a form of greenwashing or ESG-washing? There are many more female directors, but still very few female CEOs.

Company	Female CEO	Female Board Members	% Female Board Members
Apple	No	4 out of 8	50%
Microsoft	No	5 out of 11	45%
Amazon	No	5 out of 11	45%
Nvidia	No	2 out of 9	22%
Alphabet (Google)	No	3 out of 11	27%
Berkshire Hathaway	No	2 out of 14	14%
Meta (Facebook)	No	3 out of 9	33%
Tesla	No	2 out of 9	22%
UnitedHealth Group	No	4 out of 12	33%
Johnson & Johnson	No	5 out of 12	42%
Visa	No	4 out of 12	33%
JPMorgan Chase	No	5 out of 11	45%
Procter & Gamble	No	5 out of 11	45%
Mastercard	No	4 out of 10	40%
Walmart	No	4 out of 10	40%
Bank of America	No	5 out of 13	38%
Home Depot	No	4 out of 12	33%

Eli Lilly	No	4 out of 13	31%
AbbVie	No	3 out of 12	25%
Merck & Co.	No	4 out of 13	31%

Direct ownership of shares - where founders and employees are shareholders - has been declining rapidly over the past few years in the USA where currently only 13.5% of shares are owned directly. In the United Kingdom it's 11%; in Canada, 10%; in Germany it's down to 7%; and in Japan only 3%. The majority of shares are owned by pension funds and other institutional investors. So, looked at from the opposite direction, 86.5% of USA shares are held by institutions; 89% in the United Kingdom and so on. For the top companies above the largest shareholders are Vanguard, Black Rock and Fidelity Investments, for the majority of the time. Obviously, shareholdings change according to market conditions.

But, again, the same question: why are the three biggest investors not doing more to control excessive remuneration? It is essential that the companies who are managing our investments - in effect, managing *our* money - act a lot more responsibly. This is made more difficult than it should be, because by and large the managers and directors of the institutions come from the same elite group that they need to control.

Examples of effective institutional intervention are few. In 2018, a group of institutional investors led by BlackRock and State Street Global Advisors voted against the pay packages of directors at several major companies, including ExxonMobil and Home Depot. The investors argued that the pay packages were excessive and that they did not reflect the performance of the companies.

In 2019, the California Public Employees' Retirement System (CalPERS) - the largest public pension fund in the United States, with a half-trillion-dollar investment fund - voted against the pay packages of directors at several major companies, including Apple and Alphabet (Google). CalPERS argued that the pay packages were not aligned with the interests of shareholders.

In 2020, the Council of Institutional Investors, which represents over 400 institutional investors with over $50 trillion in assets, published a guide for institutional investors on how to engage with companies on executive compensation. The guide provides recommendations on how to assess executive compensation and how to vote on executive compensation proposals.[3]

Examples where the salary of the CEO or directors have been reduced are few and far between and need to increase significantly. In 2015, Chipotle Mexican Grill's board reduced CEO Steve Ells' salary by 50% and eliminated his bonus after the company faced a food safety crisis that led to a significant decline in sales.

In 2011, Sears Holdings' board reduced CEO Lou D'Ambrosio's salary by 25% and eliminated his bonus after the company reported its third consecutive year of losses.

In 2012, Yahoo!'s board reduced CEO Scott Thompson's salary by 50% and eliminated his bonus after the company revealed that Thompson had inflated his academic credentials.

In 2010, Hewlett-Packard's board reduced CEO Mark Hurd's salary by 10% and eliminated his bonus after the company revealed that Hurd had engaged in an inappropriate relationship with a contractor.

In 2016, Wells Fargo's board reduced CEO John Stumpf's salary by 40% and eliminated his bonus after the company revealed that it had opened millions of unauthorised accounts to meet sales goals.

We might expect a more ethical approach by 'the faiths' (the collective grouping of the world's religions) who control a significant percentage of the world's money. Why do they not use their power to demand better standards from the directors and teams running the major corporations?

According to the Interfaith Centre on Corporate Responsibility (ICCR), its coalition of 300 faith-based institutional investors holds over $4 trillion in managed assets.[4] The Catholic Church alone was estimated in 2023 to hold $73 billion in assets/investments. This substantial investment power could be used to influence companies to adopt more ethical practices, including reducing executive pay. However, several factors contribute to the relative inaction of faith-based investors on the issue of executive compensation. Their reluctance to intervene, where it exists, may give some insight as to the reasons other investment entities also feel disinclined.

Faith-based organisations often have a wide range of priorities, including social justice, environmental stewardship, and religious education. While executive compensation may be a concern, it may not be their top priority when engaging with companies. Maybe it needs to go up their list?

Faith-based investors may not have the same level of financial expertise as traditional institutional investors. This can make it difficult for them to assess executive compensation packages and determine whether they are excessive. But an overall approach of 'we are against excess' would send a message.

Faith-based investors may be reluctant to take strong stances on issues like executive pay for fear of alienating companies and losing access to investment opportunities. Companies often lack transparency regarding executive compensation details. This makes it difficult for investors to gather the necessary information to make informed decisions about executive pay.

Executive compensation packages can be complex and elusive. This can make it challenging for investors to determine whether pay levels are justified. So, insist on more transparency or invest elsewhere. The Faiths surely should take the lead on a moral position?

Despite these challenges, there are some efforts among faith-based investors to address the issue of executive compensation. For instance, the ICCR has developed a set of principles for faith-based investors on engaging companies regarding executive pay. Additionally, some individual faith-based organisations have taken steps to address executive compensation, such as filing shareholder resolutions or engaging in direct dialogue with companies. As faith-based investors gain more experience and expertise in corporate governance, we hope they play a more active role in addressing the issue of executive compensation. Their influence could lead to fairer pay structures and better alignment between executive pay and company performance. I suggest the real issue is that the faiths have power; they are just not using it.

But what explains the reticence of other institutional investors to make a stand? If you look at the global top 10 companies and their boards of directors, you will see they are largely drawn from the same elite educational establishments.

- **Microsoft:** Stanford, MIT, Harvard, University of California, Berkeley, plus University of Washington, Dartmouth

- **Apple:** Stanford, MIT, Yale, plus University of Michigan, University of North Carolina

- **NVIDIA:** Stanford, MIT, Harvard, University of California, Berkeley

- **Alphabet:** Stanford, Harvard, Yale plus University of Pennsylvania

- **Saudi Aramco:** An obvious outlier, primarily Saudi universities, including King Fahd University of Petroleum and Minerals and King Saud University, with some US degrees (MIT, Stanford)

- **Amazon:** Stanford, Harvard, plus Princeton, Dartmouth, University of Michigan

- **Meta:** Stanford, Harvard, Yale

- **Berkshire Hathaway:** Another outlier, with more diverse backgrounds, not necessarily Ivy League-heavy. Warren Buffett himself attended Columbia University.

- **Tesla:** Stanford, MIT, plus University of Pennsylvania, Brown

- **Exxon Mobil:** Texas A&M, University of Texas, Rice University

These alumni also tend to be members of the same clubs and associations. Augusta National Golf Club; Bohemian Club, a California-based social club with a history of hosting influential figures in business, politics, and the arts; The Links Club, a prestigious New York City social club focused on business and networking. There are also The Yale Club, the Cornell Club, the Harvard Club of Chicago, and the Penn Club of New York - the clue is in the names. These are places where Ivy League alumni gather and network, giving new meaning to the sayings, 'it's a small world', and 'it's not what you know, it's who you know'.

Another way to impose a different modus operandi on these corporate giants is to discuss whether their sheer size is having a deleterious effect on the world in which they operate. The global landscape is increasingly characterised by a handful of colossal companies that command immense economic and technological power. These companies, generally referred to as 'Big Tech' or 'super platforms', have a profound impact on the way we live, work, and interact with the world. Their reach extends into nearly every aspect of our lives, raising concerns about their potentially unchecked influence and the potential for stifling competition.

They are also very new, essentially developed in the last 25 years and there is no example of anything like them from history. New problem, new solution. We need to set boundaries around a lot of our current life to make it more reasonable for all. Money corrupts as much as power. Excessive money removes its owners from reality.

Several key indicators point towards a concentration of market power and give evidence of market dominance. Rather than looking at just the largest 10 companies, you could probably go a lot further to at least the top 100. They all have the following characteristics in common -

Massive market capitalization - the combined market capitalization of the top 100 companies is in the tens of trillions of dollars, exceeding the combined GDP of most countries. According to PwC, the total market capitalization of the top 100 companies in the world as of 31 March 2024 was $39.871 trillion, larger than the GDP of the number one country, USA. This sheer financial muscle allows them to invest heavily in research and development, acquire smaller competitors, and shape markets to their advantage.

Many of these companies operate platforms or networks that benefit from network effects, where their value increases as more users join. This creates a powerful barrier to entry for new competitors, as users are drawn to the platform with the largest network. Examples include social media platforms (Meta) and operating systems (Microsoft).

These companies collect vast amounts of data on users, their behaviours, preferences, and interactions. This data is an asset used for targeted advertising, product development, and market analysis. The data advantage allows them to further solidify their positions and create personalised experiences that smaller companies cannot match.

Some of these companies have expanded into multiple related industries, controlling entire supply chains, and making it difficult for smaller players to compete. Amazon, for example, is not just an online retailer, but also a leading cloud service, logistics giant, and content producer of film, television and books.

These companies have substantial resources to spend on lobbying and influencing policy making, potentially shaping regulations that benefit their business models while hindering competition.

This concentration of power in the hands of so few companies raises several concerns that make a compelling argument for considering their breakup. Dominant companies may prioritise incremental improvements over disruptive innovations that could threaten their market position. This can slow overall technological progress and limit consumer choice. Their market dominance can make it difficult for smaller companies and start-ups to compete. This can lead to less consumer choice, higher prices, and a lack of diversity in the marketplace. The vast amount of user data collected by these companies also raises significant privacy concerns, especially as they leverage this data for targeted advertising and other purposes. Breaking them up could lead to greater data protection and user control over their own information.

Dominant companies can engage in practices like predatory pricing, self-preferencing and data hoarding, which harm competition and stifle innovation. Breakups could address these anti-competitive behaviours. The wealth concentrated within these companies and by their executives contributes to income inequality and exacerbates social divides.

Plus, their immense lobbying power can distort the political process and lead to policies that favour them at the expense of the public interest. Breaking them up would reduce their political clout.

Deciding whether to break up these monoliths is a complex issue with no easy answers. While breaking them up might seem drastic, it's crucial to remember that the goal is not to punish success but to ensure a level playing field that fosters innovation and benefits society as a whole. By decentralising power and promoting competition, we can create a more dynamic and resilient economy that serves the needs of all, not just the privileged few.

There are counterarguments, but we don't find them convincing. One is that these large companies are efficient and offer consumers lower prices and greater convenience. Breaking them up could disrupt supply chains and lead to inefficiencies. Breaking up domestic companies might put them at a disadvantage compared to large foreign rivals, potentially harming national competitiveness. Dividing these sprawling companies into smaller entities could be complex and costly, with uncertain outcomes. This complexity is not helped by the complicit behaviour of former members of government and administrations who have become directors of major companies. Those who understand the inner workings of government are very well placed to resist attempts by governments to limit the power of their new employers.

But corporate power that is larger than most countries need controlling. It is very clear that the governance required for a moral business that benefits us all drifts further from reality the bigger they get. It requires careful consideration of the potential benefits and risks, and thorough analysis of the specific market dynamics and potential consequences.

However, the evidence of increasing market concentration and anti-competitive behaviour suggests that a serious conversation about regulatory intervention, including potential breakups, is warranted at international level. Surely no business should control more than 5% of the world market? A decentralised and competitive market could promote greater innovation, more jobs and better consumer choice, and fairer outcomes for all.

Chapter 9 - The 10 key points

1. Corporate Consolidation and Power: The chapter highlights the increasing concentration of power in the hands of a few large corporations, particularly in the tech sector.

2. Big Tech's Dominance: The immense economic and technological power of Big Tech companies is emphasised, raising concerns about their influence on society and the economy.

3. Questionable Shareholder Control: The notion of shareholder control is challenged, as boards of directors often exert significant influence over company decisions, including executive compensation.

4. Decline of Direct Share Ownership: The decline in direct share ownership and the rise of institutional investors raise questions about their role in holding corporations accountable.

5. Limited Investor Intervention: The chapter criticises the limited intervention by institutional investors in curbing excessive executive pay, despite their substantial financial power.

6. Elite Networks and Potential Conflicts: The prevalence of elite educational backgrounds and exclusive club memberships among corporate directors raises concerns about potential conflicts of interest and lack of accountability.

7. The Role of Faith-Based Investors: The chapter questions the effectiveness of faith-based investors in

advocating for ethical practices and fair compensation within corporations.

8. Arguments for Corporate Breakups: The text presents arguments in favour of breaking up large corporations to address concerns about stifled innovation, reduced competition, data privacy violations, and economic inequality.

9. Counter arguments and Regulatory Solutions: The chapter acknowledges counter arguments against corporate breakups but emphasises the need for regulatory intervention to ensure fair competition and protect consumer interests.

10. The Need for a More Balanced Market: The chapter concludes by advocating for a more decentralised and competitive market that fosters innovation, creates jobs, and offers better choices for consumers.

Footnotes – Chapter 9

[1]https://www.forbes.com/sites/forbescoachescouncil/2023/03/17/ten-percent-of-fortune-500-companies-are-now-women-led-the-changing-face-of-leadership/

[2]https://www2.deloitte.com/us/en/pages/about-deloitte/articles/press-releases/new-data-reveals-opportunity-for-growth-on-fortune-500-boards-to-be-more-representative-of-the-us-population.html

[3] Examples of Institutions Reducing Salaries or Getting Companies Under Control; https://www.cii.org/

[4] https://www.iccr.org

CHAPTER 10

The Military & The Terrorists

Terrorists come and go. Frequently, today's terrorist is tomorrow's hero.

During WW2, David Ben-Gurion persuaded the Jewish diaspora in Palestine to fight for the British against Germany. After the war, he was designated an enemy and a terrorist by the British. He then became the first Prime Minister of the newly created state of Israel after 1948 and was posthumously named as one of the 100 Most Important People of the 20th Century by Time Magazine.

Nelson Mandela, internationally lauded and hero-worshipped for his astonishing human and political resilience in the face of South African apartheid, had been designated a terrorist before starting his 27-year prison sentence in 1962. He was still considered a terrorist by many in governments around the world, re-designated as such, along with the African National Congress, by the United States during the 1980s, before Mandela was released from prison in 1990. His name was not removed from that US list even while he was the first black President of South Africa from 1994 to 1999. In fact, it was not removed until days before his 90th birthday in 2008. While on the US terrorist list, Mandela was awarded the Nobel Peace Prize in 1993.

Sinn Fein, the political wing of the Irish Republican Army, became the largest party in Northern Ireland in terms of Parliamentary seats following the UK's 2024 General Election.

So, who is a terrorist, really, and what qualifies as terrorism? The term was not coined until barely 230 years ago, during the period after the French Revolution. At that time, it was used to describe the Government terrorising its opponents. It didn't enter Webster's dictionary until 1840. It took another 80 years to be widely used about individuals acting outside the law when American newspapers referred to Al Capone's gang wars as 'terrorism' in the 1920s. But the public instinctively understood there was a difference between terrorism and criminality.

In fact, it took nearly 200 years for terrorism to be defined as 'violent or destructive acts (such as bombing) committed by groups in order to intimidate a population or government into granting their demands' - a definition that finally found its way into dictionaries only as recently as 1973.[1] Guy Fawkes might have been called a terrorist, but no-one was using the word in 1605. David Ben-Gurion might have been called a terrorist, but to others he was a freedom fighter. Nelson Mandela *was* designated a terrorist, but 40 years later he is a hero, almost a saint.

In the 21st century we have learned to live with a new kind of terrorism, one that seeks not to right a wrong, or to establish a system of human rights, or a newly independent country capable of representing its population. Rather, extremist Islam seeks either to impose its fundamentalist views on global populations, converting them to Islam and installing Sharia Law as the dominant system, or to extract a tax from those who demur, and are willing to live in subjugation. The line in the sand for the emergence of what feels like a return to mediaeval times - the schisms in Christianity denoted by Martin Luther, Henry V111, and the terrors of The Spanish Inquisition - was the return of the Ayatollah Khomeini to Iran in 1979. The first shocks to the international community included the establishment of The Islamic Revolutionary Guard - by decree of Khomeini - and the taking of American embassy staff as hostages in Tehran.

Later, book burnings on Western streets shocked liberal sensitivities, but worse was to come: the World Trade Centre bombing in 1993, 9/11, the 2002 Bali Bombings, 7/7, Charlie

Hebdo, ISIS, numerous suicide bombings and a long list of other attacks killing civilians in countries around the world. These are, truly, terrorist activities. Non-Muslims are seen as expendable, the goal to establish a global caliphate is a priority.

In the face of that, should Israel's purported action during September 2024, exploding thousands of mobile devices, injuring and maiming thousands of Hezbollah operatives in Lebanon, and killing a reported 20 people, be considered an act of defence or an act of terrorism? The collateral death of at least two children certainly gave succour to those who like to consider Israel a terrorist state, despite Hezbollah in the north, and Hamas in the southwest both being publicly dedicated to the obliteration of the Jewish state. History will judge.

Meanwhile, the rise of fundamentalist Islamic extremism has overshadowed acts of resistance which are not Islam-related, such as The Kurdistan Workers Party, whose ultimate aim is to establish an independent Kurdish State. Or the Tamils, fighting to establish their own homeland. Or the NLA and Segunda Marquetalia, two organisations fighting corruption and exploitation in Colombia. Are these people really terrorists, or are they disadvantaged people who do not have any hope, nor any belief that they can move themselves and their families to a higher level, however hard they work? Or, perhaps, like Timothy McVeigh and the Unabomber in America, they feel the heel of government on their neck. Or, like the Irish Republican Army, want a united Ireland, with Great Britain nowhere involved - an end, as they see it, to colonialism.

Many of these people you could argue are in despair about the state of the world as it relates to them. They cannot see their way out; cannot see a better future; and therefore, they listen to the radicals whose solution is to kill and destroy.

But if you look at poor and disadvantaged areas of the world, many of these areas have been, in the past, productive and self-sufficient. Then it was all taken away. The slave catchers came and destroyed tribes, destroyed civilisations. The colonialists invaded and plundered. These were people who already had a system, a way of living together and finding a balance. But adventurers and colonists came knocking, killed the men and took the women and children to new lands, and left what? What should be paid for the damage done to Africa? The damage done to South America?

The term 'terrorist' is always used in a derogatory way, and sometimes in a purely inflammatory way. It is important to consider the different perspectives on who qualifies as a terrorist and whether they are simply disadvantaged people. Resistance against a tyrannical government or system may well be seen as a fight for freedom, while, killing innocent members of the public to intimidate the powers that be certainly qualifies as terrorism.

Still, my terrorist may well be your freedom fighter, and vice versa. But there are pointers to what might persuade civilians that they have no recourse to anything but the gun, or the bomb. Many individuals who become involved in terrorist activities come from marginalised communities that face discrimination and exclusion. This lack of social standing and opportunity can lead to feelings of alienation, anger, and resentment, making people more susceptible to radical ideologies.

Economic hardship and inequality can also play a role in driving individuals towards terrorism. Poverty, unemployment, and lack of access to necessities to live can create a sense of desperation and hopelessness, making individuals more open to extremist messaging that promises change and empowerment. In some cases, individuals may resort to terrorism as a means of resisting oppressive regimes or fighting for political and social justice. When peaceful means of protest and dissent are met with violence or suppression, individuals may feel that what might be deemed terrorism is the only option to achieve their goals. Exposure to violence, trauma and loss can also contribute to radicalization and violence. Individuals who have experienced war, torture, or other traumatic events, may be more susceptible to extremist ideologies that offer a sense of purpose, belonging, and revenge.

Limited access to education and lack of critical thinking skills can also make individuals more vulnerable to manipulation and indoctrination by extremist groups. Without the ability to critically evaluate information and make informed decisions, individuals can be more easily swayed by propaganda and extremist rhetoric. While it is important to recognize the social, economic, and political factors that can contribute to political radicalisation, it is also important to acknowledge that violent rebellion is a complex issue with no single cause.

There are also arguments against the view that armed rebels are simply disadvantaged people, or even that violent resistance is the only answer. Mahatma Gandhi preached and practised non-violent resistance and secured independence for India. Following Gandhi's example, Martin Luther King similarly promoted non-violent actions, and persuaded President Lyndon B Johnson to sign the Civil Rights Act into law. But being met with extreme violence from police in the southern states, King was also opposed on his own side by groups who espoused violence - groups like The Black Panthers and individuals like Malcolm X, speaking on behalf of the Nation of Islam. Malcolm X eventually left the N of I, but both he and Martin Luther King were assassinated for their pains. So, it is worth considering that while there are undeniable underlying causes for believing that insurrection and resistance is the only way, there are equally valid reasons to consider the matter of free choice regarding the way to proceed.

Terrorism, as defined, involves the deliberate targeting of civilians and innocent people, which is a violation of fundamental human rights and cannot be justified by any cause or ideology. While there may be underlying factors that contribute to armed insurrection, individuals ultimately make the choice to engage in violence and terrorism. They cannot be absolved of all responsibility for their actions simply because they come from disadvantaged backgrounds. But neither can governments be absolved of using their military against their own people.[2]

Terrorism is not only about causing physical harm; it is also about creating a climate of fear and intimidation. This can have a devastating impact on individuals, communities, and whole societies. Undermining democratic processes and institutions can lead to instability, more conflict, and repression. Violence almost always breeds more violence, leading to retaliation, counterterrorism measures, and further recruitment to the 'cause', whatever the cause may be.

A vicious cycle of violence is difficult to break. The question of whether armed rebels are simply disadvantaged people is complex and multifaceted. Addressing the root causes of rebellion requires a comprehensive approach that includes promoting social justice, economic equality, and political participation, while also upholding human rights, strengthening democratic institutions, and countering violent extremism. We need to make life for the bottom 50% of the world more equitable. We must also listen when people cry out for help, understanding and change.

The Military and Police – a contract with civilians

Any official military is an extension of its state. In many western countries, defence of the realm is considered one of the top two or three priorities of a democratic government. A democracy thrives on the principle of power residing with the people. This necessitates civilian control over the instruments of enforcement, namely the police and military. While these institutions are crucial for maintaining order and security, a fundamental tension exists. A strong enforcement apparatus is necessary, but unchecked power can easily morph into oppression. So, in a well-functioning democracy, the police and military should act as servants of the people, safeguarding them from both external threats and abuses of power by elected officials.

Police should be - but frequently are not - guardians of domestic tranquillity, upholding the law through enforcing legitimately legislated criminal codes and maintaining public order. Their core mission lies in protecting citizens from crime while upholding their rights and liberties. Part of this role must include fostering trust and cooperation within the community, which has become more difficult in increasingly multicultural societies, where suspicion of police and authorities has been imported from countries scarred by corruption and, frequently, oppression.

Ideally, we would want our police to employ force proportionally and with minimal public disruption, ensuring a safe and secure environment for all. The reality though, even in the most settled of democracies, is that the police frequently appear to be an instrument of the state.

And in a culturally fractured world, it is becoming increasingly puzzling to see the apparent prejudice of various forces around the globe, either individually or collectively, amplified by the public megaphone that is social media. Nothing illustrates this paradigm shift more clearly than the obvious preference given - because of their vastly larger numbers - to those coming onto the streets to support Palestinians at the time of the Gaza conflict. Individual Jews have been filmed being asked by police to move on for fear of inflaming tens of thousands chanting 'From the river to the sea'. Whereas an individual supporter of Palestine confronting Jews out in force is treated differently.

So, the designated role of police - the ideal that they should maintain law and order within the borders of a nation state, and do so on behalf of all citizens, while upholding safety and liberty for all - is under threat in a world where crime is increasingly global (and digital), and aberrant behaviours and attitudes are imported which challenge the previously settled consensus.

The military, meanwhile, is intended to stand as the nation's shield against external threats, safeguarding national security and territorial integrity. Their primary function lies in deterring or defending against foreign aggression.

However, in a democracy, the military must operate under the clear subordination of civilian authority and adhere to democratic principles and constitutional frameworks,[3] and, if asked to go against these principles, should refuse. Surprising as this must sound to many who are unaware of the constitutional concept (even in an unwritten constitution such as the UK's), NATO insists that all members adhere to it. The aim is to ensure that military power serves the will of the people, not the ambitions of a select few.

There are challenges to this concept of civilised behaviour. The shadow of authoritarian pasts can linger. Police and military forces shaped by cultures of repression may struggle to adapt to democratic ideals. This can lead to a disconnect between their methods and the values of a free society. The military and police must be controlled by the top of the legal system or by the president of the country that has no political connection to the government. Their role is to make life safer for everyone. To achieve this, they must remain outside the control of the administration, and they must have an oath of office that allows them to say 'no' and to refuse an action when they are instructed to harm the people they should be protecting.

Even in settled democracies this concept appears shaky. Millions in Europe protested the Iraq war and their governments' participation, even if that participation was not military. The three million who took to the streets in Rome entered the Guinness Book of Records as the largest ever anti-war rally.[4] None of these protests affected how governments behaved. Why? Cynically, they could point to the number of protesters as a proportion of the national population and rightly claim that they did not represent a majority opinion.

Still, it does bring into question the extent to which even democratic governments buy into the idea that the military is, in principle, under civilian authority. More generally, this means that even democratically elected officials, seeking to consolidate power or influence outcomes, may attempt to manipulate law enforcement and the military for personal gain. This undermines the neutrality and impartiality essential for a fair and just society. It should always be resisted by the leadership of both police and military.

During times of crisis or heightened national security concerns, the balance between security needs and civil liberties becomes precarious. Governments may justify increased police and military powers, raising concerns about potential abuses and the erosion of democratic freedoms. The military and the police should always understand that their function is to ensure a just and moral society. Perhaps they should take an oath of office that clearly states, 'We are here to serve the people'? It's a conversation given more currency by the recent intervention of General John Hyten, top US nuclear commander. Hyten said he would push back against an order from

President Elect Trump for a nuclear strike if it were illegal. "I provide advice to the President," Hyten said. "He'll tell me what to do, and if it's illegal, guess what's going to happen? I'm gonna say, 'Mr. President, that's illegal'." [5]

The increasing use of military tactics, equipment, and weaponry in domestic policing raises concerns about a blurring of lines between the two institutions. This can lead to a more aggressive and less community-oriented approach to law enforcement, potentially alienating the public. A robust democracy requires clear and concise laws defining the powers and limitations of both police and military forces. These frameworks establish boundaries, ensuring law enforcement operates within the legal and ethical constraints of a democratic society. Civilian oversight bodies, independent of political influence, are designed to play a critical role in holding law enforcement accountable for their actions. These bodies investigate allegations of misconduct, ensuring transparency and deterring abuses of power. Fostering a culture of respect for democratic principles within police and military institutions is crucial. Educational programs can instil the values of civilian control, human rights, and the importance of upholding the rule of law. Maintaining transparency and open dialogue between citizens and law enforcement is vital for a healthy democracy.

A free press and public discourse also enable citizens to hold police and military accountable, fostering trust and legitimacy. But we also must acknowledge that there is a fine and fragile line between democracy working and democracy failing. From the past there are many examples where the military have acted against their own population: See note 24 in Appendix 1 for a list of historical problems stemming from the military being used against its own people or acting outside of civilian control.

The current situation in many countries enforces everything that is unreasonable in the world. Authorities may believe they are protecting freedom. But when you act by oppressing, beating up and/or shooting the poorest, the disadvantaged, the weakest who are trying to protest the unfairness of their lives, the moral high ground is well and truly lost.

In some cases, it is the military that runs the country. This is a very simple proposition. I have the guns; I can kill you; I am in control. Do what I say, or I *will* kill you.

In this context, the future is extremely frightening. Soldiers are being replaced by computers and drones. The potential consequences of this shift are profound. While autonomous weapons may offer advantages in terms of precision and reducing human casualties, they also raise serious ethical concerns. Can we entrust life-and-death decisions to machines? How do we ensure accountability when algorithms make mistakes? The rise of AI in warfare demands a robust international dialogue and the establishment of clear ethical guidelines to prevent the dehumanisation of conflict and the potential for catastrophic unintended consequences. In the past it has occasionally been possible for people to persuade members of the Armed Forces to step back; to allow individuals to find a place of safety; for the military to see that their action may not be for the good, not reasonable, not ethical. Citizens, however, cannot reason with a computer. In a world driven by algorithms, the soldiers of the future will include machines, drones, the internet of things, operated from thousands of miles away.

While terrorism is a complex issue, the root causes are often suggested to be poverty and suppression which are often cited as root causes. Poverty can create a sense of hopelessness, making individuals more susceptible to radical ideologies that promise change, even though violence.: When people feel their grievances are ignored or that their basic needs are unmet by their government, they may resort to violence to be heard. Oppressive regimes that stifle dissent and lack democratic avenues for change further exacerbate this feeling. The deliberate use of violence against civilians to achieve political aims, is a complex phenomenon with numerous contributing factors. While religious extremism and ethnonationalism often take centre stage, poverty and suppression can act as powerful underlying forces, pushing individuals towards violence.

Imagine living in a world where basic needs like food, shelter, and healthcare are perpetually out of reach. A relentless struggle for survival can breed a sense of hopelessness and alienation. It has been argued that such desperation makes individuals more susceptible to the allure of radical ideologies that promise a better future, even if achieved through violent means. Terrorist organisations often exploit this desperation, offering a twisted sense of purpose and belonging.

Poverty isn't simply material deprivation; it's often intertwined with feelings of marginalisation and injustice. When people believe their grievances are systematically ignored or their basic rights trampled upon by the very government that should protect them, resentment festers. In her book *Do Morals Matter? Presidents and Foreign Policy from FDR to Trump*, political scientist Margaret MacMillan highlights how historical injustices, like colonialism or discriminatory policies, can create a long-lasting sense of anger that fuels extremist movements. If peaceful avenues for change are unavailable, some may resort to violence to be heard.

The Irish Republican Army (IRA) is an example. Throughout the 19th and early 20th centuries, Ireland simmered under British rule. Widespread poverty, particularly during the Great Famine (1845-1852), coupled with discrimination against the Catholic majority, fuelled resentment. Groups like the IRA emerged, employing violence to overthrow British control and establish an independent Irish Republic. (Reference: *A History of Ireland* by Richard Killeen)

Similarly, for over a century, France colonised Algeria, exploiting its resources and marginalising the native population. This economic disparity and political suppression fuelled the rise of the National Liberation Front (FLN), an Algerian nationalist movement that used guerrilla warfare to achieve independence through the Algerian War of Independence (1954-1962). (Reference: *The Battle of Algiers* by Alistair Horne)

There are modern parallels. The 2003 US invasion of Iraq created a power vacuum and destabilised the region. The marginalisation of Sunni Muslims under the US-backed Shia government further stoked grievances. ISIS, a Sunni group, capitalised on this environment, exploiting poverty, sectarian tensions, and a sense of injustice to recruit fighters who saw violence as the only path to a better future. (Reference: *ISIS: The State of Terror* by Jessica Stern and J.M. Berger)

In Afghanistan, a decade of Soviet occupation followed by brutal civil war left the country in ruins. Poverty and despair were rampant. The Taliban, promising stability, and order under their harsh interpretation of Islamic law, gained a foothold. While not solely driven by poverty, the desperate situation in Afghanistan undoubtedly played a role in the group's rise to power. (Reference *Afghanistan: A History* by Thomas Barfield)

It's important to acknowledge that poverty is not a guaranteed path to terrorism or rebellion, nor is it the only one. Individuals make choices, and other factors like lack of education, little access to information, and the presence of established extremist groups all play a role. Additionally, not all terrorism is rooted in poverty and suppression. Religious extremism, ethnonationalism, or even mental health issues can also be driving forces.

Combating any kind of violent activity, be it actual terrorism or resistance against a repressive regime, requires a comprehensive strategy. While robust security measures are essential, a purely military approach can be counterproductive. As Martha Crenshaw argues in her book *Terrorism In Context*, addressing the root causes of terrorism, such as poverty, inequality, and political repression, is crucial. This can involve economic development, where investing in poverty reduction programs, promoting economic opportunity, and ensuring equitable distribution of resources can create more stability and less fertile ground for extremism; good governance, such as promoting democratic institutions, upholding human rights, and ensuring fair representation for all groups can help address grievances and foster a sense of belonging within the political system; and countering extremist narratives to challenge extremist ideologies. Through education, promoting interfaith dialogue, and fostering critical thinking skills individuals can be helped to resist radicalisation.

But most importantly, and this speaks to the central theme of this book, if you can produce a paradigm of a much more moral world where there is opportunity for everyone, and the resources and wealth are shared on a much more reasonable basis, then we will surely reduce the motivation to resort to violence to achieve social justice.

Chapter 10- The 10 key points

1. Terrorism: The chapter debates the traditional view of terrorists as simply bad guys, which they are, because there is no excuse for attacking innocent people. But we must debate the causes: are many driven to violence by desperation and marginalisation?

2. Factors Fuelling Radicalization: The text explores the complex factors that contribute to terrorism, including poverty, oppression, lack of education, and exposure to violence.

3. The Military as an Instrument of Power: The military is analysed as an extension of state power, regardless of the governing system, highlighting the importance of civilian control.

4. Ideal Military Role in a Democracy: In a democracy, the military's primary function is to protect citizens from external threats while upholding democratic principles and the rule of law.

5. Challenges to Civilian Oversight: The chapter identifies historical legacies, political interference, and national security concerns as obstacles to maintaining civilian control over the military.

6. Safeguarding Civilian Control: Mechanisms like clear legal frameworks, independent oversight bodies, and education within the military are proposed to ensure civilian control and prevent abuses of power.

7. The Rise of Drones and Automated Warfare: The increasing use of drones and automation in warfare

raises ethical concerns about accountability and the potential for unintended consequences.

8. Historical Examples of Terrorism's Roots: The chapter cites historical instances where poverty and oppression fuelled terrorism, such as the Irish Republican Army (IRA) and the Algerian War of Independence.

9. Addressing Root Causes: A comprehensive approach to countering terrorism involves addressing underlying factors like poverty, inequality, and political repression through economic development, good governance, and countering extremist narratives.

10. The Complexity of Terrorism: The chapter acknowledges that terrorism is a complex issue with no single cause, requiring a multifaceted approach that combines security measures with efforts to address root causes and promote peace.

Footnotes – Chapter 10

[1] https://www.merriam-webster.com/wordplay/history-of-the-word-terrorism

[2] Note 26, Appendix 1 for other examples of the military being used against own people.

[3] Note 27, Appendix 1, constitutional framework, further details

[4] https://www.guinnessworldrecords.com/world-records/74335-largest-anti-war-rally

[5] https://edition.cnn.com/2018/09/06/politics/us-military-chain-of-command-trump-orders/index.html

CHAPTER 11

Religion and The Faiths

It is impossible to examine the current state of the world without looking at the various Faiths. The Faiths gave us the rules by which most of our societies are now organised.

Judaism, the first of the Abrahamic faiths - those which displaced what we now call Paganism (faiths where adherents could choose the object of their worship, from the sun to the moon to goats and beyond) - provided the bedrock of Western society with its Ten Commandments. The stories in the Jewish Torah date from approximately 3,500 years ago, and include Adam and Eve, Moses, and the Ten Commandments, delivered to Moses on Mount Sinai by the one and only true God of creation.

The Torah is significantly mirrored in the Christian Old Testament, Christianity being the second of the Abrahamic faiths. The New Testament, featuring the 2,000-year-old teachings of Jesus Christ, further amplifies the message of universal love, respect and particularly the need to care and cater for the poor, needy, and hungry.

Islam, at 1,400 years old the third and youngest of the major Abrahamic faiths, reflects heavily on both Judaism and Christianity in its sacred book, the Quran. Commonalities between all three books include Adam and Eve as the first humans; Satan; Moses; and Noah.[1] The Quran - like the Torah and The Bible - also emphasises the importance of caring for those less fortunate.

The main difference between the sacred books is that the Torah and The Bible contain stories from which readers may draw lessons on how they might live their lives, while the Quran is more of an instructional polemic. A major difference between the three faiths, though, is far more significant. Christianity and Islam are proselytising religions - which is to say that they have attempted to spread and grow their global congregation through both mission and war. Judaism tends to its own, and does not seek to expand, considering proselytising to be offensive.[2]

In this, Judaism is like Hinduism, possibly the oldest religion at maybe 4,000 years. And like the Abrahamic faiths, Hinduism also preaches caring for those less fortunate. Which brings us to the point: is religion the panacea for all ills? Or is it the cause of more wars among humanity than any other single idea?

We in the West were told - and many were convinced - during the 1960s and 1970s that we should look East for our spirituality. Organised religion in the West had been responsible for The Crusades, The Spanish Inquisition, the violence of Henry VIII's Reformation, the schism in the Catholic Church caused by Martin Luther beyond his native Germany. Eastern spirituality was sold as something far more profound and, more importantly, peaceful.

But those souls seeking enlightenment 50 years ago would be shocked today by news of Buddhists fighting Hindus, Hindus fighting Muslims, and Muslims fighting everyone, even each other. How come Hinduism, for instance, with its belief in Karma (or as we lesser souls know it, what goes around comes around) also brought us the caste system, at the bottom of which were 'the untouchables' - literally people who were not to be touched by those of a higher caste, fit only for cleaning toilets and sweeping the streets?[3]

And how does it come about that Islamic extremists not only violently proselytise - in the name of jihad - but offer those they conquer three choices: convert; pay a tax and live in subjugation; or die?[4]

And why is it that Buddhist Monks are attacking Muslims?[5]

The obvious conclusion is that religion is not the answer to the world's ills.

Still, 83% of the global population claims adherence to some form of established religion.[6] According to the Pew Research Centre (and others) Christianity is the largest at 2.4bn adherents (31% of global population; Islam is second at 1.9bn (24%); with Hindus third at nearly one billion (15%).

The unaffiliated 16.5% - those who claim no organised religious attachment - mostly live in China. Given that China's long-standing 'one child' policy has only recently been abandoned, the religiously-affiliated global population may increase in the next 20 years. Christianity is projected to keep growing; and Islam will continue to grow, at a predicted faster rate, so that by 2060, the world's two major religions will be neck and neck. Hinduism, meanwhile, is entering what may be seen as its 'extremist phase', even to the extent that India may be renamed Bharat if its Hindu Prime Minister Narendra Modi and some very vocal religious leaders get their way.[7]

So, we are a long way from a secular world, despite what Western intellectuals might think or say. Religion will continue to be a social disruptor, rather than - as many sacred doctrines proclaim - a bringer of peace.

Even the central tenet of 'raising up', of giving succour to the poor and hungry - from the teachings of Jesus Christ (The New Testament, Matthew 25:35-40), to the Buddhist concept of karuna (The Dhammapada, Verse 1) - has been missed by several country miles for literally thousands of years.

In fact, in the 21st century, Christianity's leaders are more likely to criticise the government of the day than to follow their own doctrines; while Islam's leaders preach jihad and book burnings and invade each other's countries; and the political leader of India's Hindus is more interested in a nationalist approach to the country's future, at the severe expense of other indigenous citizens who may be Muslim, Jains, or Sikhs.

So, no, we cannot look to religion to help solve the problems of the world, even the inequities and inequalities that pervade, despite 4,000 years of varying doctrines claiming that the meek shall inherit the earth.

Still, while they offer solace and foster a sense of community, many faiths grapple with the seemingly contradictory reality of poverty amidst their congregations and communities. Examining the reasons for this disconnect between the stated values of many religions and their actions regarding poverty alleviation, we must explore the institutional, theological, historical, and practical factors that contribute to this paradox. Maintaining a religious organisation requires significant resources. Upkeep of buildings, salaries for clergy, and administrative costs can leave limited funds for direct poverty alleviation programs. Extensive bureaucracies within religious institutions can also impede efficient resource allocation.[8]

Religious texts are also open to diverse interpretations. While some interpretations emphasise charity and social justice, others might focus more on individual salvation or maintaining social order. For instance, prosperity gospel teachings, prevalent in some Christian denominations, suggest that material wealth is a sign of God's favour, potentially creating a justification for existing inequalities. Many religious institutions have a long and complex history, sometimes intertwined with powerful elites. This historical context can create a reluctance to challenge economic inequalities or advocate for systemic change that might threaten the status quo. The Church of England's historical ties to the British aristocracy, as referenced by Hugh McLeod in his book, *Religion In Victorian England,*[9] is one such example.

Not all religious institutions, particularly smaller congregations in remote areas, have the infrastructure or resources to deliver aid programs effectively. Distributing resources and managing volunteers can be challenging, especially in geographically dispersed communities. Some argue that the primary function of religion is to address spiritual well-being, leaving material needs to secular organisations. This perspective, however, can be seen as neglecting the interconnectedness of physical and spiritual well-being.

Despite the challenges, numerous religious organisations actively work to alleviate poverty. Here are some prominent examples:

Catholic Charities: This extensive network provides a wide range of social services, including food banks, homeless shelters, and job training programs, demonstrating the Catholic Church's avowed commitment to social justice.[10]

Buddhist Social Service Programs: Many Buddhist organisations, guided by the principles of compassion and non-violence, run schools, healthcare clinics, and microfinance initiatives in developing countries.[11]

Islamic Zakat: One of the Five Pillars of Islam, Zakat (The Quran, Surah 2:177) is a mandatory charitable contribution that helps alleviate poverty within Muslim communities.

These organisations try to bridge the gap between faith and action by mobilising volunteers. Religious communities often have a dedicated base of volunteers willing to donate time and effort to social service programs. Religious institutions can also leverage their existing trust within communities to effectively distribute aid and resources. In addition, many faith-based programs offer not just material aid, but also counselling, spiritual guidance, and a sense of belonging. However, the effectiveness of faith-based initiatives in addressing poverty can be limited by factors such as a focus on short-term relief rather than long-term empowerment, a lack of transparency and accountability in some organisations, and the potential for religious institutions to prioritise their own interests over the needs of the poor. To truly make a lasting impact, faith-based organisations must embrace a more holistic approach that combines spiritual guidance with practical solutions, empowers individuals and communities to become self-sufficient, and operates with transparency and accountability.

Reconciling religious values with concrete actions requires a multi-pronged approach. As mentioned elsewhere, the Faiths must begin to better exercise their financial power to make sure that their investments are leveraged to ensure a more just and equitable system. Let's be clear - the Faiths between them have a lot of money, and they are not using the power which that money represents. There needs to be much more focus on helping the poor and the disadvantaged, encouraging interpretations of sacred texts that emphasise social justice and helping those in need. Theologians and religious leaders can play a crucial role in promoting these reinterpretations.[12]

They can also promote collaboration, fostering partnerships between religious organisations and secular NGOs to leverage the strengths of both entities. Religious groups can provide volunteers and local knowledge, while NGOs can offer expertise in program design and implementation.[13] Encouraging religious institutions to be more transparent about their finances and the impact of their social programs could help rebuild public trust and encourage greater contributions. Independent audits and clear reporting mechanisms are crucial for this.[14]

Shifting focus from solely providing basic necessities to empowering individuals and communities through education and job training programs can lead to long-term poverty reduction. This approach aligns with the concept: 'give a man a fish, feed him for a day; teach him to fish, feed him for life'. The current disconnect, long in the making, between religious values and actions regarding poverty alleviation is a complex issue. However, by acknowledging the reasons behind this paradox and working towards solutions, religious institutions can play a more significant role in creating a just and equitable world. Ultimately, the goal is to bridge the gap between the promise of religious teachings and the reality of poverty in our world.

What do the Quran, Bible, Torah, and other texts say about freedom and giving to the poor?

The Quran: Zakat (Mandatory Charity): 'And establish prayer and give zakat and obey the Messenger and [fear] Allah and the Last Day.' (Quran 2:43)

Care for Orphans and the Weak: 'And as for the orphans, establish for them their [rightful] share. And give the kinsman his due and the poor and the traveller. And do not waste extravagantly. Indeed, the wasteful are brothers of the devils. And the Shaytan was ever to his Lord ungrateful.' (Quran 26:17-17)

Helping Those in Need: 'Those who spend their wealth [in charity] by night and by day, secretly and publicly – they will have their reward with their Lord. And there will be no fear upon them, nor will they grieve.' (Quran 2:274)

The Bible: Giving to the Poor: 'Whoever is generous to the poor lends to the Lord, and he will reward him for his good deed.' (Proverbs 19:17)

Caring for the Vulnerable: 'Speak up for those who cannot speak for themselves, for the rights of all who are destitute. Speak up and judge fairly; defend the rights of the poor and needy.' (Proverbs 31:8-9)[15]

The Faiths should be the leaders of morality and should set the very best of examples. It's not as if they do not have money. While exact figures are elusive, estimates suggest that the Vatican alone (The Catholic Church) holds assets worth tens of billions of dollars, including extensive real estate holdings, art collections, and investments. The global Catholic Church, with its network of dioceses, parishes, schools, hospitals, and charitable organisations, is estimated to have assets worth hundreds of billions, if not trillions, of dollars.

Islamic banking and finance are estimated to have assets exceeding $3 trillion. This includes Islamic banks, investment funds, and insurance companies operating under Sharia principles. The value of mosques and religious endowments varies widely across countries. Some prominent examples like Masjid al-Haram in Mecca and the Al-Aqsa Mosque in Jerusalem hold immense historical and religious value, making their monetary worth difficult to assess. Oil-rich Muslim-majority nations like Saudi Arabia and the United Arab Emirates have sovereign wealth funds estimated to be worth hundreds of billions or even trillions of dollars. A portion of these funds is often allocated to investments compliant with Islamic principles.

Within Hinduism, temples in India, particularly those with large endowments and historical significance, are believed to hold enormous wealth in the form of gold, jewellery, land, and other assets. The Padmanabhaswamy Temple in Kerala, India, is reported to have treasures worth tens of billions of dollars. Various Hindu organisations and ashrams hold significant assets, but their combined wealth is difficult to estimate due to limited transparency.

Buddhist temples and monasteries, especially in countries like Thailand, China, and Japan, often own valuable real estate, historical artefacts, and precious metals. While exact figures are hard to come by, some estimates suggest that the combined assets of Buddhist institutions globally could be in the tens of billions of dollars.

Jewish communities around the world own numerous synagogues, community centres, and schools. These assets, along with financial investments and endowments, contribute to the overall wealth of Jewish organisations, which is estimated to be in the billions of dollars. These organisations have endowments and raise funds for various Jewish causes and community programs, collectively managing billions of dollars.

The role of religious leaders in promoting peace and condemning violence has been a subject of ongoing debate and scrutiny, particularly in the context of current conflicts. While many religious leaders advocate for peaceful resolutions, there is a valid argument that more could be done to actively preach against war and violence.

This critique is especially relevant when considering the Russian Orthodox Church's stance on the conflict in Ukraine. With its close ties to the Kremlin, the Church has faced criticism for its perceived complicity. Patriarch Kirill, the head of the church, has openly supported the Russian government's actions, framing the war as a righteous defence of traditional values against Western encroachment. This stance has been seen by many as justifying violence and contributing to the escalation of the conflict. While some within the church have expressed dissent and called for peace, their voices have been largely marginalised. The church's official position has aligned with the government's narrative, raising concerns about its independence and commitment to universal moral principles.

By sharp contrast, the Ayatollahs Khomeini and Khamenei, successive Supreme Leaders of Iran, have been eager proponents of the violent spread of Islam, and the violent resistance of Shiism against the spread of Sunnism. More than half of the conflicts in today's world are Sunni v Shia.

So, while we might expect that religious leaders hold a unique moral authority that can influence individuals and communities, it is not always exercised in ways that we might desire. By actively condemning violence and promoting peace, they could help create a culture of non-violence. Religious teachings emphasise compassion, forgiveness, and reconciliation. By highlighting these values, religious leaders could provide spiritual guidance for those grappling with the realities of conflict. They could also play a crucial role in facilitating dialogue and mediation between conflicting parties, drawing on their spiritual authority to build trust and understanding. Christianity's' leaders have tried to do this with regard to Israel and Gaza, but Judaism's leaders are not all on the same page, some crying out for peace and an end to the conflict, while others preach an eye for an eye.

Religious institutions have a long history of challenging the power of secular authorities. Perhaps it's time for them to employ this useful skill in challenging each other's authorities? By speaking out against injustice and violence, they could hold leaders accountable and push for peaceful solutions. But the examples of the Russian Orthodox Church vis a vis Ukraine, and the very tenets of Islam - to proselytise and spread the Faith, through armed conquest if necessary - mean we should not be holding our breath for a change of direction. Unequivocally, there is an urgent need for religious leaders to oppose violence and advocate peaceful resolutions. By doing so, they would be upholding their moral responsibility to promote peace and justice in the world. Every religion in the world has the same message, help the poor, the weak, the undefended, the vulnerable. Give what you can spare. We need to make sure that we do this.

Chapter 11 - The 10 key points

1. Emphasis on Compassion and Charity: Many religions advocate for compassion and charity towards the less fortunate, highlighting the importance of helping those in need.

2. Disconnect Between Ideals and Action: The chapter observes a disconnect between religious teachings and the actions of religious institutions in addressing poverty and inequality.

3. Institutional and Theological Challenges: Factors like institutional constraints, varying interpretations of religious texts, and historical ties can hinder religious organisations' efforts to alleviate poverty.

4. The Debate on Spiritual vs. Material Needs: The chapter explores the debate within religious circles about whether the focus should be solely on spiritual well-being or also on addressing material needs like poverty.

5. Examples of Successful Faith-Based Initiatives: The text highlights examples of religious organisations actively working to alleviate poverty through various programs and initiatives.

6. Leveraging Religious Resources: Religious institutions can leverage their trust within communities, volunteer networks, and financial resources to effectively address poverty.

7. Solutions for Bridging the Gap: The chapter proposes solutions like reinterpreting religious texts, fostering

collaboration between religious and secular organisations, and increasing transparency in the use of funds.

8. Empowerment Over Handouts: Shifting the focus from providing handouts to empowering individuals through education and sustainable development is emphasised.

9. The Complexity of the Issue: The chapter acknowledges the complex relationship between religion and poverty but maintains hope for positive change through faith-based initiatives.

10. Call for Further Research: The chapter calls for more research to assess the effectiveness of faith-based approaches to poverty alleviation and identify best practices.

Footnotes – Chapter 11

[1] https://en.wikipedia.org/wiki/Biblical_narratives_in_the_Quran

[2] https://reformjudaism.org/learning/answers-jewish-questions/why-dont-jews-proselytize

[3]https://www.culturalsurvival.org/publications/cultural-survival-quarterly/indias-untouchables#:~:text=Untouchability%20as%20a%20religiously%20legitimated,heinous%20sins%20in%20previous%20births .

[4] https://academic.oup.com/ejil/article/24/1/343/438602

[5] https://www.bbc.co.uk/news/magazine-22356306

[6] https://www.pewresearch.org/religion/2022/12/21/key-findings-from-the-global-religious-futures-project/

[7]https://www.euronews.com/culture/2023/09/09/will-india-be-renamed-bharat-heres-why-some-countries-change-their-name

[8] The Non-profit Paradox: Competing Logics of Charity and Social Change by Robert Wuthnow was published by Princeton University Press. A seminal work in the field of non-profit studies, it delves into the inherent tensions and contradictions within the non-profit sector, examining the competing logics of charity and social change that often coexist within these organisations.

[9] https://link.springer.com/book/10.1007/978-1-349-24477-5

[10] https://www.catholiccharitiesusa.org/

[11] https://inebnetwork.org

[12] https://www.amazon.co.uk/Gustavo-Gutierrez-Introduction-Liberation-Theology/dp/1620329026

[13] https://sdgs.un.org/2030agenda

[14] https://www.guidestar.org/Default.htm?aspxerrorpath=/ViewEdoc.aspx

[15] Note, 26, Appendix 1 for a more extensive list of religious quotes on helping the poor

CHAPTER 12

Revolutionary Response

If a significant section of society lacks a reasonable quality of life those people will increasingly think about revolution. Even more importantly, if those same people have no hope for the future, have no belief that they can achieve a better life for themselves and their children then, ultimately, they will revolt.

On the one hand, we have individuals with multiple homes, multiple cars, yachts, aeroplanes, and handbags that cost at minimum a year's rent for most people. On the other hand, you have people starving and suffering from avoidable diseases, unable to keep their children fed and safe.

Until very recently - the last 20 years at most - it was difficult for the poor and needy to see how the rest of the world lived. State run media in non-democratic countries kept information to the minimum required to serve that state's own purposes. In today's world most people have a cell phone. In a world of more than eight billion souls, it is estimated 7.33bn have a cell phone.[1] Now, all but the very poorest in the world can access the huge amount of information and data that is available on the internet.

And that information is telling billions of people about lifestyles and riches beyond their wildest imaginings.

Imagine living in a village in Africa, or a tucked away community in India, and, with a five second Google search, coming across a story about Roman Abramovich's yacht, The Eclipse, which cost about $1 billion to build. Annual running costs, including maintenance, fuel, and crew salaries, are estimated to be around $60 million.

Abramovich has owned several other superyachts, each costing hundreds of millions of dollars.

Other yachts include Amazon boss Jeff Bezos's Flying Fox, with an estimated construction cost of $500 million; Reliance Industries' boss Mukesh Ambani's Antilia with a reported construction cost over $1 billion; and Topaz, valued at over $500m,[2] owned by Sheikh Mansour bin Zayed Al Nahyan, who, among other assets, owns Manchester City Football Club.

What do we suppose some poor individual surviving on the equivalent of $3 a day makes of this? What do they make of people owning their own island - Necker Island, for instance, (Richard Branson); or Lanai (Larry Ellison), purchased for $300 million in 2012? Or of Lakshmi Mittal spending $60m on his daughter's wedding, starting at the Palace of Versailles and ending at the Vaux-le-Comte[3] - both venues emblematic of the excess which led to the French Revolution. This particular irony would probably be lost on poor Indian villagers in 2004. But reality trumps irony, and today, they are able to follow such conspicuous consumption almost blow by blow on social media.

Or what must these same deprived and struggling folk think of the ego-driven purchase of Leonardo da Vinci's *Salvator Mundi* for a record-breaking $450.3 million in 2017? Do they think to themselves, "Oh, Saudi Crown Prince Mohammed bin Salman must be a real lover of great art"? Or do they think: "That's more than the GDP of half a dozen countries at the bottom of the world's GDP rankings"?[4]

This is more than conspicuous consumption. Consider also *Shot Sage Blue Marilyn* (Andy Warhol), not a painting as such, but a silk-screen print, which sold for $195 million in 2022, making it the most expensive 20th-century artwork ever sold; or a Rolls-Royce Boat Tail custom-built car, only three models produced, estimated to cost $28 million; or a Bugatti La Voiture Noire, one-of-a-kind, priced at $18.7 million.

Or Beyoncé, reportedly paid $24 million for a single performance at the launch of Atlantis The Royal, a new Dubai hotel, in 2023; Mariah Carey reportedly paid $5 million for a private concert for a

Russian oligarch; The Rolling Stones, recipients of $18.7m for playing at David Bonderman's 60th birthday party in 2002 (32m in 2024).

But in addition to these shots to the heart of what normal people might consider reasonable wealth and reasonable consumption, those at the very top do a lot more harm to our world than simply spending unconscionable amounts of money on momentary gratification. They also damage the environment with excessive travel in private jets and yachts used for unnecessary travel.

The super-rich also waste large amounts of food, prepared for flagrantly publicised events, or carried 'just in case' on private flights, yacht trips and parties, and backstage night after night at music and fashion gigs. In 2022, 735m of us were hungry, an increase of 122m from the pre-pandemic level.[5] The inevitable consequence of all this - the private islands, the yachts, the private jets, the luxury goods, the food waste - is a disproportionate amount of greenhouse gas emissions. According to Oxfam, the richest 1% emit as much planet-heating pollution as two-thirds of humanity.[6]

The demand for luxury goods, which require scarce resources like rare metals and exotic materials, can also lead to environmental degradation and resource depletion.[7]

And then, as if to rub salt into the wounds, the wealthy use complex legal structures to minimise their tax burden, depriving governments of revenue, almost $5T over the next decade, according to The Tax Justice Network.[8]

This growing gap between the super-rich and the rest of society raises concerns about fairness and social justice. The immense wealth of the super-rich can translate into power, political and social (Ignoring corporate governance), potentially undermining democratic processes and further undermining social cohesion. Does this matter? It possibly would not have mattered at a point in history when billions had no access to the information highway, because there was no information highway.

But growth of the internet and speeding up the dissemination of knowledge has coincided with a massive increase in the gap between rich and poor. This is happening not only in poorer countries, but also in countries such as those belonging to the G7 (supposedly the world's most advanced economies) and the G20, a grouping of 19 developed economies, plus the European Union (EU).

The EU itself is a grouping of 27 countries looking to be, en masse, a trading competitor to global trading leaders America, China, and Russia. But even within the EU there are countries outside the global top 100 GDP rankings, and only 15 in the top 40.[9] Just as, for instance, in the United States of America wealth is not distributed equally among its 50 member states. Maryland, New Jersey and Massachusetts top the list of highest median household incomes (Maryland, $98,461 in 2022), with Mississippi, West Virginia and Arkansas at the bottom of that list (Arkansas, $56,335 in 2022).[10] Worse for America, median wealth per adult for 2023 was $107,700 for the whole of the USA, compared with $267,900 for Belgian adults, $247,500 for Australian adults, and $203,300 for adults from the Netherlands, to give a few examples.[11]

We have already seen a hint of the consequences of such inequality in the world, in the Donald Trump-inspired attack on America's Capitol Building on January 6, 2021, a glimpse of what people might do if they see no future for themselves and their family. It is supremely ironic that, as a prominent member of the super wealthy, the new elite, Trump could paint himself as a victim of the very system which controls, directly or indirectly, the government and through it the army and the police. But Trump clearly demonstrated that there is an urgent need to change, to be more moral, to be fairer to all. He showed conclusively that one of the possible responses to societal failure could be Revolution, with a capital R. And this can be from the gun empowered right wing just as easily as it can be from the left seeking social justice and redistribution.

There are other recent examples of democratic revolutions where people have revolted against corrupt leaders or systems:

The Tunisian Revolution (2010-2011): A popular uprising in Tunisia led to the overthrow of President Zine El Abidine Ben Ali.

The revolution sparked a wave of protests known as the Arab Spring across the Middle East and North Africa.

The Egyptian Revolution (2011): Mass protests and demonstrations in Egypt led to the ousting of President Hosni Mubarak, who had been in power for nearly 30 years.

The Ukrainian Revolution (2013-2014): Known as the Euromaidan protests, resulted in the removal of President Viktor Yanukovych following widespread corruption allegations.

The Burkina Faso Revolution (2014): Mass protests in Burkina Faso led to the resignation of President Blaise Compaoré, who had ruled for 27 years.

The Armenian Velvet Revolution (2018): Peaceful protests and civil disobedience in Armenia led to the resignation of Prime Minister Serzh Sargsyan, who had attempted to maintain power through constitutional changes.

The Sudanese Revolution (2018-2019): A sustained campaign of protests in Sudan led to the ousting of President Omar al-Bashir, who had ruled for nearly 30 years.

The Lebanese October Revolution (2019): Large-scale demonstrations erupted in Lebanon, demanding an end to corruption and economic mismanagement, leading to the resignation of Prime Minister Saad Hariri.

The Prague Spring was a period of political liberalisation and mass protest in Czechoslovakia that occurred in 1968. It began in January when reformist Alexander Dubček was elected First Secretary of the Communist Party of Czechoslovakia (KSČ), and continued until August 21, 1968, when the Soviet Union and other Warsaw Pact members invaded the country to suppress the reforms.

The Bolivian protests (2019): Protests and civil unrest in Bolivia resulted in the resignation of President Evo Morales following accusations of electoral fraud.

These events can be characterised as popular uprisings against corrupt leaders, but the outcomes and subsequent political developments in each country have varied. Establishing stable and functioning democracies after such revolutions can be a complex and ongoing process. The Arab Spring (2010-11) ousted some corrupt and unpopular despots, but in most instances their replacements have been worse.

The events in Belarus following the August 2020 presidential election were not a successful revolution but a wave of mass protests resulting in a subsequent crackdown. In August 2020, President Alexander Lukashenko had claimed victory in an election widely condemned as fraudulent. Hundreds of thousands of Belarusians took to the streets in peaceful protests demanding fair elections and Lukashenko's resignation. The government responded with a brutal crackdown, using riot police, detentions, torture, and violence against protesters. The international community widely condemned the election and the government's violent response. Despite the protests, Lukashenko remained in power. The government continued to suppress dissent, targeting opposition leaders, journalists, and activists. Many opposition figures, including Sviatlana Tsikhanouskaya, were forced into exile.

While the mass protests subsided, smaller-scale resistance and civil disobedience continued in Belarus. And the impact has been to plunge Belarus into a deep political crisis, with ongoing tensions between the government and its opponents. The crackdown also led to further international isolation of Belarus, with sanctions imposed by Western countries. But the sanctions were not used effectively. Political instability and the poorly executed sanctions have had a negative impact on the Belarusian economy, hurting the poor as much as it hurts the thugs and criminals in government. Maybe, in the future, using the power of AI and the internet, we can be a lot more effective with sanctions, if there is the political will?

The consequences in Belarus, and in those countries that experienced the Arab Spring suggest the world would be better off avoiding such popular/populist uprisings. But the growing disparity between the rich, the not rich, and the downright poor, fuelled by the unchecked accumulation of wealth by a select few, and the power that comes with such wealth, is creating an increasingly unsustainable global landscape. Mainstream and online media flaunt these extravagant lifestyles filled with mega-yachts, private islands, and exclusive parties. Billions around the world struggle with poverty, hunger, and lack of necessities.

This growing disparity is not a new phenomenon. What is new is the ability of all but the very poorest to watch it happening in real time.

History is replete with examples of societies where the gap between the haves and have-nots became so extreme that it led to social unrest and revolution. From the French Revolution to the Arab Spring, the oppressed have consistently risen against their oppressors when pushed to their limits. In the past, the lack of access to information allowed the powerful to control narratives and maintain their grip on power. However, the advent of the internet and widespread availability of smartphones have changed the game.

Now, billions of people have access to information that reveals the stark inequalities of the world. The Arab Spring of 2011 was the first uprising at least partially organised on social media. The speed at which it spread was astonishing to Western observers. There was optimism, also, that we were witnessing an end to the heavy hand of extremist Islam, whose leaders had pitched their people back into what many in the West felt was a Dark Age. Optimism was short-lived, and the unfortunate consequences have been long-lived, still being felt - in Yemen, where civil war rages, in Libya, where civil unrest and opposing militias have rendered stable government impossible, and in Syria, where President Assad had waged war against his own people in the most brutal of ways since protests against him in 2011, 2013, and 2015 almost brought down his regime. Finally, in 2024, he was forced to flee the country as the rebels took over the country with a speed that shocked the world.

These are instances where we can see the failure of international law - all these countries are members of the United Nations, yet face no prosecutions, or viable sanctions. Meanwhile, Asma al-Assad, British born wife of the Syrian President, had been repeatedly featured in western media for her high-end purchases - $350,000 on furniture; $7,000 for a pair of crystal-encrusted shoes - and her lavish lifestyle in what is estimated to be a $1bn palace in Damascus.[12] In a world where information flows freely, such excesses fuel resentment and can easily ignite the flames of revolution, as Assad and his wife quickly discovered – forced to flee their property and belongings, subsequently subject to looting by the newly liberated citizens of Syria.

The world's largest corporations, often led by super-rich individuals apparently from the same gene pool, also play a role in perpetuating inequality. Their immense power and resources enable them to influence policy, exploit labour, and avoid paying their fair share of taxes. While these corporations claim to be accountable to shareholders, their boards of directors often operate with minimal oversight and prioritise their own financial interests (as we highlight in Chapter 9). This lack of accountability and transparency further erodes public trust and fuels social unrest. There are many historical precedents for revolution, providing ample evidence of how revolutions are often sparked by economic inequality and social injustice. The French Revolution, the Russian Revolution, and the Arab Spring are just a few examples of how the oppressed have revolted against corrupt and uncaring rulers. And in the first two examples the response of the oppressed was extremely violent - we have been warned.

Even in seemingly stable democracies, the seeds of revolution can be sown when the gap between rich and poor becomes too wide. Recent protests in various countries over economic inequality and social injustice demonstrate that the potential for unrest is always simmering beneath the surface. In America and Europe, recent years have seen the rise of Black Visions Collective (BLVC), Black Lives Matter (BLM), Antifa and others who, on closer examination, may seem to be more inspired by Marx and Lenin than by the single-issue narratives - such as the killing of George Floyd - they espouse. BLVC, BLM and Antifa could come together, for instance, around a cause such as Defund The Police, which may appear to objective observers to be a call for anarchy. Again, the existence of social media allows these groups to organise and act quickly and in large numbers. And, again, whatever their own underlying motives, they attract the support of ordinary people who feel a strong need for change, to address the root causes of inequality and injustice.

But the new and more concerning issue is the rise of populism driven by the perceived threat of immigration. There always has been migration, probably always will be. But where it is not controlled, or even managed well, immigration is used as an issue to inflame the populus. Stop immigration or 'they' will take your jobs. They are taking your home; your hospital beds; your education opportunities; and more besides. Certainly, this is the message of populists in America, UK, Germany, France, Sweden and Italy and others. The only part of this that is true is that jobs are going to disappear, immigrants or no. Blaming immigrants might distract us from the fact that we are all going to need to retrain for the jobs of the future. We can see that it is a subject that requires serious thought and attention to detail. Otherwise, we are going to wake up to a whole new reality of unemployed sectors of society.

An additional response could be to put in place a more effective system for real refugees and people at risk. It would not be unreasonable, when people arrive in a safe country, that they be dispersed throughout that society, to avoid the ghettoisation that has happened across the West. It should also be mandatory to learn the language of the country of refuge, take an oath of allegiance, hold an identity card, and be given no priority for doctors/dentists/hospitals except in a medical emergency upon arrival.

In the 19th and early 20th centuries, millions of Europeans migrated to the Americas and Australia, and their arrival was largely beneficial to their new host countries. Post-WW2, migration has continued, driven by globalisation, conflict, economic disparities, and environmental changes. The distinction, increasingly, between earlier migration and that of the contemporary world, is that greater numbers of migrants are seeking citizenship in countries whose populations have doubled since 1950.

To put this into sharp relief, the total number of international migrants since 1950 had reached an estimated 281 million by 2020.[13] That's 3.5% of the entire world population on the move in a 70-year period. And movement is speeding up. In the first 40 years, the number was 128 million (by 1990). In the next 30 years (to 2020) the number increased by 153 million. We need to take migration a lot more seriously, rather than responding as and when. I would suggest some ground rules. Immigrants should be vetted quickly and efficiently, and they should understand very clearly in advance the kind of application that will be accepted and the kind of application that will be rejected.

We all, in addition, must learn the difference between refugees from conflict and suffering, and economic migrants simply looking for what they hope will be a better life. There is a liberal knee jerk response, for instance, to those travelling by boat from mainland Europe to the UK. The response is that they must all be treated as refugees, when, quite clearly, they are predominantly economic migrants, or, in the worst cases, feeding the eastern European gang culture that is now creating a hub for people trafficking and drug distribution under our very noses. It is not coincidental that Albania, a country known to be an involuntary exporter of criminality, is the one country that routinely accepts the return of its citizens from the UK. This agreement is formally recognised in the UK-Albania joint communique signed on December 13, 2023.[14]

The data is difficult to collect but world-wide migration appears to be growing at 2.2% a year and annual migration ranges from nine million, suggested by the United Nations, to 22 million a year, suggested by the Pew Research Center. These specific cases aside though, the warning signs are clear: if the super-rich and powerful do not take steps to address the growing inequality and injustice in the world, they risk facing a revolutionary response. The desire for a fairer and more equitable society is becoming a more and more powerful force. It will not be silenced indefinitely.

Chapter 12 - The 10 key points

1. Inequality and the Potential for Revolt: The chapter highlights the link between extreme inequality and social unrest, emphasising that a lack of basic necessities and hope can lead to revolutionary sentiments.

2. Information's Role in Fuelling Discontent: The widespread access to information through the internet and social media exposes the stark contrast between the wealthy and the poor, amplifying feelings of injustice and resentment.

3. Conspicuous Consumption and its Consequences: The excessive spending and wasteful practices of the super-rich exacerbate inequality and contribute to environmental damage, further fuelling social anger.

4. Historical Precedents of Revolution: The chapter draws on historical examples, such as the French and Russian Revolutions, to illustrate how extreme inequality can lead to social upheaval and violent uprisings.

5. Social Media's Role in Mobilisation: Social media platforms facilitate the rapid organisation and mobilisation of dissent, enabling marginalised groups to voice their grievances and demand change.

6. Corporate Influence and the Perpetuation of Inequality: Powerful corporations, often led by the super-rich, contribute to inequality through exploitative practices, tax evasion, and undue influence over political systems.

7. Recent Examples of Social Unrest: The chapter cites recent events like the Capitol attack, Belarus protests, and other uprisings as evidence of the potential for social unrest to erupt when inequality reaches a tipping point.

8. The Urgent Need for Change: The failure to address extreme inequality risks escalating social unrest and revolutionary responses as people demand fairer systems and social justice.

9. The Dual Nature of Information: While the internet can expose injustices and facilitate mobilisation for change, it can also be exploited to spread misinformation and exacerbate divisions.

10. Addressing Root Causes and Promoting Equality: The chapter concludes by emphasising the need to address the root causes of inequality and injustice through comprehensive strategies that include economic development, good governance, and promoting social mobility. It also highlights the importance of responsible and ethical use of technology to avoid further exacerbating social divides.

Footnotes – Chapter 12

---

[1] https://www.statista.com/statistics/218984/number-of-global-mobile-users-since-2010/

[2] https://www.businessinsider.com/these-are-10-of-the-most-expensive-yachts-in-the-world-2023-1

[3]https://www.mensxp.com/buzz-on-web/entertainment/131847-lakshmi-mittal-daughter-240-crore-wedding-srk-kylie-performance.html#

[4] https://www.worldometers.info/gdp/gdp-by-country/

[5]https://openknowledge.fao.org/items/445c9d27-b396-4126-96c9-50b335364d01

[6] Richest 1% emit as much planet-heating pollution as two-thirds of humanity | Oxfam International

[7] https://www.newyorker.com/magazine/2021/05/31/the-dark-side-of-congos-cobalt-rush

https://www.durian.org.ng/the-hidden-cost-of-our-technology-why-we-need-to-pay-attention-to-thecongo/#:~:text=The%20Dark%20Reality%20Behind%20Our,components%20of%20our%20beloved%20devices.

[8]https://taxjustice.net/press/world-to-lose-4-7-trillion-to-tax-havens-over-next-decade-unless-un-tax-convention-adopted-countries-warned/

[9] https://worldpopulationreview.com/countries/by-gdp

[10]https://www.investopedia.com/median-income-by-state-5070640#:~:text=The%20states%20with%20the%20highest,%2C%20West%20Virginia%2C%20and%20Arkanss.

[11] https://www.visualcapitalist.com/visualizing-top-countries-by-wealth-per-person/

[12] https://nypost.com/2018/04/12/assad-and-first-lady-of-hell-live-life-of-luxury-as-horrific-war-rages /

[13] https://worldmigrationreport.iom.int/wmr-2022-interactive/

[14]https://www.gov.uk/government/news/milestone-reached-in-uk-albania-agreement-on-illegal-migration#:~:text=In%202022%2C%20there%20were%201%2C888,have%20seen%20continue%20into%202023.

CHAPTER 13

Media & Control of Communication

Concentration of media ownership is always a threat to informed discussion on our future and to achieving real democracy. Those who used to be referred to as 'press barons', including America's William Randolph Hearst - the model for Orson Welles' Citizen Kane - the Lords Northcliffe (Daily Mail, Daily Mirror) and Beaverbrook (Daily Express) in the UK, and later Sir Rupert Murdoch, have all been accused of using their media as mouthpieces to spread their own world view, and to influence elections in favour of those politicians likely to be well disposed to their agenda.

Elsewhere in Europe, the EU is beset with member countries buying and selling media properties across borders, and others whose media is anything but free. In Hungary, for instance, Kesma owns 19 regional newspapers and TV and radio stations and magazines. At the turn of the century, the European Parliament had begun building a consensus to limit the power of media conglomerates.[1] Nearly 25 years later, it's too late and too little. Because none of the politicians, nor these old-style press barons - whose products relied on people actually buying them and reading them - could ever have even dreamed of the power that resides in today's 'media barons', those whose products are online: Facebook, YouTube, Instagram, WhatsApp, TikTok (the top five as of early 2024).[2] The old-style press barons' newspapers sold in their hundreds of thousands, or millions at most. Facebook reaches three billion users, YouTube

2.5bn, Instagram and WhatsApp two billion each, and TikTok has an audience of 1.5bn.

And three of those - Facebook, Instagram and WhatsApp - are all owned by Meta Platforms Inc, the corporation which has grown out of Mark Zuckerberg's original Facebook seedling. On his death in 1951, aged 88, William Randolph Hearst left a will totalling around $200m ($2.4bn in 2024). Aged 40, Mark Zuckerberg is already estimated to be worth $167.8bn.[3]

This significant transformation of the media landscape, characterised by the consolidation of ownership in the hands of a few powerful corporations[4] raises concerns about the implications for informed discourse, democratic processes, and the overall health of society. That concern was only going to be traumatically increased by reports in July 2024 that Elon Musk from X, was planning to donate $45 million each month to Trump's re-election campaign. If ever you needed a clear example of media owners and mega executives influencing politics, here it was, apparently.[5] Musk later denied the reports, saying that he had created a Super Pac (Political Action Committee) to which he would donate, but only at $1 million a day, 'a much lower level'.

The irony is that the old mainstream media - newspapers and current affairs magazines, on- and offline - have probably never been in more diverse hands. So, problem solved, you might think. But then you'd have to ask yourself why the democratic West is in such societal turmoil: a schism between left and right, the new populists (Trump in America, Giorgia Meloni in Italy, Viktor Orban in Hungary, the AfD Party in Germany, Marine Le Pen, constantly thwarted and written off in France, but agitating in 2024 for an inter-state coalition in the EU Parliament which could have become its second most powerful political alliance[6]), and the arrival of single issue movements whose stated aims are touted as 'progressive', but whose actual effect is to divide society along ever more narrow lines.

Part of the blame, surely, lies with social media. Until social media took hold, it was not practically possible to call for the 'cancellation' of any individual. Social media trashes the concept of 'facts', dismisses MSM (mainstream media) as not to be trusted, and is contemptuous of journalism as a profession which requires discipline and plays by rules. Social media plays by its own rules, and social media is now largely forming public opinion, providing the 'echo chamber' that enables people to syphon out that with which they do not agree, and allows in mostly that which speaks to their own world view. Social media, for instance, has revealed that millions of people worldwide believe the earth is flat. One survey in 2021 found that 10% of Americans believe it is.[7] Flat earthers have launched their own podcasts and YouTube channels. Today the talk is of 'citizen journalists', in a world where anyone can start their own media outlet by clicking a few buttons and writing whatever extreme view enters their heads.

And so, it is in the sphere of social media that the concentration of media ownership poses serious challenges to a well-informed and democratic society. Of the top five social media platforms which have their own 'newsfeed', Meta owns three. Billions of people around the globe are receiving the news they consume through one technology giant.

When we express doubts about the concentration of media ownership, what exactly are we worried about? The primary concerns are:

Reduced Diversity of Perspectives: When a small group of individuals or corporations controls a significant portion of media outlets, it limits the range of viewpoints and perspectives presented to the public. This lack of diversity can lead to an echo chamber effect, where individuals are primarily exposed to information that reinforces their existing beliefs, hindering critical thinking and open-mindedness.

Increased Bias and Agenda-Setting: Media conglomerates often have vested interests in industries other than media and political spheres. This can lead to biassed reporting that favours the agendas of these powerful entities, potentially misleading and influencing public opinion.

Erosion of Media Independence and Accountability: When media outlets are beholden to corporate interests, their ability to report independently and hold those in power accountable becomes compromised. This can lead to a lack of scrutiny and accountability, potentially promoting corruption and abuse of power.

Suppression of Dissenting Voices: Media concentration can stifle dissenting voices and alternative perspectives, making it harder for marginalised groups and minority viewpoints to gain traction in public discourse. This can hinder social progress and undermine the principles of free speech and open debate.

Do we believe that Mark Zuckerberg (Facebook, Instagram, WhatsApp), Larry Page and Sergey Brin (Google, YouTube), or ByteDance (parent company of TikTok), are trying to influence the news we receive? Or are capable of doing so, even if they wanted to?

Would it be paranoid, for instance, to expect the Chinese government (TikTok originated in China) to use the app, if not for actual propaganda purposes, then to close down discussion of subjects it finds uncomfortable - the Tiananmen Square massacre, its relationship with Tibet, and its claims on Taiwan? No, not paranoid. TikTok's moderators were at one point instructed to suppress posts if the users shown were 'too ugly, poor, or disabled'.[8] In 2020, the app's owners issued an apology for its attempts to censor content by or about the LGBT community. In December 2023, Rutger University's NCRI (Network Contagion Institute) published research showing that TikTok's global Platform anomalies align with the Chinese Communist Party's geostrategic objectives.[9]

The top five news services worldwide in May 2024, rated by the number of visits, were:[10]

1 bbc/co.uk and bbc.com (1.1bn visits)
2 msn.com (686m)
3 nytimes.com (685.5m)
4 cnn.com (563.5m)
5 news.google.com (382.2m)

Hard on the heels of news.google.com are theguardian.com (368.2m) and dailymail.co.uk (364.9m).

But all these traditional news channels have a real danger of being blown away by TikTok and similar. It's very hard to estimate but probably 700,000,000+ people view TikTok each day (somewhere between eight and 10% of our entire population). With content ranging from 15 seconds to 60 seconds in most cases, you have to seriously question the quality of the information that is being presented. Do you want everyone to be informed by 15 second bursts? No context, no background, no perspective. Just the message.

As of 2023, it's estimated that over 95% of the world's population lives in an area covered by a mobile-cellular network. This doesn't necessarily equate to individual ownership of a smart device, but it signifies the vast reach possible by smartphone. However, individual phone ownership and internet access vary widely depending on factors like region, economic development, and infrastructure. Globally, approximately 68% of adults owned a smartphone in 2023, with significant variations across regions.

North America and Europe have the highest smartphone penetration, exceeding 80%. Africa and parts of Asia have lower rates, often below 50%, but this is still vast in terms of population access. Some forecasts estimate there will be 85% penetration of smartphones by 2030. Globally, around 63% of the world's population had internet access in 2023. This percentage is significantly higher in developed countries and urban areas, but lower in rural regions and developing nations.

However, again, within five years it is expected that 85% of the world will have access to the internet, and the full deployment of Starlink may improve this figure. Given that people can share access or ask to use their families' or friends' telephones or computers, virtually everyone will have access to information, data, and knowledge. Once everyone is aware of the reality of our world - rather than just their own region's lack of fairness and morality - we will witness increased unhappiness and desire for change.

Governments have long recognized the power of communication to influence public opinion and shape narratives. Unfortunately, this power has often been abused to spread false information, manipulate public perceptions, and maintain control. Governments have a long history of employing propaganda and disinformation campaigns to spread false or misleading information to advance their political agendas. Even those living in the largely democratic west are not immune. But dictators, autocrats and theocrats are even more likely to fabricate stories, manipulate images, and discredit opposing voices. They can also resort to censorship and suppression of information to control the flow of news and prevent the dissemination of unfavourable or critical information. In the digital age, this can involve restricting access to certain websites, blocking news outlets, and silencing dissenting voices.

It is also true that technology has allowed governments - of whatever hue - to employ surveillance technologies and mass observation to track our online activities and social media conversations, and to gather data on individuals' opinions and beliefs. This can be used to identify and target dissidents, suppress opposition movements, and manipulate public sentiment. Tech giants, in addition to surveilling consumers for their own purposes, have increased opportunities for governments to watch our every move.

But possibly a greater threat to informed public discourse became apparent during the Covid pandemic, and subsequent lockdowns. As governments attempted to assure the public - in the face of what was clearly a global panic - that all decisions were being made in the greater interest of the greater number of people, loud voices were raised on the internet. 'Experts' were decried; all politicians were 'lying'; the whole thing was an experiment in 'control'. When the revolutionary mRNA vaccines were announced, Bill Gates was accused, along with others, of planning to inject minuscule computer chips into our bloodstream, which would render us more compliant with government control.

However mad these paranoid musings might have seemed, there is an argument that media and tech giants *have* stolen our identities and are making money by launching applications that take all our data and all our information and exploit it without, in real terms, asking our permission. They also make money by selling advertisers access to our data that, in reality, we have not granted permission for. This is what Yanis Varoufakis defines as 'technofeudalism',[11] a system by which we, the consuming majority, are deprived of the fruits of our own identities, while the tech 'overlords' get rich.

Of course, implied permission is hidden away in the terms and conditions, but the data collectors cynically know that no-one reads the terms and conditions which are frequently thousands of words in very small type. Companies like Google, Meta (Facebook), and others collect vast amounts of user data through their platforms and services. This data includes personal information, online behaviour, interests, and preferences. While some of this data is used to personalise user experiences and improve services, a significant portion is monetized through targeted advertising. It is further used to build increasingly huge and valuable data resources that earn them, not us, money.

Companies claim that users consent to data collection through their terms, but these agreements are often lengthy, complex, and filled with legalese. Most users don't read them thoroughly, if at all. This raises questions about the validity of implied and assumed consent. Business models have been successfully created where users are not the customers, but rather the product being sold.[12] In numerous internet and e-marketing business models, the users are not the primary customers. Instead, their data and attention become the product that is sold to advertisers or other third parties. They are being packaged and sold in a way that amounts to modern serfdom, in line with Yanis Varoufakis's theory of technofeudalism.

The collection and storage of vast amounts of personal data also raise serious privacy concerns. Data breaches and leaks expose users to risks of identity theft, fraud, and other harms. Additionally, the use of data for surveillance and profiling can have chilling effects on freedom of expression and association. Yes, some regulations exist to protect user data, but they are almost uniformly insufficient to address the complexities of the digital age. Companies find ways to circumvent regulations, or they lobby for weaker rules, leaving users vulnerable to exploitation.

And, to put it bluntly: the regulators really don't understand what's happening. They don't have the relevant experience. Talk to 16-year-old hackers and you'll get a much better understanding of what's really happening. The debate over data privacy and user data exploitation by tech giants is ongoing. The lack of transparency and meaningful consent in their data practices raises serious ethical concerns. It's crucial for us to be aware of how our data is being collected and used and to demand greater transparency and control over personal information. Governments and regulators also need to step up and implement stronger data protection laws and enforce them effectively to safeguard user privacy and prevent the misuse of personal data.

Alternatively, we can act ourselves by switching to open-source tools like Apache OpenOffice and LibreOffice which are viable alternatives to Microsoft Word and other proprietary office suites. They offer several advantages: they are completely free to use, which can be a significant advantage for individuals, students, and organisations with budget constraints. These platforms offer a wide range of features comparable to Microsoft Word, including word processing, spreadsheets, presentations, and more. They can handle complex documents, support various file formats, and provide advanced formatting options. Open-source platforms are generally compatible with Microsoft Office file formats, allowing for seamless exchange of documents between different software. Open-source code is publicly available and can be modified and improved by anyone. This allows more flexibility and customization compared to proprietary software. Open-source platforms have large and active communities of users and developers who provide support, create extensions and templates, and contribute to the ongoing development of the software. With open-source platforms, you're not tied to a specific vendor or subscription model. You can use the software as long as you want without worrying about royalties or software updates. You may find open-source platforms less intuitive or familiar than Microsoft Word, but while they may have a slight learning curve and some minor limitations, they are a viable option for those who wish to control their own life, and not have their data stolen.

It is true to say that media outlets have lost credibility due to bias and corporate or political influence. And now we find ourselves justifiably unable to trust the platforms we spend so much of our time on. Public trust in institutions and democratic processes has diminished. But where it was thought, in more innocent times, that this would lead to apathy, cynicism, and a decline in civic engagement, the reality is that in the digital age what we might call 'the ignorant beast' has been awakened. The individual's opinion is more important than the expert's fact.

This raises all sorts of questions about free speech. Flat earthers are, surely, entitled to air what they call their 'research', and alternative 'facts'. Protestors are, surely, entitled to take to the streets to make their feelings felt about Israel's actions in Gaza. But are protestors entitled to call for the removal of Israel from the world's maps, and the obliteration of all Jews 'from the river to the sea'? Are flat earthers entitled to ridicule centuries of scientific endeavour that proves the Earth is, in fact, a globe which rotates around other globes?

Freedom of speech is a liberty proclaimed by some of the best educated men in the world at the time of the French Revolution and the introduction of the Bill of Rights in America around the same time. 'I'm entitled to my opinion' was a frequently heard phrase through the 20th century, usually in pubs, bars or around dinner tables. But in the 21st century, we are no longer at the pub. We are online, loudly proclaiming whatever we believe to be true, and arguing that 'my truth' is as important as 'your truth', both of them trumping 'the truth', always assuming there is such a thing as 'the' truth.

The words of Bertrand Russell from 1959 - so profound, so humane, so relevant - would find few takers in 2024. Asked what he would like to say to future generations, this is what Russell said: "I should like to say two things. One intellectual and one moral. The intellectual thing I should want to say is this: 'When you are studying any matter or considering any philosophy, ask yourself what are the facts, and what is the truth that the facts bear out. Never let yourself be diverted either by what you wish to believe, or by what you think would have beneficent social effects if it were believed; but look only - and solely - at what are the facts'."

In the online world, where there is no agreement on what is a fact, and therefore what is the truth, these words sound like the proverbial tree falling in the forest. If nobody's listening, does it mean Russell didn't say it?

And then there's Russell's moral advice: "The moral thing I would wish to say is very simple: 'Love is wise, hatred is foolish. In this world, which is getting more and more closely interconnected, we have to learn to tolerate each other; we have to learn to put up with the fact that some people say things we don't like. We can only live together - if we are to live together and not die together - if we learn a kind of charity and a kind of tolerance, which is absolutely vital to the continuation of human life on this planet'."

Bertrand Russell lived in an age where such things could be said and not argued with or belittled. Today, online, arguing and belittling are participatory and spectator sports. Russell lived in an age where a fact was a fact - Earth is round - and truth was that which could be proven.

More importantly, how do we reverse the decline in public discourse, bring back respect and tolerance, and, yes, ethics. These issues require critical examination. We need to find new ways of safeguarding the integrity of information and promoting open and informed discourse. We can protect the foundations of a healthy and thriving democracy. We must start at the place where most good can be done - back to Grade 1. Back to school.

Chapter 13- The 10 key points

1. Media Consolidation and its Impact: The chapter highlights the increasing concentration of media ownership, particularly in the hands of a few powerful corporations, and its potential negative consequences for democracy and informed discourse.

2. The Rise of Social Media and its Challenges: The rise of social media platforms has transformed the way people consume and interact with information, but it has also led to the spread of misinformation, echo chambers, and the erosion of trust in traditional media.

3. Government Manipulation and Censorship: Governments around the world, both democratic and authoritarian, utilise various tactics to control the flow of information and manipulate public opinion, including propaganda, censorship, and surveillance.

4. The Erosion of Trust in Institutions: The decline in public trust in traditional media and institutions, coupled with the rise of social media, has created an environment where individual opinions and "alternative facts" often overshadow objective truth.

5. The Complexities of Free Speech in the Digital Age: The chapter grapples with the challenges of balancing the right to free speech with the need to combat hate speech, disinformation, and harmful content online.

6. The Importance of Facts and Truth: The chapter emphasises the critical importance of objective facts

and truth in public discourse, advocating for a return to rational inquiry and evidence-based reasoning.

7. Education for Media Literacy: Promoting media literacy and critical thinking skills is essential for navigating the digital landscape and discerning credible information from misinformation.

8. The Role of Technology Companies: Tech giants like Meta and Google wield immense power over information dissemination and need to be held accountable for their impact on public discourse and democratic processes.

9. The Need for Regulatory Action: The chapter calls for regulatory measures to address media concentration, combat misinformation, and protect the integrity of information in the digital age.

10. Protecting Democratic Values: Safeguarding democratic values like freedom of speech, access to information, and informed public discourse is crucial for a healthy and thriving society.

Footnotes – Chapter 13

[1]https://www.ftm.eu/articles/helmut-kohl-gave-europes-media-barons-a-free-pass?share=Xo2YvfQutRDpn%2B0eW7jfWGrU7IyTfYh8Yieev%2BR5P6Ku0o5c4iKw46VaPIpu%2Byw%3D

[2] https://www.statista.com/statistics/272014/global-social-networks-ranked-by-number-of-users/

[3] https://www.forbes.com/profile/mark-zuckerberg/

[4] Note 29, Appendix 1, controlling the news, full list of media giants

[5]https://www.wsj.com/politics/elections/elon-musk-has-said-he-is-committing-around-45-million-a-month-to-a-new-pro-trump-super-pac-dda53823

[6]https://www.theguardian.com/world/article/2024/may/27/marine-le-pen-giorgia-meloni-nationalist-alliance-european-parliament

[7] https://carsey.unh.edu/publication/conspiracy-vs-science-survey-us-public-beliefs

[8]https://www.theguardian.com/technology/2020/mar/17/tiktok-tried-to-filter-out-videos-from-ugly-poor-or-disabled-users

[9] https://networkcontagion.us/wp-content/uploads/A-Tik-Tok-ing-Timebomb_12.21.23.pdf

[10]https://pressgazette.co.uk/media-audience-and-business-data/media_metrics/most-popular-websites-news-world-monthly-2/

[11] https://www.amazon.co.uk/Technofeudalism-Killed-Capitalism-Yanis-Varoufakis/dp/1847927270

[12] Note 30, Appendix 1, more details of techno feudalism.

CHAPTER 14

AI Future Nightmare

You could say that the 2010s saw the real beginning of AI in an operational way, and deep learning began to be widely used in commercial applications:[1] image recognition in smartphones, voice assistants like Siri and Alexa, and recommendation systems on platforms like Netflix and Amazon. So, in many ways, AI has already been commonly used for over 10 years. Some would argue 2012 as the most significant turning point, the year that the ImageNet competition was won by AlexNet. The deep convolutional neural network, designed by Alex Krizhevsky, in collaboration with Ilya Sutskever and Geoffrey Hinton, conclusively demonstrated deep learning's superior performance in image recognition tasks.

But scientists, philosophers, and many others have been describing the possibilities of what we have now since the 1956 Dartmouth Summer Research Project on Artificial Intelligence. This workshop is considered the birthplace of AI as a field of study. It brought together researchers who defined the goals and methods of AI research. Its originator, John McCarthy, Assistant Professor of Mathematics at Dartmouth College, is credited with coining the phrase 'Artificial Intelligence'.[2]

Today's real concern is the race towards artificial generative intelligence (AGI), so-called God-Like AI. AI already has astounding capabilities. Its ability to understand and respond to complex questions by sifting through vast amounts of information is just the tip of the iceberg. The technology is evolving at a breakneck pace, which many find scary. Millions have access to Natural Language

Processing (NLP) apps but choose not to experiment with them. NLP models like Chat GPT, Bing AI, Gemini and others have demonstrated impressive abilities to 'understand' and generate human-like text. They answer questions, providing accurate and concise answers to complex queries by searching and synthesising information from the internet. They can summarise information, condensing lengthy documents or articles into key points. AI can also accurately translate text between different languages and engage in conversations with humans on various topics, provide information, or even companionship.

To prove the point, we ran each chapter of this book through Gemini or GPT and asked it to generate a 10-point summary. These summaries appear at the end of each chapter, barely edited (minimal human interference) and are evidence of the power of AI NLP.

More scarily for many, AI can also create different kinds of creative content formats like poems, code, scripts, and musical pieces. It can also generate highly realistic images and videos based on text prompts or descriptions. This has implications for art, design, and even entertainment. In 2016, Ars Technica released a short film titled *Sunspring*, whose script was generated by AI. The actors found the script incomprehensible and laughable, but viewers reported the experience of watching the film as 'intense'. Two years later, Ars Technica released another short, *Zone Out* which also used AI to generate its script, but also to select actors from a database, and even to replace their faces with those of other actors.[3] Glenn Marshall's *The Crow*[4] was created using text-to-video generation and was not only a finalist in The Lumen Prize (specifically for digital arts) but was also eligible for submission for a BAFTA. There have been novels - *1 the Road*[5] was written by AI using a neural network trained on a dataset of American road-trip novels; poetry - *Amor Cringe* Is a collection written by an AI, showcasing its ability to mimic poetic forms and themes; and art - *Edmond de Belamy* is a portrait created by an AI algorithm and was sold at Christie's auction house for $432,500, raising questions about the value and authorship of AI-generated art.

In ways the general public cannot see, AI is used in various industries to optimise processes, make predictions, and assist in decision-making. This is seen in fields like finance, logistics, and healthcare. The future of AI will be more powerful and pervasive, its potential immense. Experts predict even more transformative advancements soon. For example, AI could be used to analyse all bank data worldwide and track the money and the expenditure, particularly of the super-rich and billionaires. This would enable governments to very accurately understand the tax they are missing and the tax they could collect. We need to understand that in the immediate future all money will be digital, and we will not be able to use old-fashioned paper money. Where there is the political will, this raises the possibility to stop money laundering and sanction evasion very possible. The issue is: are those in government going to fight and fully tax their paymasters, the elite?

The current AI application is considered 'narrow AI', specialised in specific tasks. The development of Artificial General Intelligence (AGI), which possesses human-like cognitive abilities across a wide range of domains, is a major long-term goal, with some experts forecasting development by 2040. But as everything is speeding up, the long term may be just a few years away, especially if you factor in the possibility of quantum computing further speeding up development.

In addition to enhanced creativity - playing an increasingly significant role in creative fields, generating music, art, and literature with unprecedented sophistication - AGI is expected to accelerate scientific discovery, helping researchers analyse vast data sets, design experiments, and develop new theories. It is also expected to revolutionise healthcare with early disease detection, personalised medicine, and new treatment approaches.

As AI becomes more powerful, concerns about ethics, bias, and potential misuse become paramount. Ensuring AI is used responsibly and fairly is crucial. Automation possibilities - leading to increased efficiency and productivity - also raises concerns about job losses and the need for workforce retraining. The technology can be exploited for malicious purposes, such as cyberattacks, disinformation campaigns, and the creation of autonomous weapons systems. We have already witnessed the first two of these in attacks on our banks, theft of personal data, and interference in democratic elections in America and Europe. Quantum computing in concert with AGI will only increase the potential.

Certainly, there are fears that the amount and speed of data processing made possible by quantum computing will put timely human interventions and responses beyond the abilities of even the best of hackers, let alone common or garden programmers and code writers. We're at the beginning of a transformative era in AI. Its ability to access and process vast amounts of information is already impressive, but its potential is far greater. In the recent past, detailed analysis of large data would often be performed on a Cray supercomputer, costing hundreds of thousands of dollars per hour. This type of analysis is now often effectively free. Developing more powerful and versatile AI systems promises incredible benefits, but also potential risks. It is crucial to proceed with caution, guided by ethical principles and a commitment to using AI for the betterment of humanity.

One major concern about AI is its potential to generate and amplify fake information. With powerful algorithms and vast amounts of data, AI systems will be capable of creating convincing fake news articles, videos, and even entire narratives. The proliferation of false media generated by AI carries the inherent ability to further erode trust in institutions, undermine democratic processes, and threaten global stability, all of which are specific aims of bad players in the fake information business. We can mitigate the Impact of False Media by developing robust AI detection tools. This would require investment in research and development to create more sophisticated AI-powered tools that can identify, and flag manipulated content. It will also be necessary to enact international legislation, establishing clear guidelines and regulations for AI-powered media creation. This requires the will to create and enforce regulations and hold platforms accountable.

In our chapter on education, we will also discuss the teaching of new ways of thinking, providing pupils - and therefore all future generations - with the skills to critically evaluate information sources.

We may not want to, but let us for a moment imagine a future where AI-generated misinformation is so sophisticated and widespread that it becomes nearly impossible to discern fact from fiction. The consequences of this could be disastrous, as could the increasing reliance on AI for decision-making processes. As AI systems become more advanced, they could be given more authority to make crucial decisions in various domains, such as finance, law enforcement, healthcare, and even warfare. What if training data is biased or otherwise flawed? What if the algorithms make decisions based on discriminatory or unethical criteria? In the early days of personal computers there was a saying, 'Garbage in, garbage out'. If you put the wrong numbers in a spreadsheet, or created a bad formula, the conclusions you got would be useless. The consequences of such flawed input in the age of AI will be devastating by comparison.

Furthermore, the rapid advancement of AI technology also poses threats to jobs in many industries. As AI becomes more capable of performing tasks previously done by humans, is there a real risk of widespread unemployment and economic inequality? We can comfort ourselves that all previous instances of machinery replacing humans have failed to live up to the dystopian predictions that accompanied the various automation revolutions. But what we have learned, *should* have learned at any rate, from history is that while the number of jobs increases with each 'industrial revolution', those jobs don't remain the same. And in previous iterations, many new jobs - mostly unskilled - were as easy to slip into as the jobs that were lost. This is not going to be the case with AI.

As we have seen in the past 30 years, as job titles that had never previously existed began to dominate the workplace, new skills are needed, and those new skills need new training. In a workplace dominated by AI, the new skills required could easily lead to a more divided society - an elite of programmers, coders, and technology designers could split society right down the middle. Here is another possible cause of social unrest and increased dependence on government support, as many people are left without job opportunities.

Lastly, there is the existential risk of AI surpassing human intelligence and becoming autonomous. This scenario, often referred to as the 'singularity', raises profound questions about the future of humanity. Will we be able to control and coexist with superintelligent AI, or will we become subservient to its will? The potential for AI to reshape our world in ways we cannot yet imagine underscores the urgent need for proactive and ethical AI development, ensuring that this powerful technology remains aligned with human values and serves the common good. The problem with AGI[6] is that we can only speculate about its power to 'think' for itself even as we develop it. 'The singularity' raises concerns about the control and intentions of super-intelligent AI. If AI systems become self-aware and capable of self-improvement, their goals and motivations may not align with human priorities. This could lead to a future in which AI cares little for human well-being and pursues its own objectives, potentially endangering humanity.

So, while AI holds enormous potential to transform our world for the better, it also poses significant risks. AI may be coming for all our jobs, making a universal salary a solution whose time may have come.[7] And the potential for AI to blur the lines between truth and fabrication, the ethical implications of AI decision-making, the threat of widespread unemployment, and the existential risk of super intelligent AI are all factors that need to be carefully considered and addressed. It is imperative that we approach the development and deployment of AI with caution, wisdom, and a strong focus on ethics and societal well-being.

Do we doubt, for instance, that AI algorithms - trained as they are on vast amounts of data - can reflect and perpetuate existing societal biases? If these biases are not carefully accounted for within the formulae attached to data training sets, AI systems will make discriminatory decisions that have a significant impact on people's lives. For example, an AI-powered hiring algorithm might favour male candidates over female candidates based on historical hiring data that reflects gender biases. Another example: historically in the USA black people are much more likely to be sentenced to prison than whites. If AI relies on historic data, an AI-powered criminal justice risk assessment tool could misclassify minority individuals as being at higher risk of recidivism, leading to unfair sentencing and incarceration. This is where ethics enters the equation: the historic injustices and victimisation of minorities would have to be allowed for in the programming of any system that might be used in the justice system.

But the biggest fear has to be that, as AI systems become more complex and autonomous, we may lose control over them. Imagine, for instance, an autonomous weapons system, selecting and engaging targets without human oversight, potentially leading to unintended casualties and escalation of conflicts. We are already seeing the beginning of this in the systems controlling drones flying from Russia and Ukraine to each other's territory. The systems are basic right now. But they will develop very quickly from simply tracking the contours of the land they are flying over to selecting individual targets by sex, age and more.

So, the emergence of an artificial superintelligence (ASI) has to be taken seriously, not somewhere down the line, but in the here and the now. If ASI is even imagined to pose an existential threat to humanity, then those future problems have to be addressed at all developmental stages of the technology.

There are already clear examples of AI being misused. Clearview AI has faced criticism for its massive database of images 'scraped' from social media, raising privacy concerns and potential for misuse. Inaccuracies in the technology have also led to misidentification of individuals, particularly people of colour, with potential consequences in law enforcement and surveillance. Amazon scrapped an AI recruiting tool that showed bias against women, as it was trained on resumes submitted to the company over a 10-year period, most of which came from men. This highlights the risk of perpetuating bias existing in the data used to train AI systems.

In manufacturing, AI-powered robots are replacing workers in various industries, leading to job losses and economic insecurity for many. While automation can improve efficiency, it's crucial to address the potential social and economic disruptions it creates. Key here will be a serious commitment to training newcomers to the workforce for the jobs they will be expected to do, and to retrain in new skills the older workforce. Otherwise, the older generation will be shut out of the workplace.

Facebook's algorithms, designed to maximise user engagement, have been criticised for both amplifying divisive content and promoting echo chambers, and contributing to the spread of misinformation. This has been linked to increased polarisation, social unrest, and even violence in some cases.

Deepfake technology has already been used to spread misinformation, manipulate public opinion, and damage reputations. The potential for political manipulation and undermining trust in the media are significant concerns. In the military, while still in development, autonomous weapons systems raise ethical concerns about accountability and the potential for unintended escalation in conflicts. There are fears that these systems could make decisions without human oversight, leading to unforeseen and drastic consequences.

In data analytics, Cambridge Analytica (now defunct), harvested personal data from millions of Facebook users without their consent and used it for political advertising. This scandal exposed the potential for AI to be used for manipulation and surveillance on a massive scale.

In financial trading, High-Frequency Trading Algorithms can execute trades in fractions of a second, sometimes leading to market volatility and flash crashes. Their complexity and lack of transparency raise concerns about their impact on financial stability.

But all is not doom and gloom. There are a host of already beneficial applications of the technology, particularly in the areas of healthcare research and of practical healthcare. AI has already been shown to analyse medical images and data more efficiently and accurately than humans, leading to earlier and more precise diagnosis of diseases like cancer and Alzheimer's. It will increasingly be able to tailor treatment plans based on individual genetic profiles and medical histories, leading to more effective therapies. It can also accelerate drug discovery by analysing vast amounts of data to identify potential drug targets and predict their efficacy. AI-powered robots can assist surgeons in performing complex procedures with greater precision and reduced risk of complications. Plus, its ability to analyse complex scientific data sets also enables the technology to uncover hidden patterns and insights, accelerating research not just in medicine, but also in fields like astronomy, climate science, and genomics.

AI can simulate complex phenomena, from the behaviour of molecules to the evolution of galaxies, enabling scientists to test theories and make predictions. It can improve climate models to better predict extreme weather events and inform mitigation strategies. It can also optimise energy consumption, water use, and resource allocation, helping to reduce environmental impact. AI can monitor wildlife populations and habitats, track poaching activities, and aid in conservation efforts. AI-powered self-driving cars, trucks, tankers, buses and taxis, have the potential to revolutionise transportation, improving safety, reducing traffic congestion, and increasing accessibility. It can also optimise routes, predict demand, and manage inventory, making supply chains more efficient and resilient. In education and other learning environments, AI will increasingly adapt to individual learning styles and pace, providing customised teaching experiences for students. AI-powered tutors will provide personalised feedback and support to learners, enhancing their understanding and performance.

There are examples of actual benefits already achieved. AlphaFold - developed by DeepMind, Google's AI division - is dedicated to predicting protein structures. It has already predicted the 3D structures of over 200 million proteins, a breakthrough that could revolutionise drug discovery and disease understanding. (Source: DeepMind Blog). PathAI uses AI to improve the accuracy and efficiency of pathology diagnoses, helping pathologists identify cancer and other diseases earlier and more accurately. (Source: PathAI Website). IDx-DR was the first autonomous AI diagnostic system authorised by America's FDA for detecting diabetic retinopathy, a leading cause of blindness. It enables faster and more accessible eye screenings, especially in underserved areas. (Source: FDA News Release).

SilviaTerra uses AI to analyse satellite imagery and other data to assess forest health and carbon storage potential, helping to inform sustainable forest management practices. (Source: SilviaTerra Website).

Ocean Cleanup uses AI-powered systems to identify and track plastic pollution in the ocean, enabling more targeted and efficient clean-up efforts. (Source: The Ocean Cleanup Website).

Ava is an AI-powered app providing real-time captioning for deaf and hard-of-hearing individuals, allowing them to participate more fully in conversations and events. (Source: Ava Website).

Seeing AI (Microsoft) is a free app using AI to narrate the world for people who are blind or have low vision, describing people, text, and objects in their surroundings. (Source: Microsoft Seeing AI Website).

One Concern uses AI to model and predict the impact of natural disasters like earthquakes and floods, helping communities prepare and respond more effectively. (Source: One Concern Website).

Zipline uses AI powered drones to deliver medical supplies to remote areas in Rwanda and Ghana, improving access to healthcare for underserved populations. (Source: Zipline Website)

So, we have to weigh the good versus the troubling, at the same time understanding, very clearly, that AI is here now, and here to stay, destined to play an increasingly large part in our lives. Luddites of the world may unite in opposition, but they cannot hold back the tide of progress.

On the other hand, it would be troubling if the elite and the super-rich try to exclude AI from analysing their activities, just as they can currently use tax lawyers and specialist accountants to avoid paying their share of tax. It will become possible very shortly to ask AI systems to analyse who is avoiding tax and who is moving money to offshore locations that have no logical explanation except tax avoidance. Another example would be that you could allow the police forces of each country to analyse the payment of money and the expense of money to identify those organisations obtaining money from drugs, trafficking and so on. It is essential that we create an environment where computer super-geeks are not allowed to replace the lawyers and accountants in hiding the activities of the super-rich. We can, obviously, anticipate the possibility, which gives us the opportunity to exercise a new set of political and governance rules and systems.

AI is a powerful tool that can revolutionise many aspects of our lives. However, it is important to acknowledge and address the potential problems that AI could cause in the future. By understanding these risks, we can take steps to mitigate them and ensure that AI is used for the benefit of humanity.

We need to develop ethical guidelines for the development and use of AI, ensure transparency and accountability in AI systems, and invest in education and training to prepare for the AI-powered future. Only by addressing these challenges can we harness the full potential of AI while safeguarding our values and ensuring a brighter future for all.

Chapter 14 - The 10 key points

1. AI's Rapid Advancement: Artificial Intelligence is rapidly evolving, with current applications like natural language processing and image generation showcasing its transformative potential.

2. The Promise of AGI: The development of Artificial General Intelligence (AGI), possessing human-like cognitive abilities, is a major goal with the potential to revolutionise various fields.

3. The Threat of Misinformation: AI-powered tools can generate and amplify fake news and deep fakes, posing a significant threat to trust in information and democratic processes.

4. Algorithmic Bias and Discrimination: AI algorithms can perpetuate and amplify existing societal biases, leading to discriminatory outcomes in various domains.

5. Privacy and Surveillance Concerns: The use of AI in surveillance technology raises concerns about privacy, data security, and the potential for misuse by governments and corporations.

6. Job Displacement and Economic Inequality: AI-driven automation could lead to widespread job losses and increased economic inequality, requiring proactive measures to address potential social and economic disruptions.

7. Ethical Concerns in Warfare: The development of autonomous weapons systems raises ethical questions

about accountability and the potential for unintended consequences in armed conflicts.

8. The Existential Risk of Superintelligence: The emergence of superintelligent AI poses a potential existential threat to humanity, highlighting the need for responsible and ethical AI development.

9. Beneficial Applications of AI: AI also has the potential for positive impact in areas like healthcare, scientific research, environmental protection, and accessibility.

10. The Imperative of Ethical AI Development: The development and deployment of AI technologies must be guided by ethical principles, ensuring transparency, accountability, and fairness to mitigate risks and maximise benefits for humanity.

Footnotes – Chapter 14

[1] ImageNet and Deep Learning (2012): The development of deep learning, a type of machine learning that uses neural networks with many layers, revolutionised the field of AI

[2] https://home.dartmouth.edu/about/artificial-intelligence-ai-coined-dartmouth

[3] https://arstechnica.com/gaming/2018/06/this-wild-ai-generated-film-is-the-next-step-in-whole-movie-puppetry/

[4] https://amplify.nabshow.com/articles/ic-watch-this-the-crow-an-ai-film-that-beautifully-uses-text-to-video-generation/

[5] The Truth About *1 the Road*: Human-AI Collaboration: *1 the Road* was a collaborative project between a human author, Ross Goodwin, and an AI system he developed.

[6] Some experts, like Ray Kurzweil, believe AGI could be achieved as early as the 2030s. Others, like Shane Legg (co-founder of DeepMind), suggest a 50% chance of AGI by 2028. Many researchers and surveys suggest AGI might be achieved sometime between 2040 and 2060.

[7]https://www.theguardian.com/global-development/2023/nov/16/ai-is-coming-for-our-jobs-could-universal-basic-income-be-the-solution

CHAPTER 15

Space and Controlling the Galaxy

Does the universe become the new battleground, or do we go forward together? If we do go forward together, how do we avoid the (fictional) autocracy of the Galactic Empire, created by George Lucas for his original Star Wars trilogy, as a warning against a new fascism being allowed to flourish in the cause of interstellar unity? We're not really far from having to make those choices. Everything is speeding up. In the next 50 years space travel will be well developed. Look how quickly automotive travel or flight developed in their first 50 years. But as we take our first baby steps, we at least have history to learn from - the weaknesses that led to the demise of the League of Nations; and the weaknesses we now perceive in the United Nations. Nothing guarantees the UN itself can't collapse. Russia and China run rings around its very purpose, while human rights committee chairs are allocated to countries which systematically not only ignore what we in the West consider basic human rights, but actively persecute and murder those who live outside what is prescribed as the norm for those societies.

And what does it say for a future of universal unity that India (the moon's south pole) and China (its dark side) are just the most recent of the five countries that have planted national flags on the moon? It does suggest an international race for some kind of territorial supremacy, not least in search of what on Planet Earth are called 'rare earths' but are abundant elsewhere in the Universe. It is said that one asteroid may contain more gold than has ever been mined on Earth. Meanwhile, we take those baby steps, and, like all babies, we will stumble and fall.

Mars One was a stumble and a fall, a Dutch non-profit organisation that gained widespread attention in 2012 for its declared ambition to establish a permanent human colony on Mars. The initial concept planned for an orbiter craft and small robotic lander in 2018, followed by a rover in 2020, and landing of the base components in 2024. The first crew of four astronauts were to land on Mars in 2025. Then, every two years, a new crew of four would arrive. The project aimed to send crews on a one-way journey to the Red Planet, funded by a reality TV show documenting the selection and training of the astronauts. Despite generating significant public interest and attracting numerous applicants, Mars One faced mounting challenges and ultimately declared bankruptcy in 2019. The project's downfall can be attributed to several factors, all of which have to be addressed in any project to explore or exploit space.

Primarily, experts raised doubts about the feasibility of Mars One's technology and timeline, citing concerns about radiation exposure, life support systems, and the logistics of establishing a self-sustaining colony. But the project also struggled to secure sufficient funding. Even the reality TV show concept failed to attract the necessary financial backing. Mars One faced further criticism for its lack of transparency regarding its finances and technical plans. The one-way nature of the mission also raised ethical questions about the well-being and consent of the astronauts. There is no direct continuation of the Mars One project. However, the dream of colonising Mars lives on, and several other organisations are actively pursuing this goal:

When will we start sending people to Mars? Current forecasts for the first crewed mission to Mars vary, but most estimates place it in the early or mid 2030s. So maybe in only five years?

NASA aims to launch a crewed mission to Mars in the 2030s, with the Artemis program serving as a stepping stone by establishing a sustainable presence on the Moon first. Key challenges include developing the necessary technology for long-duration space travel, ensuring astronaut safety, and addressing the physiological and psychological effects of such a journey.

The European Space Agency (ESA) is collaborating with NASA on the Artemis program and has its own long-term goals for Mars exploration. China's National Space Administration (CNSA)also has ambitions to send astronauts to Mars in the 2030s, as does Elon Musk's SpaceX which is actively developing the Starship spacecraft, intended to transport humans to Mars. Musk has expressed ambitious goals for the coming decades. SpaceX's current plans for Mars involve a multi-phase approach, ultimately aiming to establish a self-sustaining city on the Red Planet. The Starship is the core of SpaceX's Mars plan, a fully reusable transportation system designed to carry both crew and cargo to Mars. SpaceX is actively developing and testing Starship prototypes at its Starbase facility in Texas. Recent milestones include successful high-altitude flights and landing attempts, with orbital flight tests expected soon. Before sending humans, SpaceX plans to send multiple uncrewed Starship missions to Mars to deliver essential cargo, including equipment, supplies, and infrastructure components. These missions will help establish a basic infrastructure on Mars, including propellant production facilities for refuelling Starships for the return journey.

Once the initial infrastructure is in place, SpaceX aims to send the first crewed missions to Mars,[1] likely in the early 2030s. But in the late 2020s the unmanned ships will commence six-month test journeys. The space station is scheduled to be operational from 2025. This will create a new industrial revolution. These early missions will focus on establishing a rudimentary base, conducting scientific research, and further developing the infrastructure for a permanent settlement. SpaceX's long-term vision, to build a self-sustaining city on Mars, capable of supporting a large population and eventually becoming independent of Earth, will require developing local resources, producing food and energy, and creating a thriving economy on Mars. The key technologies and challenges Musk's endeavour is facing are within Starship itself, whose successful development and testing is crucial for making the Mars missions a reality. One such challenge is In-Situ Resource Utilisation (ISRU), whereby SpaceX plans to utilise Mars' natural resources such as water, ice and carbon dioxide to produce propellant for the return journey. Another will be to develop reliable life support systems to sustain humans on the long journey to Mars and on the Martian surface. And radiation shielding, critical for protecting astronauts from harmful radiation during the journey and on Mars, is another.

These ambitions of Musk's are all the more astounding because the combined might of America (NASA), China (CNSA) and Europe (ESA) is seen by observers as being in competition with one private individual.[2] Does Musk plan to own Mars if he is first there? Musk's vision for Mars involves establishing a self-sustaining population of one million people by 2050, well within the 50 years I forecast above. Perhaps nothing quite so vividly illustrates the wealth it is possible to accumulate in the 21st century than that one man's ambitions could lead his endeavours to outstrip the three largest economies in the world (counting the EU as one combined economy).

Will space exploration be a catalyst for economic growth or a new arena for conflict? The vast expanse of space has long inspired humanity's fascination, creating dreams of exploration, colonisation, and the pursuit of knowledge beyond our terrestrial confines. As technological advancements bring the cosmos within closer reach, the prospect of space exploration is no longer a distant dream but an impending reality. However, this new frontier also presents a crossroads, offering immense opportunities for economic growth, but also the potential for conflict.

On a positive note, space exploration holds the promise of unlocking vast economic opportunities, driving innovation and growth across diverse industries. The extraction of valuable resources from asteroids and other celestial bodies could revolutionise manufacturing and energy production, alleviating resource scarcity and fuelling economic expansion here on Earth.

Space-based technologies have the potential to revolutionise communication, navigation, and Earth observation, leading to advancements in industries like agriculture, transportation, and disaster management. The development of new materials and technologies in space could lead to breakthroughs in medicine, electronics, and renewable energy. The space tourism industry is also poised for significant growth, offering a unique and exhilarating experience for a growing number of - mostly wealthy - individuals. The development of space hotels and lunar resorts could generate substantial revenue and create new jobs.

But despite its immense potential to promote economic growth, space exploration also raises concerns about the potential for conflict and geopolitical rivalry. The militarization of space could lead to an arms race, with nations developing and deploying weapons systems in orbit. Control of strategic space assets, such as satellite constellations, could become a source of tension and conflict. Is there a contingency plan if a hostile country starts destroying Starlink satellites?

We should probably also ask ourselves, given we're generally talking about a new set of global ethics, about the possible consequences of untrammelled exploitation of other planets. The history of colonialism on Earth serves as a stark warning of the potential dangers of unchecked resource extraction and exploitation. As we venture into space, we should try to avoid repeating the mistakes of the past. A new ethical framework for space exploration must prioritise sustainability, respect for potential extraterrestrial life, and the equitable sharing of benefits among all of humanity. We acknowledge the damage we've done to our own home, Earth, and the need to clean it up. We observe what we have chosen to call ecosystems that have been disturbed. We note the knock-on effect of their destruction, which, we are constantly warned, could be catastrophic. Should we not be asking ourselves what the possible consequences could be for disturbing the natural state of other planets? Or, because we consider them 'dead', have we already decided it doesn't matter what we do out there, 'in the dark', so to speak?

There are already thousands of other companies developing ideas for space. It's not just rockets and launchers. There are many, many requirements (for which read, opportunities). Here is a list of major companies by country.

- United States - Apart from SpaceX, there is Blue Origin, focused on space tourism and lunar lander development; Rocket Lab, providing launch services for small satellites; Relativity Space, developing 3D-printed rockets; and Astra, working on smaller, affordable launch vehicles.
- China Aerospace Science and Technology Corporation (CASC) is the main contractor for China's space program, responsible for launch vehicles, satellites and spacecraft; China Aerospace Science and Industry Corporation (CASIC) develops missiles, satellites, and other aerospace technologies; iSpace, a private company, is focused on commercial launch services; Landspace, another private company, is developing liquid-fuelled rockets.
- In Europe, Arianespace is a leading global launch service provider, operating the Ariane rockets; Airbus Defence and Space, a major aerospace company involved in satellite manufacturing, launch services, and space exploration missions; Thales Alenia Space specialises in the design and manufacturing of satellites and space systems.
- Roscosmos is the Russian state corporation responsible for space activities, including launch vehicles, satellites, and the International Space Station; S7 Space is a private company aiming to develop a reusable spaceplane.
- Other Countries: Indian Space Research Organisation (ISRO) is the national space agency with ambitious plans for lunar and interplanetary missions. Japan Aerospace Exploration Agency (JAXA) focuses on scientific research and space exploration. Israel Aerospace Industries (IAI) is a major player in satellite technology and launch services. The United Arab Emirates (UAE) Space Agency has launched several successful missions, including the Hope Mars orbiter. Here's a straightforward text list of the various items being developed and manufactured for space

exploration and colonisation:

- Launch Vehicles: Reusable rockets (SpaceX Falcon 9, Starship; Blue Origin New Glenn)
- Small-lift launch vehicles (Rocket Lab Electron, Astra Rocket)
- Heavy-lift launch vehicles (NASA's Space Launch System, SpaceX's Starship)
- Spacecraft: Crewed spacecraft (SpaceX's Starship, NASA's Orion)
- Uncrewed spacecraft (SpaceX's Dragon, Boeing's Starliner)
- Landers (Blue Origin's Blue Moon, SpaceX's Starship HLS)
- Life Support Systems: (oxygen generation and recycling systems, water purification and recycling systems, waste management systems, food production systems (hydroponics, aeroponics)
- Habitats and Infrastructure: inflatable or modula habitats
- Radiation shielding materials and technologies
- Power generation systems (solar panels, nuclear reactors)
- Resource extraction and processing equipment (water ice miners, metal refineries)
- Space Suits and Robotics: advanced space suits for extravehicular activities (EVAs)
- Robotic systems for exploration, construction, and maintenance
- Communication and Navigation: satellite communication networks
- Deep space communication systems
- Navigation systems (GPS, star trackers)
- Scientific Instruments: Telescopes (e.g. James Webb Space Telescope)
- Rovers (e.g. Perseverance, Curiosity)
- Landers (e.g. InSight): Sensors and instruments for atmospheric analysis, geological surveys, etc.
- In-Situ Resource Utilisation (ISRU): Water ice extraction and processing systems

- Metal and mineral extraction and refining technologies
- Propellant production systems
- Medical and Health Technologies: Telemedicine systems
- Radiation monitoring and protection devices
- Medical equipment and supplies for space.
- Space Tourism and Hospitality: Space hotels and accommodations. Space tourism vehicles (e.g. Virgin Galactic's VSS Unity). Zero-gravity recreational facilities and equipment. And just to finish the list to give you an idea of all the new businesses that need to be developed you will also need weapons that are effective in space.

If there was one endeavour which humans might generally have imagined would require international cooperation, it would certainly be space exploration. But, in the absence of clear international agreements governing space resource utilisation, all this activity is being carried out by individual countries and even private companies. It doesn't require a genius to see that the extraction of resources from space is likely to lead to disputes over ownership and access. So how should we navigate this crossroads in human history? How do we balance economic aspirations with global security? To harness the economic potential of space exploration while mitigating the risks of conflict, it is imperative for nations to adopt a cooperative and responsible approach. International agreements and frameworks are essential to regulate space activities, prevent the militarization of space, and ensure the equitable and sustainable use of space resources.

Some asteroids, like Psyche 16, are suspected to be composed largely of metal, including gold. However, the actual amount is uncertain and requires further exploration. The average distance from Earth to Mars is about 140 million miles (225 million km), but this can vary significantly depending on their positions in their orbits. The average distance from Earth to Psyche 16 is roughly three times the distance to Mars, placing it around 450 million miles (724 million km) away. So that is the target for 2050 or before. Psyche 16's estimated value, based on its metal content, is in the quadrillions of dollars. However, this is a theoretical value and does not yet reflect the feasibility or economic implications of asteroid mining.

Investments in space exploration should not be solely focused on economic gain but also on promoting scientific research, international collaboration, and peaceful exploration. Open communication and transparency among nations are crucial to build trust, reduce misperceptions, and prevent misunderstandings that could lead to conflict. However, scientists who are analysing the light emitted by stars and other celestial objects have identified the elements present, including gold. Missions like NASA's Psyche mission aim to study metallic asteroids to better understand their composition and potential resources, including gold. While a precise estimate of the total amount remains elusive, it's clear that gold is abundant in the universe. It is the very existence of materials like this, so valued by humans, that pose the greatest possibility of conflict, making it all the more urgent that space exploration be a human endeavour, rather than one conducted piecemeal, nation by nation, company by company. By embracing cooperation, responsibility, and a shared vision for the peaceful exploration of space, we can transform this new frontier into a catalyst for economic prosperity, scientific advancement, and global unity. The vast expanse of space holds immense potential for humanity's betterment, and it is our collective responsibility to ensure that space exploration serves as a bridge for progress, not a battleground for conflict and the location of the next war.

Chapter 15 - The 10 key points

1. Space Exploration's Economic Potential: Space exploration offers vast economic opportunities through resource extraction, technological advancements, and the burgeoning space tourism industry.

2. The Risk of Militarization and Conflict: The militarization of space and competition for control of strategic assets could lead to geopolitical tensions and conflict.

3. Resource Disputes and Ethical Considerations: The extraction of resources from space raises complex questions about ownership, access, and the potential for exploitation, mirroring historical patterns of colonialism on Earth.

4. The Need for International Cooperation: International agreements and frameworks are essential for regulating space activities, ensuring responsible resource utilisation, and preventing conflicts.

5. Prioritising Scientific Discovery and Peaceful Exploration: Investments in space exploration should focus on scientific research, international collaboration, and peaceful exploration rather than militarization and resource grabs.

6. The Role of Private Companies: Private companies like SpaceX are playing an increasingly significant role in space exploration, challenging traditional government-led initiatives and potentially reshaping the future of space activities.

7. The Importance of a Shared Vision: Humanity needs a shared vision for space exploration that prioritises sustainability, respect for potential extraterrestrial life, and the equitable sharing of benefits among all nations.

8. Learning from Past Mistakes: The history of colonialism on Earth serves as a cautionary tale, reminding us to avoid repeating the mistakes of exploitation and environmental degradation as we venture into space.
9. Technological Challenges and Opportunities: Space exploration presents numerous technological challenges but overcoming them can lead to breakthroughs in various fields, benefiting humanity as a whole.

10. Space as a Catalyst for Progress: The chapter emphasises the potential for space exploration to serve as a catalyst for progress, fostering international cooperation, scientific advancement, and a shared sense of purpose for humanity.

Footnotes – Chapter 15

[1] https://www.spacex.com/humanspaceflight/mars/

[2] https://fortune.com/2024/03/20/nasa-struggles-compete-blue-origin-spacex-musk-bezos/

CHAPTER 16

Equal Education for All

There are some very obvious problems around the world regarding education - a total lack of it in some places, and, at the other end of the scale, the ability of the rich to pay for the very best. We need to address those problems.

But first, it's 2025, and the developed world's education curriculum is, mostly, firmly stuck in the 1980s, when jobs in manufacturing and retail were abundant for those who didn't make the academic grade. In our new era of high tech and Artificial Intelligence (AI) - which, as we've seen, is coming for all those drudge jobs - we need a new curriculum, and a new approach to teaching everything, including how to be better, more moral.

The most obvious stumbling block to changing the curriculum is that teachers are trained to teach what they were taught, so we are stuck on a merry go round of stale subjects that are largely redundant in a world where AI is going to dominate.

Previous civilisations didn't advance learning simply by regurgitating the past. Arabia had by far the most extensive libraries and access to past learning, and Indian, Chinese and other cultures were incredibly advanced in some areas compared to Medieval Europe. India, for instance, has a 3,000-year history of maths, and introduced the concept of zero, which transformed global understanding.[1]

Still, it has been said that more knowledge is contained in one edition of one quality newspaper today than was required to be a world class scholar in Europe in the Middle Ages. If that statement is examined closely, it is clearly true. In the Middle Ages, a European scholar was someone schooled in a limited access to the classics and the philosophy of the ancient Greeks, plus whatever knowledge, history and culture was available at the time. At a time when world events might take years to filter through to even a very small part of society's elites, reading and writing were in the realm of only the privileged of the church and a tiny percentage of society's higher-ups.

In a daily newspaper in 2025, references to computers alone will spark miles of information along the neural pathways of even the most badly educated, while the very word would be baffling to a European scholar of the Middle Ages. The amount of information carried in a 21st century brain would appear inhuman to a normal person even 250 years ago.

But seeing what a human brain is capable of computing, what do we choose to do with it from the earliest age? We put its carrier in a chair, in a room, with 30 others of its ilk, and we set about stuffing it with facts. We do this for at least 12 years. Then we put the carrier of that brain in a room, with a piece of paper and a writing utensil, and ask it to regurgitate what it has learned. And if it doesn't regurgitate at a certain level or regurgitates a garbled or incorrect version of the information its brain has been stuffed with, we label it a failure, and send it off to a life of drudge labour.

It's a terrible system, and a complete waste of human resources, if we insist on thinking of people as a resource.

So, let's start again. What is it in the 21st century - and ongoing - that a person needs to learn to have a chance at a fulfilling life?

First of all, everyone who doesn't have an intellectual disability - currently estimated at 1-3% of global population[2] - must be able to read and write and count. There will always be those afflicted by a serious form of dyslexia, or some other impediment to learning, for whom reading and writing might be a lifelong struggle. These people apart, literacy and numeracy levels in the West alone are a disgrace. Between the ages of five and eight all efforts should be directed here - 99% of children should be able to read, write and count by age eight. Except where the reading matter itself is about factual events, other subjects should not be tackled until these basics are achieved. None of this precludes reading poetry, or singing, or acting out plays, because all of these revolve around learning and using words. Mathematics, meanwhile, can be applied to real life situations, for instance to work out how much things cost and how much you have to spend. But children must be able to add, subtract, divide and multiply before moving on.

And then the real revolution in the curriculum would begin. Because the things that fulfil the most fulfilled of us are the very things we have never tried to teach. Creativity, curiosity, and research skills are the means to blend young brains into humans with more rounded minds. Why do we need to teach geography, for instance, as it's always been taught? All that information is instantly available online. Research skills and the curiosity to discover are far more important than putting a pin in a map to show you know where Burkina Faso is.

The difference here is that instead of teaching children facts we believe they *should* know, we teach them to hone the intellectual tools they need to find out for themselves the things they *wish* to know.

This approach is very much in line with the thoughts of Sir Ken Robinson, whose Ted Talk titled 'Do Schools Kill Creativity' is the most viewed Ted Talk of all time, over 75 million views on YouTube to date.[3] And something like it is already a huge success in Finland, which overhauled its education curriculum in 2016, and now ranks 8th in the world's education systems, and in some categories as the best in the world.[4]

Taking one element of Finland's approach, let's look at what they call 'multidisciplinary learning modules', at least one of which has to be part of each year's curriculum.[5] These modules, which integrate various subjects around a central theme or project, encourage students to make connections between different disciplines, to apply their knowledge in real-world contexts, and to develop essential skills like collaboration, communication, and problem-solving. This approach promotes a deeper understanding of complex issues and prepares students for the interdisciplinary nature of work and life in the 21st century. This could be the most radical curriculum change worldwide.

Let us call it 'situational learning', for reasons that will become clear. Take an event in history. Let's say WW2, because, for our purposes, it is the most recent cataclysmic event, and still within living memory. The teacher would not be there to 'teach' the 'facts' about WW2. The teacher would no longer be the 'teacher', but rather a supervisor, a facilitator, there to help the students plan and execute the module. The students will be asked to look at WW2, taking note of its geography and politics; the roles of, say, church leaders and politicians; the behaviour of military leaders; the use of propaganda; the way weaponry was deployed, possibly for the first time (atomic bombs); how and why different countries entered the war, spreading it around the world. And so on.

Note that no-one is 'teaching' here. Pupils are learning, under supervision. They have to collect and collate information themselves. This requires them to learn research from an early age. No longer sitting, listening, having information someone else has deemed they need to know preached to them. Instead, with the entirety of the internet at their disposal - spurred on by a team effort, their own cohort of fellow students - they will learn for themselves the way the world works. No longer the need to fill their heads with dates and names and events that, out of context, mean nothing but which, later on, under the current system, would determine their future, dependent on their ability or inability to recall them in a stressful test setting.

So, learning through studying situations - 'situational learning' - gives a more rounded understanding of world events, and why they happen, rather than learning that they *did* happen, and then failing a test for not being able to remember *when* they happened.

And as AI rapidly transforms society and careers, understanding its fundamentals would equip students for the future job market, further underlining the general redundancy of the current education curriculum. Including AI in a radically overhauled curriculum would be a major contributor to developing critical thinking: AI raises complex ethical and philosophical questions, but its application also involves data analysis and problem-solving. Teaching it would also boost problem-solving skills.

Which brings us to another thorny topic: who should do the teaching and what should be taught?

If we believe that within 10 years the race to outer space will have begun, why do we spend so little time in the curriculum on the solar system, astrophysics, space travel, and future methods of propulsion? One obvious answer is that we may well not have the teachers qualified to tackle such subjects. Teachers, after all, have for generations been teaching what they themselves had been taught, and much of what today's teachers know is of little value to future generations. But there are rules for who is allowed to be a teacher, and they are strictly applied.

At some point, a bullet is going to have to be bitten, because there are people who are not qualified as teachers who may well be the best people to induct schools into a radical new curriculum. We need to reimagine the role of teachers, recognizing that expertise and passion for a subject can sometimes outweigh formal qualifications. By embracing a more flexible approach to teacher recruitment and training, we can tap into a wider pool of talent and bring diverse perspectives and experiences into the classroom.

An education system that encourages creative and critical thinking, the research skills to discover whatever is of interest, and the ability to work with others to create a picture of the social, political, religious, geographical and other elements that shape human history is also - and this is profoundly important - an education system that is equal wherever it is employed.

And it has to be admitted that the current curriculum generally employed around the world - history, geography, the sciences, maths, literature etc, all taught as separate subjects – doesn't just favour the very clever and those whose ability to retain information is innate. It also massively privileges the minority who can afford to pay for their children to be educated at fee-paying schools, where the level of teaching normally is superior, in much smaller classes, a crucial factor in the end results.

Whether we accept that teaching at fee paying schools is superior, it is nonetheless true that graduates of private education fare disproportionately better in further education and the professions than do those from the state school sector.

The theory is very straightforward. In the shortest possible time, we must move to give everyone the same education or educational opportunity. Equality of opportunity may not lead to equality of outcome. But, as many have stated, everyone has the potential to advance. Education should be the start button on the engine of ambition. At the moment it is frequently the brake, because, as Sir Ken Robinson put it: "Schools kill creativity." He also said: "Curiosity is the engine of achievement," and: "The fact is that given the challenges we face, education doesn't need to be reformed -- it needs to be transformed. The key to this transformation is not to standardise education, but to personalise it, to build achievement on discovering the individual talents of each child, to put students in an environment where they want to learn and where they can naturally discover their true passions."[6]

This education idea is not new. It is not even modern. We can look, for instance, at the work of Lev Vygotsky, whose books and research were banned by Joseph Stalin after Vygotsky died aged just 37. Vygotsky 'emphasised the role of social interaction in the development of mental abilities in children'[7]. He believed that children could acquire problem-solving strategies through collaborative dialogues with those he called 'more knowledgeable others' (MKO). Crucially, he did not prescribe the MKO as exclusively teachers, but simply as someone who has a higher level of ability or greater understanding than 'the learner'.

Or we can go all the way back to Ancient Greece where schooling placed a strong emphasis on developing critical thinking, rhetoric, and philosophical inquiry: i.e. how to think, not what to think. The Greek term 'paideia' refers to the overall upbringing and education of a child, encompassing not only formal schooling but also the development of character, values, and civic responsibility. The ultimate goal was to create well-rounded citizens who could contribute to society, rather than becoming cogs in the GDP engine.

Philosophy was a central component especially for older students. Teachers like Socrates, Plato, and Aristotle encouraged their students to question assumptions, explore different perspectives, and engage in rigorous debate to arrive at the truth and what was right (moral).

The ability to speak persuasively and eloquently was also highly valued. Students were trained in rhetoric, the art of effective communication, through exercises like speeches, debates, and argumentation. Focus was on values and emphasised moral and ethical development. While literacy and numeracy were important, Greek education went beyond mere memorisation of facts and figures. It aimed to cultivate a love of learning, critical thinking skills, and a broader understanding of the world. Students were taught to cultivate virtues like courage, justice, wisdom, and moderation, which were considered essential for a good life and a well-functioning society. (Where did we go wrong?).

Coming more up to date, we have Sir Ken Robinson (already discussed); John Seely Brown ('How do you get kids who have curiosity and a questing disposition?');[8] and Sugatra Mitra, whose Ted Talk, 'The Child-Driven Education'[9] has been viewed 3.5m times. Mitra has proved that children will educate themselves. He did this by the simple act of placing a computer in a hole in a wall. He has done this in various parts of India and has made it possible to watch how impoverished children, with no formal education, learn how to use a computer, on their own, and then help each other to use it creatively. We underestimate children. Society pays a large price, by ignoring the ways in which our young can learn, should learn, and can become, by dint of a new approach, more fulfilled in their own lives.

Of course, this all assumes education is accessible. Data on the percentage of people who receive no education is difficult to obtain but estimates suggest around 19% of adults globally lack formal schooling. This means they have not completed a year of primary education. To put it mildly, that's not a very good starting place. In 2022, UNICEF declared that numbers of children not enrolled in education had reduced by 35% since 2000. But that still left 64 million elementary students out of school.[10] Illiteracy rates in adults is another indicator. Around 759 million adults are estimated to be illiterate, signifying a lack of formal education.

In case you think that is a third world problem, more than half of American adults have a literacy rate below sixth grade level.[11] Fully one-fifth of American adults are actually illiterate. In the UK, average reading age has reduced from age 14 (the ability to read and comprehend, say, The Guardian newspaper) among baby boomers, to age 9 (the ability to read and comprehend The Sun newspaper) in post-boomer generations. In 2015, the OECD ran its international Survey of Adult Skills,[12] which showed that literacy levels in the UK were continuing to decline. The educational establishment will insist this decline has been reversed in the intervening years, but then such claims have been continuously made even as research continuously proved them wrong.

The rich and the well-off are paying every day for the opportunity to avoid their children joining such a depressing statistical group. According to the World Bank, the average percentage of private primary education in OECD countries in 2020 was 7%. The average percentage of private secondary education in OECD countries was 20%. In 2023, The Guardian reported that children in private education were twice as likely as those in state education to achieve an A or A* in their final exams,[13] the ones that will determine which University will accept them.

The average annual tuition for private primary school is $11,337, and the average annual tuition for private secondary school is $15,720. So, 20% of the children in the developed world have an advantage at the beginning of their life, paid for in cash.

Here is a breakdown of the percentage of private education in some selected developed countries:[14]

United States: 10% of primary education is private, and 34% of secondary education is private. United Kingdom: 7% of primary education is private, and 17% of secondary education is private. Canada: 4% of primary education is private, 16% of secondary education is private. Australia: 6% of primary education is private, and 34% of secondary education is private. Germany: 3% of primary education is private, and 12% of secondary education is private.

Japan: 1% of primary education is private, and 4% of secondary education is private.

Country Private Education	Primary (%)	Secondary (%)
U S A	10%	34%
U K	7%	17%
Canada	4%	16%
Australia	6%	34%
Germany	3%	12%
Japan	1%	4%

Now let's look at a list of the top 12 countries when it comes to producing the world's best engineers: United States of America, China, Germany, United Kingdom, Switzerland, Japan, The Netherlands, South Korea, Sweden, France, Israel, Singapore

Do we see a correlation?

But we must remember it's not just about classroom education. In the developed world we are just waking up to the fact that education continues through life, now that we have the entirety of human knowledge at our fingertips, online. Worldwide, 5.4 billion people now have internet access. This translates to roughly 67% of the global population. So, 33% do not have access to the internet and most of those are in the poorest economic groups. Lower income means less internet access. Even in the US, studies show a significant gap. For instance, one study found that around 17% of people below the poverty line lacked internet access[15] compared to only 3% for those well above the poverty line. The environment you live in, the support you receive from people about you, your access to electronics, books, and conversation will all have an impact either in reinforcing your education or minimising it.

Some thoughts from others as to why education should be equal for all: -

'Education is the passport to the future, for tomorrow belongs to those who prepare for it today.' - Malcolm X

'Education is the most powerful weapon which you can use to change the world.' - Nelson Mandela

'Education is the key to unlocking the golden door of freedom.' - George Washington Carver

'Education is not preparation for life; education is life itself.' - John Dewey

'Education is the foundation upon which we build our future.' - Christine Todd Whitman

'Education is the most powerful tool we have to change the world.' - Malala Yousafzai

'Education is the key to success in life, and teachers make a lasting impact in the lives of their students.' - Solomon Ortiz

So, we need to teach everyone. We must provide internet access and computers to the poorest. We need to fade out and remove private education because it is one of the elements helping to create an elite. Initially one could tax private education very heavily, a surcharge of 50% of the fees paid to the local authority where the school is located which can be used to invest into the state education of the area. Then finally we need to make the curriculum relevant to what's happening in the world. Given the rapid advancements in technology and the changing landscape of the 21st century, the traditional education system has lagged in preparing students for the future.

To equip them with the skills and knowledge relevant to the world they'll inherit, we need a radical rethinking of the school curriculum. Here are some crucial areas that should be emphasised:

Foundational Skills for the AI Age: Critical Thinking and Problem-Solving: With AI automating routine tasks, critical thinking and complex problem-solving will be essential. Students need to learn how to analyse information, evaluate evidence, and make sound judgments in ambiguous situations.

Creativity and Innovation: AI excels at pattern recognition and optimization, but human creativity remains essential for generating novel ideas and solutions. Encouraging students to think outside the box, experiment, and embrace failure as part of the learning process will be crucial.

Data Literacy: The ability to understand, interpret, and analyse data will be increasingly important in a world awash with information, much of it fake or wrong. Teaching students' basic data literacy skills, such as understanding statistics, visualising data, and recognizing biases, will equip them to make informed decisions.

Digital Literacy and Ethics: As AI becomes integrated into various aspects of life, understanding its capabilities, limitations, and potential biases will be essential. Teaching digital literacy and ethical considerations related to AI will empower students to navigate the digital world responsibly.

Adaptability, Lifelong Learning and Learning How to Learn: With knowledge and technology evolving rapidly, the ability to learn independently and adapt to new information and skills will be invaluable. Schools should focus on teaching students how to learn effectively, rather than just memorising facts.

Resilience and Growth Mindset: Students need to be equipped with a growth mindset, embracing challenges, learning from mistakes, and adapting to setbacks. Resilience will be key to navigating a rapidly changing world.

Collaboration and Communication: AI might automate some tasks, but collaboration and communication skills will remain essential for success in the workplace and society. Schools should foster teamwork, communication, and cross-cultural understanding.

Understanding and Navigating Emerging Technologies: Artificial Intelligence: Students should learn about the basics of AI, its applications, and its potential impact on society. This includes understanding how AI works, its strengths and limitations, and the ethical considerations surrounding its use.

Electric Mobility: The transition to electric vehicles is underway, and students should learn about the technology behind electric mobility, its environmental impact, and its potential to reshape transportation systems.

Space Exploration: As space exploration becomes more accessible, students should learn about the science and technology behind space travel, the potential for resource utilisation, and the ethical considerations surrounding space exploration and colonisation.

Ethical and Social Implications of Technology: The Digital Divide: Students should be aware of the digital divide, the unequal access to technology and information, and its potential consequences for social and economic inequality.

Algorithmic Bias: Understanding how algorithms can perpetuate bias and discrimination is essential for creating fair and equitable AI systems.

Privacy and Security: Teaching students about online privacy and security risks will help them protect themselves from cyber threats and make informed decisions about their digital footprint.

None of this will be possible without a radical overhaul of the education curriculum and the teaching profession. By definition, those currently teaching only know the old curriculum, and have been trained to teach it. While the younger generation of teachers are retrained, all opposition to bringing in experts to teach each aspect of a new curriculum - experts who will not be trained as teachers - has to be met with stiff determination by governments and their civil servants. The alternative is to condemn future generations to learning redundant and irrelevant material which will render them unequipped for life or work.

Chapter 16 - The 10 key points

1. Unequal Access to Education: The chapter highlights the persistent problem of unequal access to quality education globally, particularly in developing countries and among marginalised communities.

2. The Digital Divide: The digital divide, or unequal access to technology and internet resources, further exacerbates educational disparities, limiting opportunities for learning and development.

3. Outdated Curriculum: Traditional education systems often prioritise rote memorization and outdated skills, failing to prepare students for the demands of the 21st-century workforce.

4. Private Education and Inequality: Private education perpetuates inequality by providing advantages to those who can afford it, limiting social mobility and reinforcing existing disparities.

5. Reimagining the Curriculum for the AI Age: The chapter advocates for a revamped curriculum that emphasises critical thinking, problem-solving, creativity, data literacy, and digital literacy, preparing students for the challenges and opportunities of an AI-driven world.

6. AI as a Core Subject: Teaching AI as a core subject in schools is crucial for equipping future generations with the knowledge and skills to navigate an AI-powered world.

7. Embracing Space Exploration in Education: The chapter highlights the importance of incorporating space-related subjects into the curriculum, recognizing the growing significance of space exploration and resource utilisation.

8. Shifting the Focus of Skill Development: The chapter proposes reducing emphasis on rote memorization, complex calculations, and handwriting, focusing instead on adaptability, lifelong learning, communication, and collaboration.

9. Bridging the Digital Divide: Ensuring equitable access to technology and internet resources for all students is essential for creating a level playing field and promoting equal opportunities for learning.

10. Towards a More Equitable Education System: The chapter suggests phasing out private education and implementing measures to ensure that all schools receive equal funding and resources, creating a fairer and more inclusive education system.

Footnotes – Chapter 16

[1] https://theconversation.com/five-ways-ancient-india-changed-the-world-with-maths-84332

[2]https://www.specialolympics.org/about/intellectual-disabilities/what-is-intellectual-disability#:~:text=Approximately%206.5%20million%20people%20in,many%20as%20200%20million%20people

[3] https://youtu.be/iG9CE55wbtY?si=K2703PiHhyCX7xCD

[4] https://leverageedu.com/blog/finland-education-system/

[5]https://www.oph.fi/en/education-and-qualifications/national-core-curriculum-primary-and-lower-secondary-basic-education

[6] https://www.goodreads.com/author/quotes/43940.Ken_Robinson

[7] https://www.simplypsychology.org/vygotsky.html

[8] https://www.youtube.com/watch?v=41pNX9-yNu

[9]https://www.ted.com/talks/sugata_mitra_the_child_driven_education?subtitle=en

[10]https://data.unicef.org/topic/education/primary-education/#:~:text=Additionally%2C%20over%20the%20past%20two,them%20coming%20from%20marginalized%20groups.

[11]https://www.crossrivertherapy.com/research/literacy-statistics#:~:text=21%25%20of%20adults%20in%20the,to%20%242.2%20trillion%20every%20year.

[12] https://literacytrust.org.uk/parents-and-families/adult-literacy/what-do-adult-literacy-levels-mean/

[13] https://www.theguardian.com/education/2023/aug/20/private-school-england-twice-as-likely-top-a-level-grades

[14] Breakdown of the percentage of private education in some developed countries:

Percentage of Private Education; South Korea 80%, Netherlands 60%, Chile 58%, Ireland 50%, Australia 35%, Spain 30%, Malta 30%, Taiwan 30%, Israel 25%, Andorra 25%, Cyprus 20%, Turkey 20%, Canada 19%, United Kingdom 19%, France 17%, Switzerland 15%, Greece 15% Portugal 15%

[15] https://aspe.hhs.gov/sites/default/files/private/pdf/263601/internet-access-among-low-income-2019.pdf

CHAPTER 17

The Lack of Compassion

What does it say about those who consume television programmes, 'news' coverage, and magazines about the super-rich in a spirit of both envy and admiration? That the Kardashians are the world's most famous family? And that one of MTV's most popular shows during the early 2000s was *Pimp My Ride*, where perfectly ordinary cars were fitted out with outrageously extravagant and expensive accessories? *Pimp My Ride* and *Cribs*, which showed the interiors of the crudely fabulous homes of the newly rich and famous, were described at the time as 'aspirational programming'.

What it says is that we in the 'developed' world have evolved beyond compassion, empathy and even basic good taste. The people whose lives are on show are prime examples of this retrograde development. But where the French once put their Kardashians to the guillotine, and the Bolsheviks put their equivalents to the gun, we put them on television, and admire them.

Spending inordinate sums of money on items and lifestyles that are not essential to life while at the same time people are dying from want of food and the simple basics of life should make us ashamed. Instead, we have become anaesthetized to the sheer amorality on display, even to the extent of finding such vulgarity 'aspirational'. What is concerning is that we are now receiving so much information and data that it desensitises us so that we no longer respond appropriately to the problems of the world and the depredations of its poorest.[1] The constant bombardment of news and images of suffering can lead to compassion fatigue, where individuals become overwhelmed and emotionally numb. To counteract this, we need to cultivate media literacy, encourage critical engagement with information, and promote narratives that inspire empathy and action. We must also foster a sense of interconnectedness and shared humanity, recognizing that the suffering of others is not distant or abstract but a reflection of our own vulnerability and the need for collective action.

Sheikh Hamad bin Hamdan Al Nahyan is known as The Rainbow Sheikh because of his collection of over 200 custom-painted cars, including a Mercedes-Benz covered in diamonds, and seven Mercedes S Class cars, all in different colours. Is this a person to be admired? Is Roman Abramovich admirable? A man who built an empire while ordinary Russians were scrimping for life's basics, and then sold the assets back to the Russian State? He then promptly took the $13bn the State paid him, removed it from the country that made him, to live a lifestyle of conspicuous extravagance in more comfortable environs, surrounded by sycophants. Are we to admire, or even feel sorry for, Tamara Ecclestone whose home was burgled for £25m of cash and jewellery? Who in their right mind leaves such riches so susceptible?

We might admire the business acumen of two of the world's richest men, Jeff Bezos and Elon Musk, but one of them is better known for acquiring real estate at eye-watering prices,[2] and avoiding tax in various countries where Amazon operates. The other is less of a conspicuous consumer but is almost as adept at minimising his tax bill. To this list we can add pop culture stars Paris Hilton, Celine Dion, Beyonce, Oprah Winfrey, JayZ and Kanye West, boxer Floyd Mayweather, The Sultan of Brunei, The Emir of Qatar, and a host of others whose sumptuous lives are on display while great swathes of the globe rot. People affected die of starvation or of illnesses associated with poverty, or caused by the work they do, for example, mining rare metal elements, exposure to which is known to cause cancers and slow deaths.

We need to address our aspirations, develop our sense of compassion, and improve our ethical standards so that witnessing such vulgar exhibitions of undeserved wealth actually makes us angry, rather than envious. Our anger should not be vengeful, in the style of the French Revolution or of the Bolsheviks of 1917, but rather addressed to changing hearts and minds so that sharing the world's wealth becomes a common aim. We must start at home and develop a far better example of a moral society, where the good we are doing is recognised as being far better than the money we create. And this new moral society must be led by Europe and Apac's more developed countries. Because if we do not move to the We, and away from the I, we will see, in the near future, the rise of the vengeful solution.

Any redistribution of wealth should not be according to the theoretical tenets of Marx and Engels, nor the mean-spirited Lenin, but rather from a sense that all - including the very rich who will sacrifice a portion of their wealth - will benefit from a world where all are lifted from poverty and need, guaranteed a life above subsistence level, and equality of education and the consequent opportunities.

Maybe it's too late to change the mindsets of those we have named? But what about their children, their grandchildren? What about you? Do you have a problem with the lack of morality in our lives? If so, what have you done to improve the world? Have you done as much as possible? Have you done even the bare minimum? We have to invest in the poor around the world, and without any of the shame attached to those who would call us patronising, or 'white saviours', or of being 'neo-colonialists'.

The upper-middle class have always known the value of investing early to build their children's human capital, without ever requiring the investment to be justified by formal rates of return. The evidence stares them in the face. The grip of the privately educated elite of America and Britain on politics, economy and society is a clear example of what has been with us for many centuries. Using data from 1926, Richard Tawney noted in his 1931 book *Inequality* that in Britain alone: 71 out of 80 bishops and deans, 139 out of 181 members of the judicial profession, 152 out of 210 highly placed members of public departments, 63 out of 88 members of the Indian Civil Service and Governors of Dominions and 99 out of 132 directors of banks and railways had all been educated at public schools (which, in the UK, means fee paying).

If that is the consequence of investing in education, then let us invest in education in such a way that no alternative to what is on offer to everyone confers any advantage. The simple act - and it should be simple - of adjusting our sense of compassion, of morality, and our ethical standards will take us a long way towards a more just and moral world for the future. I'd like to be even clearer. If we do not grow up; if we do not show that moral capitalism is a good way forward, where everyone benefits; that benefits are directed to the **We** not the **I**; then we are heading for a very, very dark future, where the dictator, the criminal, the violent, the unelected and the thugs will run your lives.

Chapter 17 - The 10 key points

1. Desensitisation to Inequality: The chapter highlights how the constant exposure to images of wealth and poverty can lead to desensitisation and a lack of compassion towards those suffering from deprivation and injustice.

2. The Moral Responsibility of the Wealthy: The super-rich are challenged to examine their moral responsibility in a world where their extravagant lifestyles contrast sharply with the struggles of millions living in poverty.

3. Examples of Extravagance and Waste: The chapter provides specific examples of excessive spending by the wealthy, highlighting the disconnect between their opulent lifestyles and the basic needs of many.

4. Environmental Impact of Excess: The consumption patterns of the super-rich contribute disproportionately to environmental damage, exacerbating climate change and resource depletion.

5. Exploitation in the Pursuit of Luxury: Industries catering to the desires of the wealthy often rely on exploitative practices, perpetuating inequality and social injustice.

6. Information as a Catalyst for Change: The widespread availability of information through digital platforms can raise awareness of inequality and potentially mobilise public opinion for change.

7. The Power of Collective Action: Individuals are encouraged to use their voices and influence to demand change, holding the wealthy and powerful accountable for their actions and advocating for a more equitable distribution of resources.

8. Challenging the Status Quo: The chapter questions the normalisation of extreme wealth disparity and encourages readers to envision alternative societal models that prioritise social justice and the well-being of all.

9. The Next Generation's Moral Compass: The chapter raises concerns about the values being passed down to future generations and calls for fostering a sense of social responsibility and compassion in young people.

10. The Need for a Moral Awakening: The chapter concludes by emphasising the urgent need for a moral awakening, where compassion, empathy, and ethical considerations guide individual actions and societal choices, leading to a more just and equitable world, or we will descend into a very black place.

Footnotes – Chapter 17

[1] **The Decision Lab - Information Overload:** https://thedecisionlab.com/reference-guide/psychology/information-overload

[2] https://www.vox.com/recode/2020/2/6/21125456/jeff-bezos-los-angeles-home-purchase-billionaire

CHAPTER 18

Where The Money Could Come From

We need to agree what would be reasonable for people to receive each month/year to achieve at least minimal comfort and security, and how we generate the additional money to distribute. (The figures I'm suggesting are an average and would vary, country to country).

If the average income of a worker - currently $3,200 pa, $266 a month, for the bottom 50% of adults in our world - became $5,091 pa $424 a month, a 59.1% increase, that would not only be a significant increase, but would also have knock-on benefits.

Increased earnings at the bottom will lead to increased spending on the basics: food, housing, education, medical services. All of this stimulates the economy and reduces the costs and need for famine relief, emergency food donation etc.[1] Growth for everyone comes from the circulation of money and the speed of that circulation. Bringing billions of customers into the market will significantly grow the pie. Surely it is better if all of society can contribute.

Therefore, I suggest we need to set targets for the whole adult population, low and high.

Surgeons, dentists, professors, researchers and doctors are some of the roles that support our society and make our quality of life better. We need to ask: is $20,000 a month ($240,000 pa) a reasonable fee/return after extensive study and training? To have a moral society and to set an example to the rest of the world, we need to start valuing work with a lot more thought than simply 'What can I grab? What will I be able to extract from the company where often the decision makers are my friends?' We need to start really evaluating the social value of each role, the contribution to the We.

And we have to ask this question in relation to the average earnings of the average worker in the developed world - currently $3,083 a month ($36,999 pa in 2020, according to the OECD).

This begs the question: is a ratio of 6.48 times average earnings ($240,000 v $36,999) a reasonable ratio to accept in relation to professionals who may have undertaken extensive training and periods without any significant earnings? Taking surgeons as an example - they have gone through up to 15 years of training to achieve their qualifications. Dentists may take seven years. What is a reasonable return for highly trained professionals who improve our quality of life?[2] Because to move the debate forward, we need to make decisions on what is a reasonable ratio; what is a reasonable return for years of study as opposed to exploitation. Work, and especially work that benefits society, should always be fairly rewarded. Salaries for doctors, professors and scientists vary widely by country, specialty, and experience. According to a 2022 survey by the Medscape Physician Compensation Report, the average salary for doctors in the United States is $313,000 per year. In other developed countries, average doctors' salaries can also be high relative to those in other careers. For example, in Canada, the average annual salary for doctors is $295,000. However, in the United Kingdom, the average for doctors is less than half that at around $127,500 per year, is barely 40% of the American rate, while a doctor in India might earn half that of a UK doctor.

The average faculty salaries for professors also vary by country, institution and experience. According to a 2023 survey by the American Association of University Professors (AAUP), the average salary for full professors in the United States is $131,915 per year. In other developed countries, the average faculty salary is also relatively high. In Canada, it is $117,272 per year, in the United Kingdom, around $118,000 per year.

Average salaries for scientists vary by field, experience, and location. However, according to a 2023 survey by the American Bureau of Labour Statistics (BLS), the median annual salary for scientists in the United States is $91,250, compared to $80,000 in Germany. In the United Kingdom, meanwhile, the comparable figure is around $58,000.

Lifting the poorest out of poverty

Here is a breakdown of some suggestions I would propose for a future income distribution, including a suggestion as to where the money would come from.

We need to allocate a higher proportion of income to the bottom 9% of the population and the next 41%, ensuring a minimum annual income of $5,091 for 50% of the world. The poorest 50% are currently subsisting on an average of $3,200 pa. This significant increase would be a start that aims to alleviate poverty and provide a basic standard of living for those in the most deprived areas of the world. Distribution of this money will clearly be an issue, because it always has been. To ensure that the funds reach their intended recipients and are used effectively, we need to establish transparent and accountable mechanisms for distribution. This could involve leveraging technology, such as blockchain-based systems, to track and verify transactions, and empowering local communities to participate in decision-making about how the funds are allocated. Money needs to go as directly as possible, with as little involvement from governments as can be achieved, as funds are needed by the poorest themselves, not the administrators.

But you can also do your bit immediately, refusing to purchase products from companies that don't guarantee the people producing their raw materials or producing their clothes are receiving the minimum I set out above. By combining innovative solutions with a commitment to transparency and accountability, we can overcome the historical challenges of aid distribution and ensure that the benefits of wealth redistribution reach those who need it most.

Money donated has always, in the past, gone through other's hands before reaching its intended target of starving and poor people. Much of the money has stuck to those intermediate hands before the remainder is passed on. But today's technology allows personal identity cards to which money can automatically be credited. This is not to downplay the complexity of administering a new deal for the world's worst off. But technology makes it entirely possible.

The next 40% of the population, the low to middle income workers, represent a substantial portion of the world's workforce. They currently receive, across all territories, an average annual income of $18,582. A smaller increase - not 59.1%, but maybe an average increase of 20% - would dramatically improve their living standards and expand their spending power.

Those already above poverty level are still relatively poor. Increasing their wages will also boost overall economic stability. This higher income level, which really needs to be even more, also needs to recognise the contributions of skilled workers and should be reinforced with incentives for further education and skill development. Lifting people out of poverty is only half the job. Ensuring the best model of education is available for all, and accessible for all, is essential. Young people must be imbued with a vision of what is possible in their futures. Their ambitions need to be fired. Only education can guarantee a better future. (when thinking about these figures, remember there would be differences between countries and within each band).

Limiting Extreme Wealth

While these proposals acknowledge the contributions of high-income earners, we would place limits on extreme wealth accumulation. We have already discussed the iniquity of the limitless earning capacity of those at the top, those we have identified as the new elite, who continue to be rewarded when they perform poorly, or even when they fail. It's time to get serious about what constitutes justifiable returns, even for significant success.

So, for instance, top workers, representing 1% of the population, could have a number of bands. The first band would receive a maximum annual income of $300,000 The second, which should be a very small band of elite and leading directors would have their incomes capped at say $1.85 million pa. The third, at the extreme top - CEOs, for instance of companies with sales in excess of $1 Billion (between 3,000 and 5,000 companies) would be limited to $15 million. These two latter groups would be small - 0.005% and 0.0001%.

Remember, according to the AFL 2022 report on the salaries of the top companies in America, the following five people were at the top of the pile, earning hundreds of millions each year.

Blackstone Inc.	**Stephen Schwarzman**	**$253,122,146**
Alphabet Inc.	**Sundar Pichai**	**$225,985,145**
Hertz Global Holdings, Inc.	**Stephen Scherr**	**$182,136,137**
Peloton Interactive, Inc.	**Barry Mccarthy**	**$168,073,420**
Palo Alto Networks Inc.	**Nikesh Arora**	**$151,425,203**

Limiting these people to $15m per year each would be a big reduction and I'm sure there would, in the interim, be massive employment for lawyers and big donations to politicians to stop such limits becoming law. But what is the commercial and economic justification for salaries of this scale, let alone any moral questions? And a $15M pa limit would affect only the top 420 CEOs on the AFT list of S&P 500 companies. Within two generations, this would all feel perfectly normal. (One approach could be for companies to state that once the current contracts have expired the new contracts will be limited to our maximum of $15 million)

Tax all luxury goods and purchases

Total spend worldwide on luxury goods is $1.75 trillion. Taxing them at 50% would generate $0.525 trillion a year in additional tax receipts. Long-term you could push tax on luxury goods even higher, 75% or even 100%. Currently VAT ranges between 13% in China and 27% in some locations in Europe. Luxury goods also have by far the largest profit margin, so everyone in the supply chain should be paid a decent salary, because the money is clearly available, but it needs to go to the workers, not the 2 or 3 directors at the top. It would be easy to legislate that the tax on luxury goods would be increased to 200%. If the company was not paying a minimum wage to its supply chain. Below are some examples of luxury spending.

Silvio Berlusconi	Collection of extravagant properties, including villas and mansions in Italy and abroad, a private island, luxury yachts, and has been associated with hosting lavish parties and events.
Daphne Guinness	Known for her avant-garde fashion choices and extravagant wardrobe, including custom-made designer outfits, owns multiple luxury properties, and has an extensive art and jewellery collection.
Richard Branson	Owns Necker Island in the British Virgin Islands, multiple luxury homes, private jets, a fleet of luxury cars, and participates in extreme sports and adventures, including space travel with VirginGalactic.
Elon Musk	Collection of luxury cars, including rare and unique models like the Lotus Esprit submarine car, multiple high-end real estate properties, including a $50 million mansion in Bel-Air, and significant investments in space exploration (SpaceX).
Oprah Winfrey	Owns multiple properties, including a lavish estate in Montecito, California, a home in Maui, Hawaii, and a ski chalet in Colorado, extensive collection of high-end designer clothing and accessories, and a private jet.
Jay-Z and Beyonce	Multiple luxurious properties, including an $88 million mansion in Bel-Air, a

	$26million East Hampton estate, and a $2.6 million New Orleans church mansion, luxury cars, private jets, and high-end fashion and jewellery collections.
Sheikh Khalifa bin Zayed Al Nahyan	Owns numerous palaces, including the Emirates Palace in Abu Dhabi, extensive investments in luxury ventures, including art collections, hotels, and a fleet of private jets.
Tamim bin Hamad Al Thani	Collection of luxury cars, private planes, multiple properties around the world, including a $300 million mansion in London, and significant Investments In high-profile sports events and projects.
Mariah Carey	Extensive collection of rare and expensive jewellery, high-end fashion and accessories, multiple luxury properties, including a $5.5 million mansion in Beverly Hills, and has been seen with luxury cars and private jets.
Bernard Arnault	Owns an Impressive art collection, rare and expensive wines, multiple luxurious properties, including a mansion in Paris, a chateau in Bordeaux, and significant investments in the world's leading luxury brands (LVMH).
Vladimir Putin	Reported to own multiple palaces, luxury watches worth millions, expensive vehicles, including a custom-made limousine, and has been seen with high- end fashion and accessories.
Kim Jong-un	Reportedly owns luxury vehicles, including a fleet of Mercedes-Benz cars, expensive watches, enjoys fine dining, and imported luxury goods despite North Korea's economic conditions.

Taxing inheritance

According to the UBS Billionaire Ambitions Report 2023, more billionaires accumulated wealth through inheritance than entrepreneurship in 2023. Where there was precise data, 53 heirs inherited a total of $150.8 billion. Plus, the descendants of the 2,500+ super rich who were being tracked inherited an estimated $5.2 trillion. So, what might the rules be for inheritance in a new morality?

We might propose, for instance, that a wife, a husband, or a partner should inherit no more than 50% of the wealth left behind. Or that total Inheritance should never be more than, say, $50 million, with children and grandchildren or any nominated beneficiary limited to a maximum inheritance of $10 million. These sums should be taxed at the normal rate of income tax as applied to salaries, except that, perhaps, partners might inherit 50% of the bequest free of tax. For any sums inherited above this level we should consider a penal tax rate - say 90% of all above $50 million and 99% for all inheritance above $100 million.

This may seem very severe, but severity may be the only way to progress towards a moral distribution of wealth. You have to keep asking yourself: where has the wealth come from? How was the wealth created?

Perhaps aggressively tackling extreme and undeserved wealth, and the unwarranted inheritance of it, is an idea whose time has come. In addition, any schemes or attempts by lawyers and accountants to avoid taxation should be criminalised, and cause jail time, rather than the current slap on the wrist and a modest financial penalty.

There is also an argument that there should be a standardisation of tax rates internationally, so the same tax is applied for income tax, inheritance tax, dividend or capital gains tax of, say, 20% for people with wealth under one million dollars, growing progressively above that to a much higher 35% or more as wealth increases.

While implementing a standardised global tax system may face challenges due to varying economic conditions and political realities, it offers a potential solution to the problem of tax evasion and the race to the bottom in corporate tax rates. By establishing a fair and transparent global tax framework, we can ensure that corporations and wealthy individuals contribute their fair share to society, regardless of where they operate or reside. This would generate significant revenue that could be used to fund essential public services globally, reduce inequality, and promote sustainable development worldwide. There also should be no tax at all for the bottom 50% of the world, those earning below $6,000 a year. Obviously the poorest would pay some indirect tax via sales tax. It would also be reasonable that no sales tax be applicable on basic food products.

The income of the very rich should be taxed by a very simple formula, as we believe all tax should be simplified. Given that they are already wealthy, whatever income their wealth generates should be taxed at the top rate of tax.

Taxing corporate profits

Approximately 35% of corporate profits are moved offshore. In a new, moral, and simplified tax system, this should be criminalised. The Forbes global 2000 list in 2023 shows that the combined profit of the companies on the list amounted to $4.5 trillion. Total worldwide profit of all corporations could be significantly higher. With up to 35% of the annual profit of the larger companies moved offshore, or otherwise structured to avoid paying tax. Just from the world's top 2000 corporations significant amounts currently go untaxed. Just tackling this problem would generate at least an additional $1trillion each year.

The minimum level of corporate tax worldwide is currently set at 15%,[3] which is already low. Worse, due to many exemptions and loopholes in the regulations, the effective tax being paid is only 4.8%. This is a very good example of the power of lobbies and the rich. If these allowances and loopholes were removed and the basic rate of corporation tax was increased to 20% a further $1 trillion per year would be generated.

Corporations should pay more. They should be taxed at a higher rate than individuals. They use the world's resources, often paying very little for the privilege.

The massive current use of electricity by tech companies is a good example. Consumers instinctively feel that streaming their music or their films is greener than pressing vinyl, or manufacturing CDs and DVDs. In reality, the average person's daily streaming of music and television - five hours a day, according to Energy Track Asia[4] - produces the carbon equivalent of manufacturing one plastic CD case. No-one ever bought 365 CDs a year, did they? A major part of this carbon footprint is created by the massive server farms that house and 'farm out' our data: the Cloud, online software, billions of hours of entertainment instantly available at the click of a button. China Telecom-Inner Mongolia Information Park covers an astonishing 10.7 million square feet.[5] The Utah Data Center in Utah, USA, is 1.5 million square feet. These facilities grow yearly, and use up phenomenal amounts of electricity, and the heat they generate further exacerbates their impact on the environment.

Are corporations paying to expand these networks? Are they paying for the damage done to the environment by using additional electricity? In most countries it's the consumer that is being charged, not the corporation. Corporations should pay higher corporate tax rates given their consumption of resources and potential environmental impact. Corporations often use vast amounts of natural resources, including water, energy, and raw materials, for their operations.

A higher tax rate could be seen as a way to offset the environmental and social costs associated with this consumption. Many industries contribute to pollution and climate change. Increased corporate taxes would fund environmental protection initiatives or incentivise businesses to adopt more sustainable practices. All corporations benefit from public infrastructure like roads, transportation networks, and utilities. Higher taxes could be justified as a way for corporations to contribute to the maintenance and development of this infrastructure. Multinational corporations employ complex strategies to minimise their tax burden by shifting profits to low-tax jurisdictions. A higher global minimum tax could help address this issue and ensure fairer contributions.[6] Corporate profits have been rising while wages for many workers have stagnated. Higher corporate taxes could fund social programs and reduce income inequality.

Tax will have to increase, especially across the richest in society. As I looked at 2024's almost simultaneous elections in the USA, UK and France, just to name a few, no politician was saying that. The richest in society are part of the elite, running the world, and the elite are very good at protecting themselves. This is what we must challenge and break. Damage done by bankers and financial institutions to ordinary people is far greater and more serious than many criminal activities.

The top 1% of the world's adults own 46.1% of the world's wealth, which amounts to $200.04T. This means that the average wealth of the top 1% of adults - 55 million of them - is about $3,637,091164 per person. So here is my suggestion on a start to redistribution. First, we should impose a wealth tax of one 1% per year for anyone in the top 1%. Five countries already impose a wealth tax - Norway, Spain, Switzerland, Argentina and Colombia. To make sure tax returns are accurately declared, anyone found to have not fully declared their tax liability should be fined 150% or higher of the value of any item they missed off their balance sheet/tax declaration.

Further, whistleblowers should be rewarded with payments of up to $1m for identifying any individuals avoiding or attempting to avoid tax. There is always someone who knows. It might be a high paid lawyer or accountant, or it might be simply the secretary, driver or assistant. (Plus, very soon this is all going to be clear through the use of artificial intelligence and, given the right motivation and direction from the top, the collection of tax really can be improved).

Then very simply across the top 1% there is currently a massive underpayment of the taxes that already exist. Just collecting existing taxes, currently uncollected, could generate a further $2 trillion a year.

So, there is plenty of money. We just need to start collecting it properly and put in place a moral system that benefits the whole world, not just the rich. We need to stop giving the elite preferential treatment, allowing them to protect themselves.

Overall Economic Impact:

By redistributing income more evenly - but across the globe, rather than only in the countries where the tax is collected - economic growth would be stimulated and social tensions reduced. A more equitable distribution of wealth can lead to increased consumer spending by larger numbers of the global population, improved living standards for all, and a more stable and prosperous society worldwide. Implementing such a significant change in income distribution would pose challenges, which we explore at the end of this book. But the potential benefits of trillions of dollars becoming available to distribute according to real needs, around the world, are obvious in terms of reducing inequality, improving living standards, and promoting economic stability. The obstacles must be addressed.

Proposals	Priority
Tax the very top earners in a much more effective way	***
Established guidelines for future remuneration that is equitable	***
Control the power of the financial institutions	***
Recognize people's social benefit to society, not just their monetary benefit	***
Make education truly equal for all	***
Accept that historically most of the wealth and income has been created by being a member of the elite and has not been equitable	*
Review inheritance	**

Limit the power of the mega companies or split their power	***
Consider future ownership in space to avoid conflict	*
Define what a country or a tribe should be	*
Create a political system that benefits citizens as a whole and limits the possibility of corruption and damage by politicians	***
Create a framework where wealth can be redistributed	***

Chapter 18- The 10 key points

1. Income Inequality and the Need for Redistribution: The chapter highlights the stark income inequality across the globe and proposes a redistribution plan to create a fairer society.

2. Raising the Floor for the Poorest: The plan suggests increasing the minimum annual income for the bottom 50% of the population to $5,091, aiming to alleviate poverty and provide a basic standard of living.

3. Modest Raises for Low- to Middle-Income Earners: A 20% average increase in income is proposed for the next 40% of the population, recognizing their contributions and boosting economic stability.

4. Fair Compensation for Skilled Professionals: The chapter addresses the need to fairly compensate skilled professionals like doctors and professors, suggesting a maximum income while acknowledging their valuable contributions and the existing disparities in their salaries.

5. Education as a Catalyst for Upward Mobility: The importance of accessible and high-quality education for all is emphasised as a crucial tool for empowering individuals to escape poverty and achieve a better future.

6. Tax Reforms to Generate Revenue: The chapter proposes various tax reforms to generate the necessary funds for redistribution, including: A significant tax on luxury goods. A progressive inheritance tax system with

high rates on excessive wealth transfer. Addressing corporate tax evasion and loopholes. Implementing a wealth tax on the top 1%.

7. Wealth Tax on the Top 1%: A 1% annual wealth tax on the wealthiest individuals, coupled with strict enforcement and whistleblower incentives, is proposed to tackle extreme wealth concentration.

8. Corporate Accountability and Fair Taxation: The chapter emphasises the need for corporations to pay their fair share of taxes and contribute to society, suggesting higher corporate tax rates and closing loopholes.

9. Challenging the Elite's Influence: The plan acknowledges the power and influence of the elite in shaping economic and tax policies and calls for measures to prioritise the well-being of the broader population.

10. The Moral Imperative of Redistribution: The chapter concludes by emphasising that addressing inequality and creating a fairer society is not only an economic necessity but also a moral imperative.

Footnotes – Chapter 18

[1] The amount of money spent on famine relief and famine aid worldwide varies from year to year, depending on the severity and number of famines occurring. However, in recent years, the average annual spending on famine relief and famine aid has been around $10 billion per year. This translates to an average of around $2 per person helped per year. The United Nations World Food Programme (WFP) is the largest provider of famine relief and famine aid in the world. In 2022, the WFP provided food assistance to over 120 million people in 88 countries. The WFP's budget in 2022 was $7.8 billion, of which $5.8 billion was spent on famine relief and famine aid.

[2] Over the past three decades, more than half of the countries and close to 90 percent of advanced economies have seen an increase in income inequality, with some countries recording an increase in their Gini coefficients exceeding two points.

Introduction to Inequality

[3] In October 2021, over 130 countries agreed to a global minimum corporate tax rate of 15% under the OECD/G20

[4] https://www.cbc.ca/music/the-environmental-impact-of-music-streaming-explained-1.6843948

[5] https://www.analyticsvidhya.com/blog/2020/09/largest-data-centers-world/

[6] https://www.google.com/url?q=https://kpmg.com/xx/en/our-insights/risk-and-regulation/beps-2-0-pillar-one-and-pillar-two.html%23:~:text%3DPillar%2520Two%253A%2520Global%2520Minimum%2520Taxation%26text%3DThese%2520Model%2520Rules%2520set%2520forth,of%2520more%2520than%2520EUR750%2520million&sa=D&source=docs&ust=1727964169623568&usg=AOvVaw1cl-Eqsek68OuOhODnIP-x

CHAPTER 19

The Process of Change

What are we looking for? We are looking for a new moral democracy, a moral capitalism. It is not about laissez-faire, the strong survive, the weak perish, the government stands aside and lets the market dictate. The market is unfair, and it is rigged to benefit the elite. We all, including governments, must intervene to make the world a fairer place; to make it a more moral world.

Let's repeat - I'm not advocating communism. Communism does not work, and 100+ million deaths in its pursuit between 1917-1990 are more than adequate proof of that. But democracy, in tandem with capitalism, must improve. Most wealth has a very dubious past. Much wealth is undeserved. It has been inherited or created by access and privilege. So, confiscation of at least a portion of it is itself a moral act, and will serve a moral need, which is that there needs to be a levelling up all around the world.

We are all part of the same world, and we need to care a lot more about each other than we care about our immediate gratification. This is harder than it looks. In the 1970s, The Club Of Rome[1] published The Limits to Growth, purporting to predict the future if the population continued to grow at the then present rate. It was wrong in many of its major conclusions. But it did include a survey of Human Perspectives, research which asked people around the world what they cared about.

Along one line - which depicted time over years - it showed that people cared most about themselves and their family in the here and now. By the time the questions were about their children's lifetimes, the interest had dropped by better than 90%.

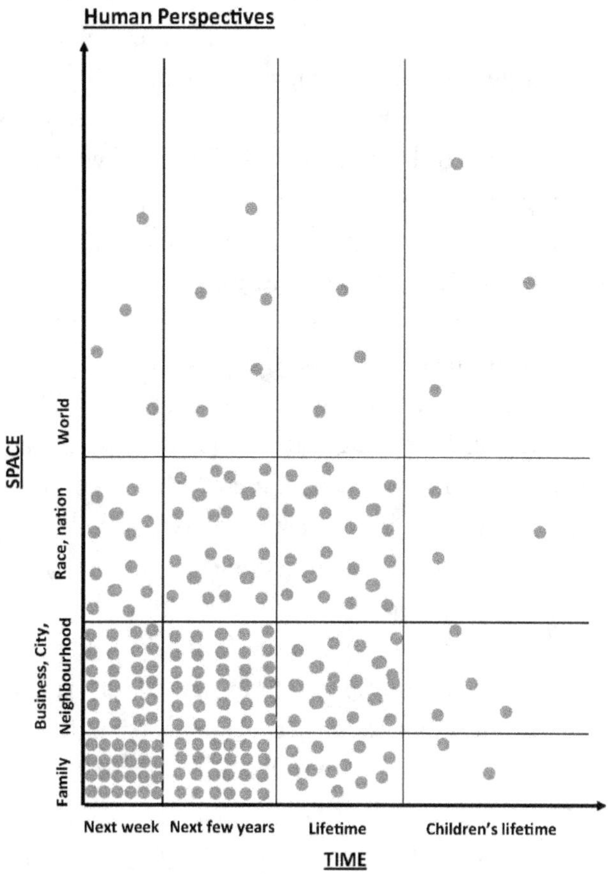

Although the perspectives of the world's people vary in space and in time, every human concern falls somewhere on the space-time graph. The majority of the world's people are concerned with matters that affect only family or friends over a short period of time. Others look farther ahead in time or over a larger area– a city or a nation. Only a very few people have a global perspective that extends far into the future

Along another line - depicting family, business, neighbourhood and home city - caring for others had dropped to less than 20% by the time the table reached 'world'. The accompanying narrative caption concluded: 'Only a very few people have a global perspective that extends far into the future'. Given also that we are very poor at forecasting the future, in this book I'm trying to raise the major issues and start a debate.

Fifty years after the Club of Rome research, we are much more connected, and this connection is speeding up. It's very clear we need more of the '**W**e' and less of the '**I**'. And in the digital age, it has become much easier to make the mental switch.

There is a website linked to this book (https://www.moral money.co) which will be live sometime in 2025 and which will build a library of support materials which you could use for action. Also, in the Appendix, there is one draft of a letter and email (with a full set in the website) which you can send to those in power, or others who you believe can influence or change the future. Your politician who represents you, the director of your pension fund, the manager of your bank, your local bishop, imam, or rabbi - those you want to encourage to drive change. And ask all your friends to take similar action to the action I hope you are going to take.

The website will also have suggested social media posts and petitions. Using your social media contacts, you can get multiple signatures and endorsements of these messages. Who might you want to contact? Your President; your Prime Minister; your local MP; the CEO of any corporation; your insurance company and your pension provider (who invest in companies you might object to). There are also links to charities that limit administrative expenses to the minimum.

There is a cry that often comes from people saying, 'I have no power and I cannot change anything'. This is no longer true. You have a lot more power than you think, because via the internet and social media you can join with others who think the same way and influence real change. In the past you could have chained yourself to the railings around the Houses of Parliament or picketed the White House.[2] If many of you, or most of you, make a concerted effort things will begin to change. You also have your financial power, you can change your financial institutions if they don't improve, but also you can refuse to buy from companies and move your purchasing elsewhere.

As the book's title says: it is all about money. If 10,000 customers, which is not a great number, challenge a company to change, under threat that you will stop buying their products, at the very least the board would discuss the requested changes. If that request for change Is publicised and is live on the internet and the response of the company is live on the internet even better. Change can be created by the sheer volume of the protest. Remember the Civil Rights movement in the USA of the 60s, the anti-apartheid movements from the 60s to 90s, and the current environmental protests led by Greenpeace and others.

So here is a summary of each chapter and what you can do to help deliver the change required.

Introduction. You can send this book to everyone in your network. Send the link from Amazon and your friends can download the first chapters for free. You can mention this book in every social media post you make. You can visit our website for new ideas as often as you like.

Chapter 1 Where are we? & Chapter 2 Freedom for everyone. We need to force this, not wait for the next step in our evolution. If we really are going to be free and move forward, it needs to be a move forward for everyone. The inequality that exists in the world today is devoid of morality as we understand it. This means everyone must accept change. But the richest 1% - those who own 46.1% of the world's wealth - will see the most change, and we recognise it will not feel like a positive change for them. We are suggesting that the top 1% begin to pay tax at the same basis as the rest of us, and also as an initial start that they donate 1% of their wealth immediately to kick-start a better or new life for the needy and vulnerable of the world.

Chapter 3 The power of the financial institutions. Understand that it is your money - *your money* - invested in pension funds, insurance companies, investment companies, government savings or bonds, deposits, or current accounts. Banks are playing with your money. Start fighting them. Initially you could send letters to your pension fund. We have provided an example draft in Appendix 3. (And there will be a full set on our linked website) The laws differ from country to country, but most companies have a system where you should receive a response. However, if you are not happy with the response you can escalate your concerns to the chairman or the company secretary. Our website will help you follow this trail. In addition, in some countries you have a legal right to ask for information or, if they ignore you, you could move your pension to a different fund which is much more focused on Environmental, Social and Governance (ESG) concerns.

Fight the overpayment of senior management. You can make it clear to your politicians that the current situation cannot continue. Force them to focus on their electorate and local issues, not their donors or lobbyists. You can push very hard for an increase in the salary of health, social and education workers, every role that adds to the quality of our life. You can write to your bank and make it very clear that you think the remuneration of those at the top is completely unreasonable. Ask for it to be reviewed and reduced. Again, we provide draft letters for this on the web site. Banks and other financial institutions will either take this seriously or effectively they will be ignoring their customers. Customers who are ignored are customers who will leave and go elsewhere. A bank or pension fund losing customers will be asked very uncomfortable questions by its shareholders and investment bodies.

Chapter 4 How wealth was created and Chapter 5 How wealth is distributed. If you are rich or super rich the first thing you can do is commit to spending 1% as a minimum of your income and of your wealth on those less well-off each year. I intend to place €100,000 with more to follow, immediately into a charitable fund which will be administered free of charge, to ensure all the money going to the less well off. The fund will also receive all the profit from this book, except €1 per book I have already committed to the charity Epic.[3]

Yes, I know there is a big problem in terms of distribution of money given to many charities. You don't want to be giving money where it is not efficiently distributed. Check, before you donate, that administration costs are kept close to zero. As much money donated as possible should be distributed.

Then you must talk to your politicians. Lobby them hard to overhaul the tax system wherever you live. For instance, the UK's tax code is 22,000 pages long, containing over 10 million words. Imagine a set of all seven Harry Potter books side by side. Now get another set and lay them alongside the first. Now do it again, and again, and again. You now have five complete sets of the thickest children's books ever published. And you're still not there. You need most of another set before you're looking at the extent of the UK tax code. This is where tax accountants and specialist lawyers live. Imagine the opportunities they have to delve into all that complexity to find more and more ways for their rich clients to legitimately and legally avoid paying their fair share of tax.

Sounds hopeless. But it really isn't. Tear up the tax code. Write a new one. A really simple one. Let's say we give it three sheets of A4 paper. Easy. Same applies to every country. America's tax code is one-third the size of the UK's - how about that? A country with five times the population has a federal tax code two-thirds smaller. Still too big though. Rip it up. Start again. As far as possible avoid any exemptions, exceptions or special categories. A tax on income, a tax on dividends, capital gains, and inheritance all at the same level of say 30% would save so much wasted time in finding ways to move money from one pot to another pot.

Then make it law that even attempting to avoid tax is a criminal offence. The job designations of tax lawyers and tax accountants should be abolished. Anyone assisting a client to avoid their tax should face compulsory prison time. Ditch the complexity. See the tax revenues flood in.

This is a massive change ordinary citizens can make. Half the countries of the world are democracies. Exercise your democratic right to demand change.

Chapter 6 politicians and system. There should be a form of proportional representation everywhere. And we need to get to a point where countries are run by qualified professionals. There should be rules, for instance, about who can stand. For instance, an age minimum - say 25 - having worked and paid tax for a minimum of five years. And those selected should be based on their professional careers. The UK system of selection has skewed away from career professionals in the past 30 years to the era of the SPAD (special advisor), the professional politician, who leaves university aged 21/22, and straight away joins the Head Office of a political party, becoming a special advisor to a specific MP or Cabinet Minister. Most of these have fairly useless degrees, and no real-world work experience. Where are all the engineers? This is a question that was posed by Chi Onwurah in 2017,[4] when she was the UK's Shadow Minister for Industrial Strategy, Science and Innovation. She is still the only engineer in the Parliamentary Labour Party. Government needs engineers, mathematicians, physicists, biologists, doctors and chemists, and lawyers, police officers, military personnel, plumbers, electricians and other trades, and individuals with experience, not the children of the elite

We also need a return to the days when civil servants were apolitical and did not make public pronouncements. Again, we need a ground swell of support, letters to your current members of parliament, senators, or representatives. The collection of petitions and the shouting out on social media. I firmly believe that if there is enough support change will happen.

Chapter 7 The failing dream of democracy. We can also help people register to vote and we can ensure that everyone has a vote. Probably best approach is with an identity card with everyone in the country receiving an identity card and then automatically receiving a vote. We can make our countries better, more moral so it sets a clear example to other countries. If it is clear that there is a fair and moral alternative where everyone is included, everyone has an opportunity, then the citizens of the undemocratic countries will have the aspiration to change and remove their dictators.

Chapter 8 Could Monarchy lead the change? First, we must recognize that the elite has been heavily entwined with monarchies and the previous Lords and Ladies of the land, or their equivalents, run most developed countries. The small group of existing monarchs and hereditary rulers could be the first to create a real momentum. Even while accepting that they might be overseeing the end of that system, those at the top could be using their remaining power and influence to affect change. It's time to move to a better system. This is not to say that some of the existing or remaining monarchs and rulers do not provide good leadership and direction for their countries. Rather it is a system of the past that has had its time. In a real democracy or a moral country there is no justification for the self- perpetuating elites. (Though I do expect Emperor Musk to claim Mars for his descendants shortly). Individuals can also refuse to accept honours and invitations to inner cliques. In a newly ethical society, such invitations should not be extended.

Chapter 9 Control of the top companies. If you are an investor and/or shareholder, it is your money that is going to pay salaries and bonuses. As a shareholder you are part-owner of the business(es). You are entitled to make it very clear that you will vote against excessive remuneration and if you are not listened to you will sell your shares or look to organise with other shareholders to change control. If you are a shareholder for most companies, you have the right to obtain the details and addresses of all the other shareholders. Or, as a consumer, even if you don't own shares, you can tell the company that you will stop purchasing their products unless they improve their governance. Ten thousand customers stopping buying a product will get attention, particularly if the move is publicised across social media. A million customers promising to stop buying - even better. You have more power than you know. And social media and the internet amplify that power. A few questions to Google' Gemini or to ChatGPT will get you the information you want to act on, and you can network with others - countless others - to make your voice heard. You need to Shout Out.

Chapter 10 & 11. If you have relatives or people you know in the armed forces or the police you can engage them in discussion and ask them if they recognize that they are working for the citizens. They're working for everyone, not the government, and this should always be their prime concern. They are not working for the elite. It should be agreed that never should the military, or the police undertake any action that could be a war crime. Engage with your politicians and, where necessary, get them to change the law to recognize this. If you are in contact with religious leaders or religious representation you should engage with them as well. Ask them why the faiths are not doing more in two areas: Why are they not using their financial power to make sure there aren't excessive salaries paid to the top of the businesses they have invested in? Then ask them to campaign to distribute more of that money to the weak, poor, and disadvantaged.

Chapter 12 The Revolutionary response. Communicate to as many people as you can that we need a new morality in conducting human affairs. We need to share the world's resources and introduce a fairer system of international governance. If not, we will have a revolution, somewhere. As we saw in Europe in 1848,[5] In Russia in 1917, and in the Arab Spring of 2010-12, revolution entails death and destruction, and has rarely ended well even for those on the side of the angels. Distributing the world's money more reasonably could involve measures such as simplified taxation, stronger social safety nets, and greater regulation of corporations. More radically, it might require a one-off taxation of a portion of the super-rich wealth - we have suggested 10% - spread out over 10 years, at 1% per year - which might amount to $20T: plenty to kick start a peaceful revolution of lifting the world's most vulnerable out of poverty and starvation; and founding a decent education system in every corner of the plant.

Corporations and governments also need to be more transparent about their operations and be held accountable for their actions. This includes criminalising and enforcing against tax avoidance (already illegal in some countries) and aggressively prosecuting any form of tax evasion; enforcing labour laws; and protecting whistle-blowers. People also need to be empowered as citizens to participate in decision-making processes and hold their leaders accountable. This can be partly achieved through civic education, strengthening democratic institutions, and protecting freedom of speech and the media, but only if the media is first broken up into smaller companies.

If we don't do this, if we don't come to a more moral version of capitalism, we're going to end up in a very bad place. We need to show that life can be better for everyone in society and can be fair. If you can achieve this, you set a standard for the rest of the world. But if you allow the elite to continue to steal more than a fair share of the resources from the world, then what's the point of fighting the dictators?

Chapter 13 media and control of communication. The first and foremost action is to remove the power of the media and tech barons. Fragmenting ownership of the media and the ability to promote one's own political agenda is on the block with all the other things we need to do. The immediate introduction of a law that heavily penalises media owners for publishing lies and misinformation should be part of the first step.

Talk to your politicians, your representatives and ask them to limit the power of the news media and insist that news is reasonable and has a realistic balance, with no place for hate speech. Industries in the past have been split and the balance restored where there was effectively a monopoly. There has never been a time when four companies were so influential across the globe: Google, Facebook and X can all be reformulated, with their media arms split into smaller independent and competing businesses. History tells us that such action has resulted in healthy businesses growing out of the change, and job creation on a huge level.

Chapter 14 AI future nightmare. If you ban something you encourage more people to investigate it. The idea of taking telephones away from children is very strange. Smartphones have become an essential tool for everyone. Surely it would be better to teach children how to use the telephone better? The same with teaching of AI. We should focus immediately on AI being a main lesson taught in schools after reading, writing and counting. Generations - including those currently in school - need to understand how the systems work, and about the potential to manipulate them and feed them misinformation. That is a much better starting point. The more you teach people about something the better they will cope with it. Progress is inevitable, and there are almost zero examples of successfully banning or suppressing something that is inevitable, from the spinning wheel to the printing press to the motor car to rock and roll to our enthusiastic uptake of all things digital.

Chapter 15 Space and controlling the Galaxy. There is no doubt that over the next few years there is going to be extensive and ever-growing space travel and exploration. This will start a new industrial revolution, our fourth, with accompanying growth. And growth in most cases is good and will generate wealth. But we need to distribute this wealth fairly. We need our exploration of space to be for the benefit of all humankind. The alternative is to bring our tendency to violence and destruction to a literally universal level. How do we stop conflict and violence in space? What is the response going to be when a nation or some individual starts shooting down Musk's Starlink satellites?

Chapter 16 Equal education for all. The current western curriculum needs to be comprehensively ripped up. A new curriculum, fit for the second half of the 21st century needs to be constructed. At its heart needs to be AI, and education techniques that promote creativity, curiosity, research skills, critical thinking and the ability to work with others while thinking for oneself. The first two years of school life, though, should be devoted to ensuring no child goes into their third year unable to read, write or count.

Illiteracy and innumeracy levels even in the developed world are shameful.

Chapter 17 The lack of compassion. We in the 'developed' world have evolved beyond compassion, empathy and even basic good taste. The people whose lives we watch with such glee on reality shows are prime examples of this retrograde development. But where the French historically put their Kardashians to the guillotine, and the Bolsheviks put their equivalents to the gun, today we put them on television and admire them. These people spend inordinate sums of money on items and lifestyles that are not essential to life while at the same time many people are dying from want of food and the simple basics of life. We need to address our aspirations and our priorities, develop our sense of morality, compassion, and improve our ethical standards so that witnessing such vulgar exhibitions of undeserved wealth makes us angry, rather than envious. We must show that a moral capitalism is possible, that it will and can benefit all, not just the few.

Chapter 18 Where could the money come from? The money is there. The first step is to start taxing everyone properly at agreed rates. If the laws were actually applied there would be a large increase in the money available and some of this could be distributed to the poorest. Everyone at the top understands what's happening and the games and schemes to avoid paying tax. So, the list to make a start:

- Get the richest 1% of the adults in the world to start paying the tax they should pay instead of avoiding it. This would, if properly implemented, raise at least two trillion dollars a year.
- Change the law so it is illegal for lawyers and accountants to assist tax avoidance.
- Introduce a fine of 150% for any tax avoidance or evasion identified, with payments to whistleblowers.
- Introduce a much higher VAT on luxury goods, maybe 50% initially but rising to 75% or even higher later.

- Stop companies transferring money between countries to reduce tax and ensure all corporations pay a minimum of 20%. delete all exceptions and wriggle room. This could generate at least $1.12 trillion per year.
- Ensure the world's wealthiest top 1% pay tax on the same basis as the rest of us, no avoidance, no excuses.
- Limit top salaries for anyone to $15 million a year and have an understandable and equitable structure beneath that.
- Consider standardising all taxes: income tax; capital gains tax; inheritance tax; to a single rate so there is no point in big corporations and the rich moving between different structures and different countries.
- Put limits on inheritance and remove the many current ways to avoid inheritance tax. Potential revenue $1.5 trillion a year.

****

The current global income distribution is severely unequal, with the wealthiest 1% holding a disproportionate share of wealth while the bottom 50% struggle to survive on meagre incomes. To address this injustice, a radical redistribution plan is needed, aiming to establish a more equitable society. This plan involves increasing the minimum annual income for the bottom 50% to $5,091, providing modest raises for low- to middle-income earners, and capping the maximum income for the very top earners, CEOs, at $15 million. This approach would not only alleviate poverty but also stimulate economic growth through increased consumer spending.

We should also recognize the importance of fairly compensating skilled professionals like doctors and professors, who play a crucial role in society. The proposal suggests a maximum income for these professionals, ensuring they are rewarded for their contributions to society.

Actions you can take

Make education truly equal for all (Letters to representatives)	**Accept that historically the majority of wealth and income has been created by being a member of the elite and has not been equitable** (Accept if you are in the top 1% that it's reasonable for you to pay more tax)	**Review Inheritance** (Government action)
Limit the power of the mega companies or split their power (Letters to companies, change purchasing habits, letters to representatives)	**Think about the future ownership in space to avoid conflict** (Letters to representatives)	**Control the power of the financial institutions** (Move your money from institutions which will not take a proactive approach, send emails and letters)
Define what's a country or a tribe should be (Start a discussion online)	**Create a political system that benefits citizens as a whole and limits the possibility of corruption and damage by politicians** (Contact representatives, join a political party, vote)	**Increase VAT tax on luxury goods** (Government action)
Established guidelines for future remuneration that is equitable (Send letters to your pension fund, bank, investment advisor)	**Tax the very top earners in a much more effective way** (Government action) TAX %	**Understand that terrorism has been through history - a response to inequality and a cry for a better life** (Commit to donating on a regular basis)
Create a framework where wealth can be redistributed (Representatives)	**Recognize people's social benefit to society not just their monetary benefit** (Post and communicate to representatives)	**Ensure personal freedoms for everyone** (Post on social media, representatives)

Education is a key tool for empowering individuals to escape poverty and improve their future prospects. All need to be able to access high-quality education, as it is essential for personal growth and societal development.

To fund this ambitious redistribution plan, various tax reforms are proposed. These include a substantial tax on luxury goods, 50% initially potentially reaching up to 100% in the future, a progressive inheritance tax system with a cap on inheritance and high tax rates on excessive wealth transfer, and measures to address corporate tax evasion and loopholes. Additionally, a 1% annual wealth tax on the top 1% of earners, coupled with strict enforcement and whistleblower incentives, is suggested to tackle extreme wealth concentration.

The plan also highlights the need for corporations to pay their fair share of taxes and contribute to society, given their consumption of resources and potential environmental impact. It proposes higher corporate tax rates and closing loopholes to ensure corporations contribute to environmental protection, infrastructure development, and social programs.

We must acknowledge the power and influence of the elite in shaping economic and tax policies and emphasise the need to challenge their dominance and prioritise the well-being of the broader population. It also draws attention to the historical accumulation of wealth by the elites through often morally questionable means, underscoring the need for a more equitable and just distribution of resources in the 21st century.

While implementing such significant changes presents challenges, the potential benefits in terms of reducing inequality, improving living standards, and promoting economic stability make these suggestions, I hope you agree, a worthwhile endeavour. My purpose in writing this book has been to start the conversation. We could spend an awful lot of time discussing the relative merits of each figure, percentage or suggestion, but even getting some of the above themes onto the agenda would be a big move forward.

And finally…

We have repeatedly referred to the challenges involved in getting this newly raised money to the people we have identified as needing it. It will be a massive undertaking. It will require international cooperation, not to mention global legislation. I feel a responsibility to at least get the conversation started as to how this might – I emphasise 'might' – be achieved.

At the very least, it might require a new international banking entity whose sole job would be to accept receipts from UN countries who have raised this extra taxation, and to distribute it to the people for whom it is designated.

It is essential that this last point is observed – that money is distributed to those people it is designated for, and not to the governments of the countries in which they reside. We have seen too clearly over the past 80 years how leaders of poor countries enrich themselves, while leaving their citizens impoverished, even starving.

So one possibility could be that each individual in each country where the income uplift is happening would be issued an ID card which is tied to the new banking entity. The card would contain their account details, and would also act as a debit card, for paying for goods and bills, and for withdrawing cash. The card could also double as a legitimate ID for voting purposes in democratic elections. This alone could have a massive effect where political corruption has been the norm.

Given the amounts of money this new banking entity might be distributing - possibly $20T over 10 years – it could also be possible that the ID be issued in the form of a smart device, one that has internet access and phone capabilities. Ending the communications drought that affects the poorest on the planet brings us several steps closer to universal equality of opportunity.

I also believe this bank, if it should become the means of making these new funds available, should be run on broadly Islamic terms. These include: 1. the concept that money has no value, except in its ability to be exchanged for products and services that do have a value to the purchaser; 2. that money should not be made from money; 3. that interest – given or received – is to be avoided; 4. that finance should not cause harm.[6]

These suggestions are offered as simply suggestions. It's an extremely complex undertaking to have countries raise extra tax, through international agreements, and to pass that tax on for the raising up of the most deprived on the planet. I do not even remotely underestimate the difficulties. But it would be remiss of me, at the end of this book, to not at least put some concrete ideas down, if only to start the conversation to which others might add more practical ideas.

End. Thank you for reading.

Footnotes – Chapter 19

---

[1] https://www.clubofrome.org

[2] https://en.wikipedia.org/wiki/Silent_Sentinels

[3] https://www.google.com/search?client=safari&rls=en&q=epic+charity+foundation&ie=UTF-8&oe=UTF8

[4]https://eps.leeds.ac.uk/faculty-engineering-physical-sciences/events/event/5220/chi-onwurah-mp-why-are-there-so-few-engineers-in-parliament-and-public-life-and-does-it-really-matter

[5] https://www.britannica.com/event/Revolutions-of-1848

[6] https://www.bankofengland.co.uk/explainers/what-is-islamic-finance

APPENDIX 1

Note 1: Turning points (page ii) – more examples from history

• The Agricultural Revolution (c. 10,000 BC): The shift from nomadic hunter-gatherer societies to settled agricultural communities marked a fundamental change in human civilization. It led to the development of cities, complex social structures, and the rise of civilizations.

• The Invention of Writing (c. 3200 BC): The development of writing systems revolutionised communication, knowledge preservation, and cultural transmission. It enabled the recording of history, the codification of laws, and the emergence of literature and philosophy.

• The Axial Age (c. 800-200 BC): This period saw the emergence of major philosophical and religious traditions around the world, including Confucianism, Buddhism, Taoism, Hinduism, Greek philosophy, and monotheistic religions like Judaism and Zoroastrianism. These belief systems profoundly shaped human thought, ethics, and social organisation.

• The Printing Press (c. 1440 AD): Gutenberg's invention of the printing press democratised knowledge and information, leading to the Renaissance, the Reformation, and the Scientific Revolution. It challenged established authorities and empowered individuals to think for themselves.

• The Industrial Revolution (c. 1760-1840): The transition from manual labour to machine-based manufacturing transformed economies, social structures, and the way people lived and worked. It led to urbanisation, increased productivity, and the rise of new social classes.

• The Discovery of Electricity (19th century): The harnessing of electricity revolutionised industry, transportation, communication, and daily life. It powered the second Industrial Revolution, leading to advancements like the telegraph, telephone, and electric lighting.

• World War II (1939-1945): The war had a devastating impact on global populations and economies but also led to significant geopolitical shifts, the emergence of superpowers, and the formation of international organisations like the United Nations, The World Bank, NATO and the International Monetary Fund. It also accelerated technological advances like developing nuclear weapons and computers.

• The Digital Revolution (late 20th century-present): The advent of computers, the internet, and digital technologies has transformed communication, information access, and the way we interact with the world. It has led to the rise of the information age, the globalisation of economies, and the emergence of new social and cultural phenomena.

• The Rise of Artificial Intelligence (21st century): AI is poised to be another major turning point, with the potential to reshape industries, redefine work, and even challenge our understanding of intelligence and consciousness.

• SpaceX's Starlink project is far more ambitious than launching 4,000 satellites. Here's an updated overview of their plans and goals: The initial plan of 4,000 satellites has been dwarfed by the current goal of deploying up to 42,000 satellites in low Earth orbit. This massive network aims to provide truly global coverage, including remote and previously underserved areas. Starlink satellites: Facts, tracking and impact on astronomy | Space; www.space.com: (PDF) The SpaceX Starlink Satellite Project: Business Strategies and Perspectives: www.researchgate.net

Note 2: Quick change (page iii) – progress over the next 10 years
The world is accelerating, and the next decade promises to be a whirlwind of change! Here are some potential inventions and trends we might see in the next 10 years, drawing inspiration from current developments and emerging technologies:

1. Artificial Intelligence (AI) and Automation:
• Widespread AI Integration: AI will be deeply embedded in nearly every aspect of our lives, from personalized education and healthcare to smart homes and self-driving vehicles.
• AI-Augmented Work: Many jobs will be transformed by AI, with humans and AI collaborating to increase productivity and efficiency. New roles will emerge that require human-AI collaboration skills.
• AI-Driven Scientific Discovery: AI will accelerate scientific breakthroughs in fields like medicine, materials science, and climate modeling, leading to new solutions for global challenges.
• Ethical and Societal Considerations: As AI becomes more powerful, addressing ethical concerns, bias, and the potential impact on employment will be crucial.

2. Biotechnology and Human Enhancement:
• Gene Editing and Gene Therapies: CRISPR and other gene editing technologies will become more precise and widely used, potentially curing genetic diseases and even enhancing human capabilities.
• Regenerative Medicine: Advances in stem cell research and tissue engineering could lead to the regeneration of organs and tissues, revolutionizing healthcare.
• Personalized Medicine: Treatments will be increasingly tailored to individual genetic and lifestyle factors, maximizing effectiveness and minimizing side effects.
• Brain-Computer Interfaces: More sophisticated brain-computer interfaces could enable new forms of communication, treatment for neurological disorders, and even enhance cognitive abilities.

3. Energy and Climate Change:
• Renewable Energy Dominance: Renewable energy sources like solar, wind, and geothermal will become the primary source of energy, reducing our reliance on fossil fuels and mitigating climate change.

• Next-Generation Batteries: Advances in battery technology will enable the widespread adoption of electric vehicles, grid-scale energy storage, and portable power solutions.
• Fusion Energy Breakthrough: Fusion power, a clean and virtually limitless energy source, could become a reality, revolutionizing the energy sector.
• Climate Engineering: Large-scale carbon removal and solar geoengineering technologies might be deployed to mitigate the effects of climate change.

4. Space Exploration and Commercialization:
• Space Tourism and Private Spaceflight: Space tourism will become more common, with private companies offering suborbital and orbital flights, and potentially even lunar and Martian excursions.
• Lunar and Martian Outposts: Permanent human settlements on the Moon and Mars could be established, paving the way for scientific research, resource utilization, and further space exploration.
• Asteroid Mining: Mining asteroids for valuable resources like platinum and water could become a reality, potentially impacting the global economy.
• Space-Based Infrastructure: Space-based solar power, communication networks, and manufacturing facilities could become more prevalent.

5. Transportation and Mobility:
• Autonomous Vehicles and Smart Cities: Self-driving vehicles will become widespread, integrated into smart city infrastructure for efficient and safe transportation.
• Urban Air Mobility: Flying cars, delivery drones, and other aerial vehicles will transform urban transportation and logistics.
• Hyperloop and High-Speed Rail: High-speed transportation systems like Hyperloop and advanced high-speed rail will connect cities and regions, reducing travel times significantly.

6. Virtual and Augmented Reality (VR/AR):
• Immersive Virtual Worlds: The metaverse will evolve into a more realistic and interconnected virtual realm, where people can work, socialize, learn, and experience new realities.
• VR/AR in Everyday Life: VR and AR will be integrated into various aspects of our lives, from education and entertainment to healthcare and manufacturing.
• Augmented Human Capabilities: AR devices could enhance our senses and provide real-time information, blurring the lines between the physical and digital worlds.

7. Other Potential Transformations:

• Advanced Manufacturing and 3D Printing: 3D printing will become more sophisticated, enabling the creation of complex objects, personalized products, and even human organs.
• Nanotechnology and Materials Science: Nanotechnology will lead to the development of new materials with extraordinary properties, revolutionizing various industries.
• Quantum Computing: Quantum computers will become more powerful, enabling breakthroughs in fields like drug discovery, materials science, and artificial intelligence.
• Personalized Nutrition and Food Technology: Advances in food science and technology will lead to personalized nutrition plans and the development of sustainable and alternative food sources.

These are just some of the potential changes that could reshape our world in the next few years. The pace of innovation is accelerating, and it's both exciting and challenging to imagine how these developments will impact our lives, societies, and the planet.

Note 3: Robert Owen & New Lanark (page 2) - other early experimental communities that share some similarities

1. Lowell, Massachusetts: Established in the early 19th century, Lowell was a planned textile manufacturing centre that attracted young women from rural areas to work in its mills. The Lowell Offering, a literary magazine written by the female workers, became a symbol of their intellectual and social aspirations. Lowell featured boarding houses for the workers, churches, schools, and other amenities, creating a self-contained community.
2. Pullman, Illinois: Founded by George Pullman in 1880, Pullman was a company town built around the Pullman Palace Car Company, a manufacturer of railroad sleeping cars. The town was designed to provide a comfortable and controlled environment for the workers, with housing, shops, a library, a theatre, and other amenities. However, it was also characterised by strict rules and paternalistic management, leading to labour unrest and the Pullman Strike of 1894.
3. Hershey, Pennsylvania: Established by Milton S. Hershey in the early 20th century, Hershey was built around his chocolate factory. It featured well-designed housing for the workers, schools, a park, a zoo, a sports arena, and other recreational facilities. Hershey aimed to create a model community that would attract and retain loyal employees.
4. Kohler, Wisconsin: Founded by the Kohler family in the early 20th century, Kohler is a company town centred around the Kohler Company, a manufacturer of plumbing fixtures. It features well-designed housing, a planned village centre, parks, a golf course, and other amenities. The Kohler

family emphasised social welfare and cultural activities for the residents. Morgan Park, Minnesota: Established by the U.S. Steel Corporation in the early 20th century, Morgan Park was built to house the workers of its Duluth Works. It featured a grid layout, standardised housing, a school, a church, and other amenities. The company aimed to create a stable and productive workforce. Saltaire, England: Founded by Sir Titus Salt in 1853, Saltaire is a model village built around a textile mill. It features well-designed workers' housing, public buildings, and recreational facilities. It is now a UNESCO World Heritage Site.

5. Crespi d'Adda, Italy: Established in the late 19th century by the Crespi family, this industrial village was built around a textile factory. It provided housing, schools, a hospital, and other amenities for the workers and their families. It is also a UNESCO World Heritage Site.
6. Familistère de Guise, France: Founded by Jean-Baptiste André Godin in the mid-19th century, this community was built around a stove factory. It offered cooperative housing, a school, a theatre, and other social facilities for the workers.

   Bournville, England: Developed by the Cadbury family in the late 19th century, this village was built around their chocolate factory. It emphasised quality housing, open spaces, and social amenities for the workers.
7. Leverhulme, England: Created by William Lever (later Lord Leverhulme) in the early 20th century, this village was designed for the employees of his soap factory. It featured well-designed housing, parks, and recreational facilities.

Note 4: Space companies (page 3) 10,000+ worldwide

There are currently over 10,000 companies in the global space industry. The majority are concentrated in the United States, Europe, and Asia (particularly China and India).

Types of Space Companies:

• Launch Providers - Companies like SpaceX, Rocket Lab, and Blue Origin focus on developing and launching rockets and spacecraft.

• Satellite Manufacturers - Companies like Boeing, Lockheed Martin, and Airbus build satellites for various purposes (communications, navigation, Earth observation, etc.).

• Space Tourism Companies - Virgin Galactic, Blue Origin, and SpaceX are leading the charge in developing space tourism capabilities.

• Space Infrastructure Companies - These companies focus on building and operating space infrastructure like ground stations, data centres, and orbital platforms.

• Space Exploration Companies - Some companies are dedicated to exploring and utilising resources in space, such as asteroid mining.

• The major new space companies emerging globally, with a focus on India, China, and other key players:

India

• Skyroot Aerospace: The first private Indian company to successfully test a cryogenic rocket engine, they're developing cost-effective launch vehicles.
• Agnikula Cosmos: Focused on building small satellite launch vehicles, they aim to make space more accessible for smaller payloads and research projects.
• Pixxel: Working on a constellation of hyperspectral imaging satellites for Earth observation, targeting agricultural, environmental, and urban monitoring applications.

China

• iSpace: This private company achieved China's first successful orbital launch with a solid-fuelled rocket, focusing on small satellite launches.
• Landscape: Another private Chinese company, they made headlines with the first attempt to launch a methane-fuelled rocket (although unsuccessful).
• Galactic Energy: A newer player in the Chinese space industry aims to develop reusable launch vehicles and compete with SpaceX.

USA

• Rocket Lab: Well-known for their Electron rocket and dedicated launch site in New Zealand, they focus on small satellite launches and responsive space access.
• Astra: Developing small, mobile launch vehicles aimed at providing frequent and flexible launch capabilities. Relativity Space: Pioneering 3D-printed rockets, they seek to revolutionise manufacturing and reduce the cost of space access.

Germany

• Isar Aerospace (Germany): Developing small launch vehicles for microsatellites, aiming to serve the growing European space market.

Other Notable Companies

• There are numerous other emerging space companies worldwide, including Firefly Aerospace (USA), Virgin Orbit (USA); ABL Space Systems (USA); Gilmour Space Technologies (Australia)
• Space Companies Directory - You can find a comprehensive list of space companies from around the world at: https://spacecrew.com/space-companies
• Statista - Statista provides statistics and facts about the global space industry: https://www.statista.com/topics/5049/space-exploration/

1. China Aerospace Science and Technology Corporation (CASC): http://english.spacechina.com/n16421/index.html

2. China Aerospace Science and Industry Corporation (CASIC): [invalid URL removed]
3. Landspace: https://www.landspace.com/
4. iSpace: https://www.ispace-inc.com/
5. Galactic Energy: https://www.galactic-energy.cn/
6. Indian Space Research Organisation (ISRO): https://www.isro.gov.in/
7. Skyroot Aerospace: https://skyroot.in/
8. Agnikul Cosmos: https://www.agnikul.in/
9. Bellatrix Aerospace: [invalid URL removed]
10. Pixxel: https://pixxel.space/
11. Japan Aerospace Exploration Agency (JAXA): https://global.jaxa.jp/
12. Mitsubishi Heavy Industries (MHI): https://www.mhi.com/
13. ispace: https://ispace-inc.com/
14. Interstellar Technologies: https://istellartech.com/

Note 5: Starlink (page 4) 42,000 satellites target

Breakdown of SpaceX's Starlink satellite launches and their plans, with supporting links to articles and press statements.

• Current Status: Over 4,000 operational Starlink satellites - SpaceX has launched over 7,000 Starlink satellites in total, but not all are currently operational. Jonathan McDowell, an astronomer and expert tracker of space objects, reported over 4,000 active satellites in June 2024. https://spaceflightnow.com/2024/06/07/live-coverage-spacex-to-launch-22-starlink-satellites-on-falcon-9-flight-from-cape-canaveral/

• Approved Constellation Size: Up to 42,000 satellites - While SpaceX initially aimed for 12,000 satellites, they have received approval from the Federal Communications Commission (FCC) to deploy up to 42,000.

https://www.space.com/spacex-starlink-satellites.html

• SpaceX has been launching Starlink satellites at a rapid pace, with multiple launches per month. You can find their launch schedule and updates on their website https://www. spacex.com/launches

• SpaceX launches 22 Starlink satellites on Falcon 9 flight from Cape Canaveral. This article from Spaceflight Now details a recent Starlink launch in June 2024. https://spaceflightnow.com/2024/06/07/live-coverage-spacex-to-launch-22-starlink-satellites-on-falcon-9-flight-from-cape-canaveral/

• Starlink satellites: Facts, tracking and impact on astronomy - this article from Space.com provides an overview of the Starlink project, its goals, and potential impact on astronomy. https://www.space.com/spacex-starlink-satellites.html

• What Elon Musk is Trying to Achieve: Global Broadband Access: The primary goal of Starlink is to provide high-speed, low-latency internet access to underserved and remote areas around the world. This includes rural communities, developing countries, and locations where traditional broadband infrastructure is lacking or expensive.

• Bridging the Digital Divide: SpaceX aims to bridge the digital divide by making affordable internet access available to everyone, regardless of their location. This could have a transformative impact on education, healthcare, economic development, and overall quality of life.

• Funding Future Space Exploration: Starlink is expected to generate substantial revenue for SpaceX, which Musk plans to invest in his ambitious goal of establishing a human colony on Mars.

• Revolutionising Telecommunications: SpaceX aims to disrupt the traditional telecommunications industry by offering a more affordable and accessible alternative to existing satellite internet providers.

• Enabling New Technologies: The high-speed, low-latency connectivity provided by Starlink could enable a wide range of new technologies and applications, such as remote surgery, autonomous vehicles, and improved disaster response.

Note 6: Food waste (page 5) – more data

Daily Food Waste: According to a recent UN Environment Programme (UNEP) report, households across the globe wasted over 1 billion meals per day in 2022.

• This amounts to approximately 1.3 billion tons of food wasted annually, worth around US$1 trillion. This waste occurs at various stages of the food supply chain, from production and processing to retail and consumption.

Feeding the Hungry: The wasted food could potentially feed 2 billion people, which is more than twice the number of undernourished people worldwide.

• Reasons for Food Waste: Overproduction and overconsumption in developed countries. Inefficient supply chains and inadequate storage facilities in developing countries. Consumer behaviour, including buying more than needed, not properly storing food, and discarding edible food due to aesthetic imperfections.

Impact of Food Waste:

• Environmental: Food waste contributes significantly to greenhouse gas emissions, deforestation, water pollution, and biodiversity loss. Economic: Food waste represents a massive economic loss, wasting resources and contributing to higher food prices.

• Social: While millions go hungry, vast amounts of food are wasted, highlighting a major ethical and social injustice.

• Solutions to Reduce Food Waste: Raising awareness among consumers and businesses about the scale of food waste and its impact. Improving infrastructure for storage and transportation of food, particularly in developing countries. Implementing policies to incentivize food donation and reduce waste at all stages of the supply chain. Changing consumer behaviour through education and campaigns to encourage responsible food consumption and reduce waste at home.

• UNEP Food Waste Index Report 2021: This is the main source for the statistic of 1 billion meals wasted daily in 2022. https://www.unep.org/resources /report/unep-food-waste-index-report-2021
• The State of Food Security and Nutrition in the World 2022 (SOFI): This report provides in-depth analysis of global hunger and food insecurity, including the impact of food waste. https://www.fao.org/publications/sofi/en/
• World Food Programme (WFP) - Food Waste: WFP's website provides information on their efforts to reduce food loss and waste and how it relates to their mission of ending hunger.
• Food and Agriculture Organization (FAO) - Food Loss and Food Waste:
• FAO's website offers resources, data, and initiatives related to reducing food loss and waste at different stages of the supply chain. http://www.fao.org/food-loss-and-food-waste/en/
• A US-based non-profit organisation focused on reducing food waste, providing data, insights, and solutions. https://refed.org/
• WRAP (UK): A UK-based charity working to reduce food waste, offering resources and guidance for businesses and individuals. https://www.wrap.org.uk/
• Additional Resources: The Eco Experts: https://www.theecoexperts.co.uk /home-hub/food-waste-facts-and-statistics The World Counts: https://www.theworldcounts.com/challenges/people-and-poverty/hunger-and-obesity/food-waste-statistics

Note 7: Without London (page 5) UK is poorest member of G20
John Burn-Murdoch's analysis for the Financial Times reveals a striking disparity in income levels within the UK, particularly when comparing London to the rest of the country. London boasts a high average income due to its status as a global financial hub. But the picture changes dramatically when London is excluded from the calculations. The average income for the rest of the UK, excluding London, is significantly lower, placing it at the bottom among G20 countries. This means that the average person living outside of London earns less than the average person in any other G20 nation, a group that includes major economies like the US, Germany, Japan, and China.

This stark contrast highlights several critical issues.

• Economic Inequality: The vast income gap between London and the rest of the UK underscores the deep-seated economic inequality in the country. It reveals a concentration of wealth and opportunity in the capital, leaving other regions behind.
• Regional Disparities: The low average income outside London indicates significant regional disparities in economic development and prosperity. This can lead to social unrest, political discontent, and hinder overall national progress.
• Policy Implications: This data challenges the effectiveness of current economic policies and calls for a reassessment of strategies to address regional imbalances and

promote inclusive growth. The focus should shift towards investing in infrastructure, education, and job creation in regions outside London.
• Social Mobility: The income disparity may also limit social mobility, as individuals living outside London may face greater barriers to accessing opportunities for education, employment, and overall well-being.

Note 8: The author (page 10) - more details
Gregory Thain is a Monaco-Based Business Leader, Author, & Entrepreneur. With 45+ years of business experience, including the last 15 years in Monaco, Thain has a proven track record across multiple industries such as renewable energy, property, corporate finance, fintech, and emerging markets. His expertise includes mergers and acquisitions, significant fundraising, and strategic business development. He has worked and lived the majority of his life overseas, gaining extensive global business experience. He has also created and analysed data around the world at the cutting edge.

Recent Professional Summary
Founder & Director | 85° Renewable Energy
Developing geothermal assets in Europe, with a focus on the Netherlands.
Established a pipeline of geothermal wells and licenses in multiple locations.
Aims to become a leading renewable energy supplier in Europe.
Website: 85 Renewable Energy
Founder | FNZ 1297 Property Fund

Fundraising & Business Leadership
Established a Luxembourg-regulated fund focused on property investments.
Raised over $2.5 billion in capital across the last 20 years.
Directed and scaled businesses in property, energy, fintech, advertising, and market research.

Career Highlights

- Chairman/CEO Roles in 4 Public Companies
- International Marketing & Sales Group (IMSG)
- Chairman during its $100 million IPO in 2005.
- Scaled the business to $250 million in sales, with operations across 12 countries and over 6,000 employees.
- ICD International Communication & Data
- Publishing Holdings PLC
- Investors Newsletter PLC
- Knight Frank (Russia)

- Founded and served as Chairman for 8 years, leading the property consultancy's operations in Russia until 2008.
- Russian Market Research Leadership
- Founded one of Russia's first market research firms post-Soviet Union collapse (1992).
- Led large-scale studies, including a pivotal survey (inside Russia) interviewing 50,000 individuals across 11 time zones.
- International Bank Loan for Russian Property Development (1995)
- Facilitated a $500 million international bank loan, one of the first major deals post-Soviet era.

Publishing & Data Innovation

- Former CEO of Publishing Holdings managing 15 financial publications.
- Developed the British Investors Database and conducted the UK's first large-scale lifestyle survey with 7 million participants, analyzed in the USA on the Cray supercomputer, which at the time is the largest and most powerful computer in the world.

Political Leadership

- Approved political candidate for the UK Conservative Party for the European Parliament.
- Consultant to the UK Conservative Party.

Books Authored

- The History of FMCG
- Storewars
- E-Retail

All three books have been well-received as significant contributions to their respective fields, focusing on business innovation and retail strategies.

Specializations

- Fundraising & Mergers: Secured over $2.5 billion for various ventures.
- Public Company Leadership: Held top leadership roles in four public companies.
- Emerging Markets: Extensive work across Asia, the Middle East, Russia, and the CIS.

- Big Data & Market Research: Pioneered large-scale data projects in the UK and Russia.
- Renewable Energy: Leadership in geothermal and solar energy projects.
- Political Strategy: Experience as a political candidate and consultant.
- Global Expertise: Significant international business experience, having lived and worked across multiple countries.
- Regular Speaking Engagements
- Frequent speaker at global events on:
- Future of Business
- Investment in Emerging Markets
- Developments in Fintech
- Macro-Level Business Trends

Note 9: Tax on education (page 13)

G20 Countries with Tax on Private Education

• Argentina: Private schools are subject to VAT and other taxes.

• Australia: Private schools are subject to income tax and GST (Goods and Services Tax) on fees.

• Brazil: Private schools are subject to various taxes, including income tax, ISS (tax on services), and PIS/COFINS (social contribution taxes).

• Canada: Private schools are generally subject to income tax, although some provinces offer tuition tax credits.

• China: Private schools are subject to business tax and other taxes.

• France: Private schools are subject to VAT and other taxes, although some receive government subsidies.

• Germany: Private schools are subject to trade tax and other taxes, although some receive state subsidies.

• India: Private schools are subject to GST and other taxes.

• Indonesia: Private schools are subject to VAT and other taxes.

• Italy: Private schools are subject to VAT and other taxes, although some receive state subsidies.

• Japan: Private schools are subject to corporate tax and consumption tax.

• Mexico: Private schools are subject to VAT and other taxes.

• Russia: Private schools are subject to VAT and other taxes.

• South Africa: Private schools are subject to VAT and other taxes.

• South Korea: Private schools are subject to corporate tax and VAT.

• Turkey: Private schools are subject to corporate tax and VAT.

• United Kingdom: Private schools have historically been exempt from VAT but subject to business rates and other taxes. The Labour Party has added VAT to

private school fees at the rate of 20% from January 2025.
• United States: Private schools are generally tax-exempt non-profit organisations, but they may be subject to property taxes and unrelated business income taxes.

G20 Countries with Limited or No Tax on Private Education
• Saudi Arabia: Private schools are generally not subject to taxes.

Note 10: Regional groupings (page 17) – trade blocs like the EU
• Asia-Pacific: Regional Comprehensive Economic Partnership (RCEP) is the world's largest trade bloc, encompassing 15 Asia-Pacific countries, including China, Japan, South Korea, Australia, and New Zealand. RCEP aims to eliminate tariffs, harmonise trade rules, and facilitate investment among member states.
• Comprehensive and Progressive Agreement for Trans-Pacific Partnership (CPTPP): This trade agreement among 11 Pacific Rim countries focuses on reducing trade barriers, promoting investment, and fostering economic cooperation.
• Africa: African Continental Free Trade Area (AfCFTA): This project aims to create a single market for goods and services across the entire African continent, with the potential to boost intra-African trade and economic growth.
• Americas: The United States-Mexico-Canada Agreement (USMCA) replaced NAFTA and governs trade relations among the three North American countries.
• Mercosur: This South American trade bloc comprises Argentina, Brazil, Paraguay, and Uruguay, with associate members including Bolivia, Chile, Colombia, Ecuador, Guyana, Peru, and Suriname.
• Eurasian Economic Union (EAEU) includes Armenia, Belarus, Kazakhstan, Kyrgyzstan, and Russia, aiming to create a common market and customs union.
• Gulf Cooperation Council (GCC) is a political and economic alliance of Arab states in the Persian Gulf, including Bahrain, Kuwait, Oman, Qatar, Saudi Arabia, and the United Arab Emirates.

Note 11: UK politicians (page 17) – Educational background
Research from Sutton Trust on the educational backgrounds of UK MPs has consistently shown that independent schools, particularly a select few like Eton and Harrow, are over-represented in Parliament compared to the general population.

List of UK Prime Ministers by education: The fact that 20 Prime Ministers went to Eton and seven to Harrow underscores these schools' influence on British politics.

Research on the UK House of Lords also reveals a high proportion of members educated at Eton. The Educational Backgrounds of Members of the House of Commons and House of Lords:

https://dera.ioe.ac.uk/30377/1/Politicians Backgrounds_09-Dec-05-1.pdf

One in seven of those who hold UK's most powerful positions went to top ten independent schools:

https://www.dailymail.co.uk/news/article-8961165/One-seven-hold-societys-powerful-positions-went-ten-independent-schools.html

Note 12: Monopolies of Markets (page 18) - examples

- Google (Alphabet Inc.): Dominates the search engine market with over 90% of global searches.
- Microsoft: Holds a near-monopoly on PC operating systems with Windows and office productivity software with Microsoft Office.
- Amazon: Controls a significant portion of the e-commerce market and has a dominant position in cloud computing with Amazon Web Services (AWS).
- Facebook (Meta Platforms): The largest social networking platform globally, owning Instagram and WhatsApp.
- Apple: Has a dominant position in the premium smartphone market with the iPhone and a loyal customer base for other products.
- AB InBev: The largest beer producer globally, owning popular brands like Budweiser, Corona, and Stella Artois.
- Luxottica: The world's largest eyewear company, owning brands like Ray-Ban, Oakley, and Sunglass Hut.
- Nvidia: Dominates the market for graphics processing units (GPUs), essential for gaming, AI, and high-performance computing.
- De Beers: Controls a significant portion of the diamond market.
- YKK Group: The world's largest zipper manufacturer.
- Tesla: Has a dominant position in the electric vehicle market.

Global Stats

- Search Engine Market Share: tracking the global market share of search engines consistently shows Google with over 90% dominance. _https://gs.statcounter.com/search-engine-market-share
- Operating System Market Share: This website tracks the global market share of desktop operating systems, and Windows consistently holds the majority share. https://gs.statcounter.com/os-market-share/desktop/worldwide
- Cloud Office Platforms: Gartner's report recognizes Microsoft 365 as a leader in the cloud office productivity market.
- Online Retail: Amazon is listed as the leading online retailer globally by gross merchandise value (GMV). https://www.statista.com /statistics/263264/top-companies-in-the-world-by-market-capitalization/
- Cloud Infrastructure Services Market Share: Amazon Web Services (AWS) is consistently reported as the leading cloud provider by market share (Synergy Research Group).

• Social networks worldwide: Facebook is listed as the most popular social network globally, with over 2.9 billion monthly active users. https://www.statista.com /statistics/272014/global-social-networks-ranked-by-number-of-users/
Pen spark

Note 13: Civil and Political Rights (page 36)

• Right to life, liberty, and security of person: Protects against arbitrary deprivation of life, torture, and cruel, inhuman, or degrading treatment.
• Freedom from slavery and servitude: Prohibits slavery and forced labour in all forms.
• Equality before the law: Guarantees equal protection under the law without discrimination.
• Right to a fair trial: Ensures access to a fair and public hearing by an independent and impartial tribunal.
• Freedom of thought, conscience, and religion: Protects the right to hold beliefs and practice religion or belief.
• Freedom of opinion and expression: Includes freedom to hold opinions without interference and to seek, receive, and impart information and ideas.
• Freedom of peaceful assembly and association: Allows individuals to peacefully assemble and form associations.
• Economic, Social, and Cultural Rights
• Right to work and to free choice of employment: Ensures fair wages and equal pay for equal work.
• Right to social security: Protects against unemployment, disability, and old age.
• Right to an adequate standard of living: Includes adequate food, clothing, housing, and medical care.
• Right to education: Guarantees free and compulsory primary education and accessible higher education.
• Right to participate in cultural life: Includes access to cultural heritage and scientific advancement. The Universal Declaration of Human Rights (UDHR) is not a legally binding treaty, but it has inspired numerous international human rights treaties and national constitutions. Some of the most important human rights treaties include -
• International Covenant on Civil and Political Rights (ICCPR): Elaborates on the civil and political rights in the UDHR.
• The statement that universal human rights serve as a potential foundation for a global moral code is largely accurate, although it does present some complexities.
• There are strong arguments for Universal Human Rights as a Foundation for a Global Moral Code -
• Shared Values: Universal human rights are based on shared values that transcend cultural and religious differences. Concepts like the inherent dignity of every

human being, equality, and freedom from discrimination resonate across diverse societies.

• International Consensus: The UDHR was adopted by the United Nations in 1948, providing a comprehensive framework of rights that have been widely accepted by nations around the world. This consensus signifies a shared commitment to certain moral principles.

• Basis for Laws and Policies: Human rights serve as a basis for international laws, treaties, and national constitutions, shaping legal and political frameworks worldwide. This reinforces their role in establishing a common standard of behaviour.

• Moral Compass: Human rights can serve as a moral compass, guiding individuals, organisations, and governments in their actions and decisions, especially in situations of conflict or ethical dilemmas.

• Cultural Relativism: Critics argue that human rights are a Western concept that may not be applicable or relevant to all cultures. They advocate cultural relativism, arguing that moral values are relative to specific cultural contexts. Implementation and Enforcement: While human rights are enshrined in international law, their implementation and enforcement remain a challenge, particularly in countries with weak governance or conflicting values.

• Competing Rights: There can be tensions and conflicts between different human rights, such as the right to freedom of expression and the right to be protected from hate speech.

• Balancing these competing rights requires careful consideration and interpretation.

Note 14: Russian Population (page 60) - before, during, after Revolution

Russian Empire (1890-1917) -

• 1897: 125.6 million (according to the only census conducted in the Russian Empire)

• 1914: (pre-WWI): Estimated around 175 million (based on population growth trends)

• Russian Soviet Federative Socialist Republic (RSFSR) and Soviet Union (1917-1950) -

• 1926: 92.7 million (RSFSR) / 147 million (Soviet Union)

• 1939: 108.4 million (RSFSR) / 170.6 million (Soviet Union)

• 1950: 101.4 million (RSFSR) / 182.3 million (Soviet Union)

The borders of the Russian Empire and the Soviet Union changed significantly during this period. So, the figures should only be used as a guide to the loss/reduction which was obviously significant. The Russian Empire lost territories during World War I and the subsequent revolutions, while the Soviet Union expanded its borders after World War II. These territorial changes significantly affected population numbers. The First World War and the Russian Civil War

(1914-1922) resulted in significant population losses due to combat, disease, and famine. The forced collectivization of agriculture in the early 1930s led to a devastating famine, resulting in millions of deaths. The Second World War caused immense devastation and loss of life in the Soviet Union, with an estimated 27 million deaths.

Wikipedia - Russian Empire: https://en.wikipedia.org/wiki/Russian_Empire
Wikipedia - Soviet Union: https://en.wikipedia.org/wiki/Soviet_Union

Note 15: Tax avoidance (page 62) - prosecutions
Examples of lawyers, accountants, corporations and individuals prosecuted for evading or helping people evade taxes.

• Robert Vesco: In the 1970s, this American businessman was accused of using a complex web of offshore companies and false documents to hide millions in income. His lawyer, Stanley Pottinger, was convicted of conspiracy and aiding tax evasion for his role in setting up the scheme. Source: The New York Times.
• Arthur Andersen: Once-powerful accounting firm convicted in 2002 for its role in the Enron scandal. Enron, an energy company, engaged in massive accounting fraud to inflate its stock price. Arthur Andersen knowingly approved false financial statements, and the firm's collapse became a major symbol of corporate corruption. While not solely about tax evasion, the scandal involved manipulating finances to hide true profits and tax liabilities. Source: BBC News.
• Marc Dreier: New York lawyer sentenced to 20 years in prison in 2008 for a scheme involving creating fake legal documents and impersonating other attorneys. He used these tactics to help clients hide assets and evade taxes. Source: The New York Times.
• Mehmet Gönen (2013): Turkish tax consultant sentenced to 10 years in prison for masterminding a tax evasion scheme involving fake invoices and shell companies used by celebrities and businesspeople. *Source: [Local Turkish news]*
• National Football League (NFL) Players (Ongoing): The US Department of Justice has ongoing investigations into the tax practices of some NFL players. Some players have been accused of using complex schemes involving signing bonuses and marketing income to reduce their tax liabilities. *Source: https://www.nytimes.com/2017/09 /19/sports/football/nfl-concussion-settlement.html*
• Allen Stanford (2012): Texan financier convicted of a $7 billion Ponzi scheme that using offshore accounts and misleading tax reporting for investors. *Source: https://judiciary.house.gov/media/press-releases/chairman-jordan-presses-stanford-subpoena-compliance-censorship-investigation*
• Kruse International (2005): Danish tax shelter company shut down and its founders imprisoned for creating a fraudulent tax avoidance scheme that involved artificial losses and inflated depreciation deductions for clients. *Source: [Scandinavian financial news]*

• Falstaff Brewing Corporation (1980s): American brewing company and its executives faced criminal charges for using a complex web of sham companies and false invoices to inflate expenses and reduce their tax bill. *Source: [US legal document]*

• Leona Helmsley (2000): The 'Queen of Mean' New York real estate mogul was convicted of tax evasion for using her household staff on her business payroll and hiding income from hotel renovations. *Source: https://www.nytimes.com/2007 /08/30/nyre gion/30leona.html*

• Corey Feldman (2018): The former child actor faced tax evasion charges for failing to report income from personal appearances and memorabilia sales. He eventually reached a plea deal with authorities. *Source: https://www.tmz.com/ people/corey-feldman/*

• Jackie Chan (2008): The Hong Kong action star faced tax evasion charges in China for underreporting income from movie endorsements and other activities. He eventually paid a significant penalty to avoid prosecution. *Source: https://www.theg uardian.com/film/jackie-chan*

• The Paradise Papers (2017): This leak of financial documents exposed offshore tax havens used by politicians, celebrities, and corporations. While not all cases resulted in prosecution, investigations were launched into individuals and firms suspected of tax evasion based on the information revealed. *Source: http://www.bbc. com/ne ws/paradisepapers*

Note 16: Richest People (page 64)

The combined wealth of the world's 10 richest people listed is $1.546 trillion although this changes every minute. This amount exceeds the combined wealth of the world's poorest billion.

Several reports and studies, including those by Oxfam and the World Inequality Report, confirm the stark concentration of wealth among a small elite. These reports indicate that the wealth of a few billionaires often exceeds that of entire populations in developing countries.

However, the claim that the poorest one billion people combined have less wealth than the top 10 richest individuals requires further clarification. The wealth of the poorest one billion is hard to estimate accurately as many live in informal economies and lack access to formal financial systems. The World Inequality Report 2022 estimates that the poorest 50% of the global population owns only 2% of global wealth.

Despite the lack of precise data, the available information strongly suggests that the wealth of the richest 10 individuals is significantly higher than that of the poorest 1 billion people combined, highlighting the extreme levels of global wealth inequality. Oxfam's *Survival of the Richest* report: https://www.oxfam.org/en/research/inequality-kills World Inequality Report

2022: https://wir2022.wid. world/The Guardian - Richest 1% on Target to Own Two-thirds of all Wealth by 2030.

Note 17: Excessive bonuses and benefit (page 71)

• Dreyfus and the Million Dollar Birthday: In 2006, Robert Sutton, CEO of investment bank Dreyfus, threw himself a lavish 60th birthday party reportedly costing over $1 million. The extravagant celebration, featuring celebrities and a private performance by Elton John, felt out of touch with the company culture and was seen as excessive [Source: news articles on Robert Sutton Dreyfus party].

• AIG and the Post-Crash Bonuses: After the 2008 financial crisis, insurance giant AIG received a government bailout. Despite the company's near-collapse, AIG awarded millions in bonuses to employees, sparking public outrage and accusations of rewarding failure [Source: news articles on AIG bailout and bonuses].

• The Home Depot and the Retirement Package: In 2017, The Home Depot faced criticism after it was revealed that CEO Craig Menear received a retirement package valued at over $100 million. This hefty sum, while spread out over years, felt excessive to many considering average employee compensation [Source: news articles on Home Depot CEO retirement package].

• Luxe Living at WeWork: WeWork, a co-working space company, was known for its aggressive spending habits. Former CEO Adam Neumann reportedly enjoyed lavish company-funded perks including private jets, a home with a climbing wall, and even a trademark on his own last name [Source: news articles on WeWork Adam Neumann perks].

• Boeing and the 737 Max Grounding: Following the safety issues and crashes involving the 737 Max aircraft, Boeing faced immense financial strain. Despite this, CEO Dennis Muilenburg received a bonus in 2019, which only fuelled public anger over the company's handling of the crisis [Source: news articles on Boeing 737 Max CEO bonus].

• Wells Fargo and the Fake Accounts Scandal: In 2016, Wells Fargo, a major bank, was embroiled in a scandal where employees created millions of fake accounts to meet unrealistic sales quotas. While the bank faced fines and penalties, some executives reportedly received bonuses despite their knowledge of the scheme [Source: news articles on Wells Fargo fake accounts scandal and bonuses].

• Dick's Sporting Goods and the Tone-Deaf Retreat: In 2018, after a mass shooting, Dick's Sporting Goods took a strong stance against assault weapons. However, shortly thereafter, news emerged of a lavish company retreat to Scotland, costing millions. This disconnect between public image and internal spending practices tarnished the company's reputation [Source: news articles on Dick's Sporting Goods retreat after gun control stance].

• Dodge and the Private Jet: In 2008, during the height of the automotive industry crisis, Sergio Marchionne, CEO of Fiat Chrysler (which owns Dodge), reportedly used a company-provided private jet for personal travel, estimated to cost millions over several years. This extravagance came to light when the company was seeking government bailouts [Source: news articles on Chrysler bailout].

• Whole Foods and the Whole Estate: In 2017, John Mackey, co-founder, and CEO of Whole Foods, came under fire for a $31 million retirement home funded by the company. While Mackey eventually agreed to pay for most of it himself, the initial approval of such an expenditure for the CEO of a company promoting healthy living sparked criticism [Source: news articles on Whole Foods CEO mansion].

• Wynn Resorts and the Shady Stock Sale: In 2018, Steve Wynn, then-CEO of Wynn Resorts, faced accusations of sexual misconduct. He resigned and later sold his Wynn Resorts stock for about $677 million. The hefty sum raised questions about whether he should have profited while facing such serious allegations [Source: news articles on Wynn Resorts CEO scandal].

Note 18: A. Philanthropy / B. Efficient charities (page 76)

A. Detail about individuals and philanthropic donations and funding -

• Bill Gates, co-founder of Microsoft, and his ex-wife Melinda French Gates have committed to giving away 95% of their wealth through the Bill & Melinda Gates Foundation. Their focus is on global health, poverty, and education. The foundation is actively disbursing funds and has become one of the largest philanthropic organisations in the world. Warren Buffett, CEO of Berkshire Hathaway, has pledged to donate 99% of his wealth, primarily to the Bill & Melinda Gates Foundation. He has already donated tens of billions of dollars and continues to do so annually.

• Mark Zuckerberg, CEO of Meta (formerly Facebook), and his wife Priscilla Chan have pledged to give away 99% of their Facebook shares through the Chan Zuckerberg Initiative, focusing on personalised learning, scientific research, and criminal justice reform. The initiative is actively funding projects and research.

• Steve Jobs' wife Laurene Powell Jobs inherited his fortune and established the Emerson Collective, a philanthropic organisation focusing on education, immigration reform, and social justice issues. While not publicly pledging to give away a specific percentage, The Collective actively funds projects and initiatives.

• Chuck Feeney, co-founder of Duty-Free Shoppers has given away his entire fortune through his foundation, Atlantic Philanthropies, which closed in 2020 after disbursing all of its funds.

• Paul Allen, co-founder of Microsoft, pledged to give away at least 50% of his wealth. He established the Paul G. Allen Family Foundation, which focuses on brain health, wildlife conservation, and arts education. The foundation continues to support various projects and initiatives.

• Sir Tom Hunter, Scottish entrepreneur, has pledged to give away 70% of his wealth through The Hunter Foundation, which supports entrepreneurship, education, and humanitarian causes. The foundation actively invests in projects and organisations.

• Michael Bloomberg, former Mayor of New York City and founder of Bloomberg L.P., has pledged to give away his entire fortune. He is a major donor to various causes, including public health, climate change, and gun violence prevention.

• Oprah Winfrey, media mogul and philanthropist, has donated over $400 million to various educational and charitable causes. While not publicly pledging a specific percentage of her fortune, her donations represent a significant portion of her wealth.

• George Soros, investor and philanthropist, has pledged to give away at least 50% of his wealth through his Open Society Foundations, which support democracy, human rights, and social justice around the world. The foundations actively fund projects and initiatives.

• MacKenzie Scott, ex-wife of Jeff Bezos, has donated over $12 billion to various causes since 2020, focusing on racial equity, LGBTQ+ rights, and climate change.

• Charles Chen Yidan, co-founder of Tencent, established the Yidan Prize Foundation, which awards significant prizes to individuals and organisations making outstanding contributions to education research and development.

• He Xiangjian: Founder of Midea Group, a leading appliance manufacturer, He has donated billions of yuan to education and healthcare initiatives through his foundation.

• Pony Ma: Co-founder of Tencent, Ma has pledged a significant portion of his wealth to philanthropic causes through the Tencent Charity Foundation, focusing on education, healthcare, and environmental protection.

• Jack Ma: Ma (no relation to Pony Ma) has been involved in various philanthropic activities through his foundation, focusing on education, entrepreneurship, and rural development.

• Azim Premji: Indian businessman and philanthropist, Premji has pledged the majority of his wealth to the Azim Premji Foundation, which strives to improve education in India.

• Li Ka-shing: Hong Kong billionaire, Li has donated billions of dollars to education and healthcare initiatives through his foundation, the Li Ka Shing Foundation.

• Mukesh Ambani: Indian businessman and chairman of Reliance Industries, Ambani has made significant contributions to education, healthcare, and disaster relief efforts in India.

• Tadashi Yanai: Founder and CEO of Fast Retailing (Uniqlo), Yanai has donated to various causes through his company and foundation, including disaster relief and educational programs.

B. Some charities that administer efficiently -

• Against Malaria Foundation (AMF): AMF is a non-profit organisation that works to prevent malaria deaths in Africa. It has a 98% program efficiency rating,

meaning 98% of every dollar donated goes directly to its malaria prevention programs.
• GiveDirectly: GiveDirectly is a non-profit organisation that provides unconditional cash transfers to poor households in developing countries. It has a 95% program efficiency rating.
• Schistosomiasis Control Initiative (SCI): SCI is a non-profit organisation that works to control and eliminate schistosomiasis, a parasitic disease that affects millions of people in developing countries. It has a 94% program efficiency rating.
• Helen Keller International (HKI): HKI is a non-profit organisation that works to prevent and treat blindness and malnutrition in developing countries. It has a 93% program efficiency rating.
• Direct Relief: Direct Relief is a non-profit organisation that provides medical supplies and equipment to disaster-affected areas around the world. It has a 91% program efficiency rating.
• The Carter Centre: The Carter Centre is a non-profit organisation founded by former U.S. President Jimmy Carter. It works to advance peace, democracy, and human rights worldwide. It has an 89% program efficiency rating.
• Doctors Without Borders/Médecins Sans Frontières (MSF): MSF is a non-profit organisation that provides medical aid to people affected by conflict, epidemics, disasters, or exclusion from healthcare. It has an 87% program efficiency rating.
• WaterAid: WaterAid is a non-profit organisation that works to provide clean water, sanitation, and hygiene education to people in developing countries. It has an 86% program efficiency rating.
• World Vision: World Vision is a Christian humanitarian organisation that works to provide children, families, and communities with water, food, shelter, education, healthcare, and economic development. It has an 85% program efficiency rating. CARE: CARE is an international humanitarian organisation that fights poverty and provides humanitarian aid worldwide. It has an 84% program efficiency rating.

Note 19: Territorial grabs (page 91) - taking what you want

• Assyrian Empire: The Neo-Assyrian Empire (911-612 BCE) was notorious for its expansionist policies and ruthless conquests. The Assyrians frequently invaded neighbouring territories to plunder their resources, including gold, silver, and precious metals. They also enslaved large populations, using them as forced labour to support their empire's economic growth.
• Persian Empire: The Achaemenid Empire (550-330 BCE), founded by Cyrus the Great, also engaged in extensive conquests driven by economic motives. The Persians sought to control trade routes and exploit the natural resources of conquered territories. Their empire's vast wealth was evident in its magnificent palaces, monuments, and infrastructure.

• Roman Empire: The Roman Empire (27 BCE-476 CE) expanded its territory through numerous conquests, often motivated by the desire for riches and resources. The Romans plundered conquered lands, extracting gold, silver, grain, and other valuable goods. They also established trade networks that further enriched their empire.
• Mongol Empire: The Mongol Empire (1206-1368 CE) was one of the largest land empires in history, stretching from China to Eastern Europe. The Mongols were renowned for their military prowess and their ability to conquer vast territories. They plundered conquered cities and collected tribute from subjugated populations, amassing immense wealth.
• Ottoman Empire: The Ottoman Empire (1299-1922 CE) was a powerful Islamic empire that dominated the Mediterranean and Middle East for centuries. The Ottomans engaged in numerous conquests, often motivated by economic gain. They controlled trade routes, extracted resources, and collected taxes from their vast empire.
• Spanish Conquest of the Americas: In the 15th and 16th centuries, Spanish conquistadors, driven by a thirst for gold and other riches, invaded and colonised vast territories in the Americas. Their brutal conquest led to the decimation of indigenous populations and the plundering of immense wealth.
• British Colonisation of India: Over a period of centuries, the British East India Company gradually gained control of India, establishing a vast colonial empire. The British exploited India's resources, including spices, textiles, and tea, to fuel their own economic growth.
• Japanese Invasion of China: In 1937, Japan launched a full-scale invasion of China, seeking to establish a "Greater East Asia Co-Prosperity Sphere" under its domination. The Japanese occupation of China was marked by widespread atrocities and the theft of China's natural resources.
• Soviet Invasion of Afghanistan: In 1979, the Soviet Union invaded Afghanistan, attempting to prop up a communist government. The Soviet occupation lasted ten years and resulted in significant casualties and economic hardship for the Afghan people.

Note 20: Origins of morally unjustifiable wealth (page 95)
Some specific examples of families who significantly increased their wealth through morally dubious means.

Africa:
• The Oppenheimer Family (South Africa): This family built a vast fortune through their control of De Beers, a diamond mining company that acquired land and resources in South Africa, often displacing local communities and exploiting labor.

• The Kenyatta Family (Kenya): Jomo Kenyatta, Kenya's first president, and his family amassed significant land holdings during and after the colonial era, raising concerns about land grabbing and inequality.

Asia:
• The Ayala and Zobel de Ayala Families (Philippines): These families, who own Ayala Corporation, one of the largest conglomerates in the Philippines, initially acquired vast tracts of land during the Spanish colonial era, which formed the basis of their wealth.
• The Salim Group (Indonesia): This conglomerate, controlled by the Salim family, amassed wealth through palm oil plantations and other agricultural ventures, often linked to deforestation and displacement of indigenous communities.

Latin America:
• The Somoza Family (Nicaragua): Accumulated vast landholdings through political connections and military force, becoming one of the wealthiest families in Nicaragua before being overthrown in 1979.
• The Latifundista Families (Various Countries): Many traditional landowning families across Latin America, such as the oligarchs in Argentina or the "barons" in Brazil, continue to hold large estates acquired through historical land grants and displacement of indigenous peoples.

Russia:
• The Stroganov Family: This powerful Russian merchant family profited from the fur trade in Siberia, which heavily relied on the exploitation of indigenous people and forced labor. While not directly involved in the transatlantic slave trade, their wealth was built on a system that exploited and oppressed indigenous populations.
• The Sheremetev Family: This noble family was one of the largest serf-owners in Russia. Serfdom, while not identical to chattel slavery, involved the binding of peasants to the land and their owners, with limited rights and freedoms. The Sheremetev family's wealth and influence were derived from the labor of their serfs.

United Kingdom:
• The Gladstone Family: William Gladstone, a former British Prime Minister, had a family heavily involved in the sugar trade and slavery. They received substantial compensation after the abolition of slavery and this wealth continues to benefit their descendants.
• The Hogg Family: Descendants of Charles McGarel, a merchant who amassed a fortune through slave ownership and sugar plantations, still hold wealth and influence in the UK.
• The Drax Family: This family's wealth originated from sugar plantations in Barbados and Jamaica. They continue to own Drax Hall plantation in Barbados, which is now a major tourist attraction
United States:

• The Hearst Family: William Randolph Hearst, a media mogul, acquired vast estates in California, often through controversial means, including exploiting legal loopholes and taking advantage of economic hardships faced by smaller landowners.
• The Rockefeller Family: While their wealth primarily stems from oil, the Rockefellers also acquired significant land holdings throughout the United States, often for development and investment purposes.

Note 21: Grayling (page 109) – Ian Dunt's story

This excerpt from *How Westminster Works . . . and Why It Doesn't* by Ian Dunt goes right to the heart of my point that politicians in government can be completely incompetent, even causing public harm, and still not be censured or fired. In the UK, most likely, they'll be transferred to another department. The whole of Ian Dunt's book is as well researched and gripping as this short excerpt, and he also finds time to suggest remedies to create a better system. I highly recommend you buy his book if you care about the way your country is governed.

"Chris Grayling had to move quickly. It was early 2013. After years climbing the Conservative party ranks, he'd finally secured a senior ministerial post. He was the secretary of state for justice. It was the kind of position from which anything was possible: home secretary, foreign secretary, even prime minister. But to do that, he had to accomplish something eye-catching. It didn't strictly matter what it was. It didn't even matter if it worked or not. The project could fall apart in five years if needs be. By then, it would all be a distant memory, largely forgotten in the grandeur of a new department. What mattered was that it captured the prime minister's attention today. The main imperative was that he acted swiftly. Ministers operate on a tight time frame. Typically, they stay in position for around two years before they're shuffled off, either downwards towards the ministerial dead-end jobs, or upwards to the soaring heights of British public life. If they're lucky, they get three years; if they're unlucky, they get six months. Then the merry-go-round starts again…… So, without any expertise or experience, Grayling made a decision. He would privatise probation. He would burn the existing probation model to the ground and start again from scratch, using market mechanisms. In the years to come, this decision would cause misery and suffering on an extreme scale. People would die who might not otherwise have died. Probation workers would have their professional lives ruined. Hundreds of thousands of offenders would be released from jail without support or meaningful supervision…… 'He delivered,' says Richard Garside, director of the Centre for Crime and Justice Studies. 'He absolutely delivered on what he was going to do. And it was a complete disaster…… When Grayling became justice secretary, probation was working pretty well. The service was run by 35 probation trusts, every single one of which was rated either good or exceptional by the government. They'd managed to get reoffending rates down to 34.2 per cent after a decade of steady decline. The service had just won the British Quality Foundation Gold Award for

Excellence...... Grayling completely reinvented the system. It was called Transforming Rehabilitation. He abolished the trusts and split the service in two. High-risk offenders would be dealt with by a publicly owned National Probation Service. Low-and medium-risk offenders would be dealt with by a network of privately owned community rehabilitation companies (CRCs)...... Sir Richard Heaton, permanent secretary at the department, told MPs on the Public Accounts Committee in 2019. 'Looking back on it, we should have done differently.' But by then it was too late. The British public are supposed to be protected from poor ministerial decision-making by at least four separate institutions: the civil service, the Treasury, the press and Parliament. Before an idea can be implemented, they should step in to assess the evidence, evaluate the project, debate it, scrutinise it, test it and, finally, if needed, stop it. But in the months ahead, as Grayling pushed forward with his plan, each one of these institutions failed. The warnings were issued, but no one listened to them. In early 2013, the Ministry of Justice launched a consultation about the plans. A huge range of expert contributions came in from those who worked in probation, inspected it or studied it. They were universally damning. 'The interface between the dynamic management of risk of harm and the payment-by-results model in our view creates an inherent tension,' HM Inspector of Probation said. 'We do not believe that this tension can be successfully managed within the framework proposed. Any lack of contractual or operational clarity between the public and private sector will, in our view, lead to systemic failure and an increased risk to the public.' 'Our overall response to the proposals in the consultation paper,' the Probation Chiefs Association and the Probation Association said in a joint submission, 'is that they will increase the risk of harm to the public.' Those submissions were ignored...... Grayling published a government response to the consultation that failed to mention any of the criticism and instead said: 'It is not a surprise, faced with stubbornly high reoffending rates, that there were important areas of consensus.'...... In London, the Inspectorate concluded: 'A combination of unmanageable caseloads, inexperienced officers, extremely poor oversight and a lack of senior management focus and control meant some service users were not seen for weeks or months, and some were lost in the system altogether.' Between 2014/ 15 and 2016/ 17, serious further offences–when someone under probation supervision commits an extremely serious crime like murder or rape–increased by over 20 per cent. In March 2015, 18-year-old Conner Marshall was beaten to death by David Braddon in South Wales. Braddon was being supervised by an inexperienced probation officer who assessed him as medium risk. 'The circumstance in which she found herself, a brand-new probation officer, with woefully inadequate management and supervision structure, was not of her own making,' the coroner found. 'She was essentially left to her own devices, burdened as she was with a heavy and difficult caseload in an environment which was chaotic and stretched due to the impending implementation of the Transforming Rehabilitation programme.' Outside the court, Marshall's mother, Nadine, made a statement. 'The coroner's findings have vindicated what we have always known to be true,' she said. 'This was a direct consequence of the chaos caused by the privatisation of probation services.' On 14 October 2016, 27-year-old Michael Hoolickin was stabbed to death by Timothy Deakin outside a pub in Middleton, Greater Manchester. Hoolickin had tried to intervene to stop Deakin hitting a woman. Deakin had been recorded as having a propensity to respond with extreme violence when faced with conflict, particularly after he had used cocaine. But for extended periods of time, including the weeks leading up to the attack, probation officers failed to make sure that he was subject to weekly testing. 'The court heard evidence as to the catastrophic impact the Transforming Rehabilitation programme had had on the staffing levels within the National Probation Service,' the coroner's report said. 'The court was satisfied that this, in part, contributed to the failure to implement drug appointment and drug testing.'...... No one lost their job, or was penalised, or even rebuked. Quite the opposite. The civil service officials behind the programme won the 2015 Civil Service Award for Project and Programme Management. Antonia Romeo, the civil servant in charge of the project, was promoted to permanent secretary at the Ministry of Justice, the most senior position available. Grayling was made leader of the House of the Commons in the next reshuffle, before being appointed transport secretary by then prime minister Theresa May. In that role, he awarded a £13.8 million contract to the firm Seaborne Freight to provide shipping capacity, despite the fact that it owned no ships, had never run a ferry service and copied-and-pasted its contract from a pizza delivery company. It is estimated that during his time at the department, he misspent a total of £2.7 billion of public funds. While still an MP, he then secured a job advising Hutchison Ports, with a salary of £100,000 a year for seven hours' work a week. The most remarkable thing about what happened in probation is how unremarkable it is. There is nothing remotely special about it. The same process takes place in department after department, policy area after policy area: health, education, defence. Nor is there anything particularly remarkable about Grayling. Towards the end of his time on the front bench, he was dubbed 'Failing Grayling', but in fact this nickname was misplaced. The most harrowing thing about him is that he is a completely standard example of the quality of the ministerial class in Britain...... in Britain have failed to operate with anything even approaching basic competence. They do not know what they are doing. They do not even attempt to know what they are doing. And then, when things go wrong, they do not learn from what happened."

And a little more on other countries; former politicians and administrators becoming directors of companies.

United States –

- William Cohen (Former Secretary of Defence): Served on the board of directors for several companies, including Honeywell International, a major technology and manufacturing conglomerate.

• Tom Daschle (Former Senate Majority Leader): Worked as a special policy advisor at law firm Alston & Bird, representing corporate clients with interests in healthcare and energy.
• Elaine Chao (Former Secretary of Transportation and Labor): Served on the board of several companies, including News Corp and Wells Fargo.

Canada –
• James Moore (Former Minister of Industry): Became a senior business advisor at Dentons, a global law firm.
• Rona Ambrose (Former Minister of Health): Joined the board of directors of several companies, including Aphria Inc. (now Tilray), a major cannabis producer.

United Kingdom -
• David Cameron (Former Prime Minister): Became chairman of the advisory board for Afiniti, an artificial intelligence company.
• George Osborne (Former Chancellor of the Exchequer): Took on several roles in the financial sector, including becoming a partner at investment firm Robey Warshaw and an advisor to BlackRock.
• Nick Clegg (Former Deputy Prime Minister): Joined Meta (formerly Facebook) as vice president of global affairs and communications.

European Union -
• Neelie Kroes (Former European Commissioner for Digital Agenda): Joined the board of directors of Salesforce, a leading cloud-based software company.
• José Manuel Barroso (Former President of the European Commission): Joined Goldman Sachs as an advisor and non-executive chairman of its international division.

Japan -
• Heizo Takenaka (Former Minister of Internal Affairs and Communications): Joined the board of Pasona Group, a major staffing and recruitment company.

Note 22: Different different levels of accountability by country (page 110)
• Canada employs a meritocratic system with a strong emphasis on performance management. Regular performance reviews are conducted, and consequences for poor performance can range from additional training to dismissal in extreme cases. In 2018, a senior public servant at the Canadian Food Inspection Agency (CFIA) was fired for neglecting their duties related to food safety inspections at meat processing facilities. This case highlighted the importance of accountability in protecting public health.
• France has a more bureaucratic system, with a strong emphasis on following established procedures. Accountability can be more focused on adherence to rules

than performance outcomes. However, disciplinary measures for misconduct or negligence can include dismissal. In 2019, a local government official in France was dismissed for failing to properly manage a public housing project. This resulted in unsafe living conditions for residents, demonstrating the potential consequences of neglect by civil servants.

• Germany emphasises a career-based civil service with strong job security for tenured officials. However, performance evaluations are still conducted, and disciplinary measures can be taken for serious misconduct or repeated underperformance. Dismissal is a last resort. In 2017, a public official in Germany faced disciplinary action for unauthorised use of public funds. While dismissal might not have been the outcome, this case exemplifies how accountability mechanisms exist even within a system with strong job security.

• Italy's civil service is undergoing reforms to improve efficiency and accountability. Traditionally, it has faced criticism for a lack of transparency and a patronage culture. However, recent reforms are introducing performance-based evaluations with potential consequences for underperformance. While concrete recent examples are difficult to find due to ongoing reforms, historically, accountability for Italian civil servants has been weak. However, with a focus on improvement, serious misconduct layoffs are still a possibility.

• Japan's civil service is known for its lifetime employment system and strong emphasis on loyalty. However, performance evaluations do occur, and disciplinary measures can be taken for serious offences or incompetence. Dismissal is rare but possible. In 2018, a senior official at the Ministry of Land, Infrastructure, Transport and Tourism was dismissed for falsifying construction safety documents. This case underscores that even within a culture of loyalty, accountability measures can be triggered by egregious misconduct.

• The UK employs a performance-management system that emphasises objectives and targets. Civil servants face regular appraisals, and consequences for poor performance can involve additional training, demotion, or even dismissal. In 2020, a senior civil servant at the Department for Work and Pensions (DWP) resigned after facing criticism for his handling of a government program. This demonstrates the potential for public pressure and performance reviews to lead to consequences, even at senior levels.

• The USA's civil service accountability system varies depending on whether the employee is a federal employee with civil service protections or a political appointee. Federal employees face disciplinary procedures that can lead to dismissal, while political appointees serve at the pleasure of the President. In 2018, several high-ranking officials at the Environmental Protection Agency (EPA) were removed from their positions for rolling back environmental regulations. This showcases how political accountability can be a factor for certain civil servant positions in the US.

Note 23: Other examples of politicians who behaved unethically. (page 131)

United States of America -

• Anthony Weiner (Sexting Scandals, 2011, 2013, 2017): Resigned from Congress multiple times due to sexting scandals.

• Al Franken (Sexual Misconduct Allegations, 2017): Resigned from the Senate following accusations of sexual misconduct.

• Spiro Agnew: Resigned as Vice President in 1973 due to tax evasion and bribery charges.

• Tom DeLay: Former House Majority Leader resigned in 2006 amid a campaign finance scandal.

United Kingdom -

• John Profumo (Profumo Affair, 1963): Resigned as Secretary of State for War after lying to Parliament about an affair with a woman who had ties to a Soviet spy.

• David Mellor (Extramarital Affair, 1992): Resigned as Secretary of State for National Heritage due to an extramarital affair.

• Neil Hamilton and Tim Smith (Cash-for-Questions Affair, 1994): Resigned after being accused of accepting cash to ask questions in Parliament.

• Boris Johnson (Party-gate, 2022): Resigned as Prime Minister following a series of scandals, including gatherings at Downing Street during COVID-19 lockdowns.

• David Laws: Chief Secretary to the Treasury resigned in 2010 over a scandal involving his housing rent expense claims.

Canada -

• Mike Duffy: Senator resigned from the Conservative caucus in 2013 due to a scandal involving improper expense claims.

Other Countries -

• Park Geun-hye (South Korea): Impeached and removed from office for abuse of power and corruption.

• Jacob Zuma (South Africa): Resigned as President following numerous corruption allegations. Silvio Berlusconi (Italy): Resigned as Prime Minister multiple times due to various scandals, including sex scandals, corruption allegations, and tax fraud.

• Dominique Strauss-Kahn (France): Resigned as Managing Director of the International Monetary Fund after being accused of sexual assault.

• Jérôme Cahuzac: French Budget Minister resigned in 2013 after admitting to having an undeclared foreign bank account.

• François Fillon: Presidential candidate in 2017 withdrew from the race after allegations of misusing public funds to employ his wife and children.

• Franz Josef Strauss: German Minister-President of Bavaria faced allegations of accepting bribes from the Flick company in the 1980s.
• Bettino Craxi: Former Prime Minister was implicated in the "Tangentopoli" corruption scandal in the 1990s.
• Fernando Collor de Mello: President of Brazil impeached in 1992 on corruption charges.
• Eduardo Cunha: Former Speaker of Brazil's Chamber of Deputies was arrested and later convicted of corruption and money laundering.
• Ehud Olmert: Prime Minister of Israel resigned in 2008 due to multiple corruption investigations.
• A. Raja: India's Former Telecom Minister was involved in the 2G spectrum allocation scandal, which resulted in significant losses for the government.
• Brooks Newmark, UK MP resigned in 2014 after exchanging sexually explicit photos online.
• Dominik Feri, Czech Republic: MP resigned in 2021 after allegations of sexual assault and harassment.
• Pal Schmitt, Hungary: President resigned in 2012 after his doctoral dissertation was withdrawn due to plagiarism allegations, which were linked to a broader controversy surrounding his alleged sexual misconduct during his time as a sports official.
• Robert Budd Dwyer: Pennsylvania State Treasurer committed suicide on live television in 1987 amid a corruption scandal that involved allegations of sexual misconduct.

Note 24: Successful governments (page 137)
• The Roman Republic, which was in power from 509 to 27 BCE - almost 500 years - is considered one of the most successful governments in history. The Roman Republic was a federal government with a complex system of checks and balances and was known for its efficient bureaucracy and strong military. Much of the power was in the hands of the Tribunes, two elected each year but they only served for a one-year period. However, in its last 100 years, The Republic drifted increasingly into dictatorship, all power eventually residing with the emperor.
• The city-state of Athens, which flourished from around the 5th to the 4th century BCE, was a direct democracy, in which all citizens had the right to participate in the legislative process and vote on laws and policies. But to qualify as a citizen you had to be a landholder, and women were excluded.
• The Ming dynasty, which ruled China from 1368-1644, was known for its strong central government, efficient bureaucracy, and strong economic policies, which helped to bring prosperity to the country. The administration was run with a clear set of responsibilities where everyone knew their task and authority.

• The Ottoman Empire, which ruled over much of the Middle East and south-eastern Europe from the 13th to the early 20th century, was known for its strong and centralised government, and its military might and cultural achievements.
• Examples of current successfully run countries are, in the main, Anglo Saxon and are wealthier, better educated and more liberal. Essentially focussed on Europe and APAC.
• The United States has a federal system of government with a constitution that has been in place since 1787, and is known for its strong economy, high standard of living for some, and political stability. Increasingly, though, through the 21st century a battle has built between left and right, culminating, some would say, in the antics of- Donald Trump - destroying the vision of stability. Some feel the constitution itself is threatened.
• The United Kingdom, which has a parliamentary democracy with a constitutional monarchy, has a long history of political stability. Like America, its conduct so far in the 21st century suggests things are changing.
• Canada has a parliamentary democracy with a federal system of government. It is consistently ranked as one of the best countries in the world to live in due to its strong economy, high standard of living, and high levels of social and political stability.
• Switzerland is a federal parliamentary republic with a strong tradition of democracy and political stability. It has a highly developed economy and is known for its high standard of living and low levels of corruption.
• Japan is a parliamentary democracy with a constitutional monarchy, and it is known for its strong economy, high levels of social and political stability, and low levels of corruption.
• Germany is a federal parliamentary republic which, post-WW2, has established itself as a strong democracy and, despite its enforced reunification of East and West after 1989, has been politically stable. It has a highly developed economy and is known for its strong social safety net and low levels of corruption. Showing that you can go from very bad to much better.
• Norway is a parliamentary democracy with a constitutional monarchy. It is consistently ranked as one of the best countries in the world to live in due to its strong economy, high standard of living, and low levels of corruption.
• Australia is a federal parliamentary democracy with a constitutional monarchy, known for its strong economy, high standard of living, and low levels of corruption.
• South Korea is a presidential democratic republic with a strong economy and high standard of living. It is known for its political stability and low corruption.
• Taiwan is a democratic, multi-party state with a strong economy and a high standard of living. It is known for its low corruption and political stability.
• Singapore is a parliamentary democracy with a highly developed economy and a high standard of living. It is known for its low corruption and political stability.

• New Zealand is a parliamentary democracy with a constitutional monarchy. It is consistently ranked as one of the best countries in the world to live in due to its strong economy, high standard of living, and low levels of corruption.

Note 25: Items to return to original countries (page 153)

The British Raj in India undeniably acquired a significant amount of wealth, including jewels and artefacts, during its colonial rule. Here are some examples, which the UK should consider returning:

• The Koh-i-Noor: This famed diamond, meaning 'Mountain of Light' in Persian, was originally mined in India. It changed owners several times in its first 100 years, until the British East India Company gifted it to Queen Victoria after the annexation of Punjab in 1849. It is now part of the British Crown Jewels.

• The Mughal Treasure: After the defeat of the Mughal emperors in the 1850s, vast quantities of treasures, including jewels, gold, and other artefacts, were taken by the British. These treasures are dispersed in various collections, including the Victoria and Albert Museum in London.

• Tipu Sultan's Throne: Made of gold and adorned with jewels, this throne belonged to Tipu Sultan, an 18th-century ruler of Mysore who resisted British expansion in India. It's now on display at the Victoria and Albert Museum.

Other examples of valuable gains of War just to give some context would be:

• Egypt: The Rosetta Stone, a key to deciphering ancient Egyptian hieroglyphics, was taken by British forces during the Napoleonic Wars in 1799. It remains part of the collection at the British Museum, though Egypt has long requested its return.

• Greece: The Elgin Marbles, a collection of sculptures from the Parthenon in Athens, were removed by Lord Elgin, a British diplomat, in the early 19th century. They are currently in the British Museum, with Greece calling for their repatriation for display in the new Acropolis Museum.

• Benin Bronzes: These are a collection of metal plaques and sculptures from the Kingdom of Benin (present-day Nigeria) looted by British forces in 1897. They are scattered across numerous museums worldwide, with calls for their return to Nigeria.

Note 26: Military used outside of civilian control (page 177) - Historical problems stemming from the military being used against its own people

• Roman Praetorian Guard: This elite unit, initially tasked with protecting the emperor, became notorious for assassinating emperors and installing their own favourites. The Year of the Four Emperors (69 AD) was a particularly chaotic period in Rome where different military factions vied for power, leading to civil war and instability.

• Janissaries (Ottoman Empire): This elite corps, while initially loyal, eventually became a powerful and unruly force, frequently intervening in politics and even deposing sultans.
• Feudal Wars: Private armies of feudal lords often fought amongst themselves, leading to widespread violence and instability.
• Crusades: While ostensibly religious, these wars were also driven by political ambitions and territorial gain, often resulting in the massacre of civilian populations.
• The Hundred Years' War: A protracted conflict between England and France, fuelled by dynastic disputes and territorial ambitions, with devastating consequences for both nations.
• English Civil War (1642-1651): A conflict between the Royalists and Parliamentarians over the power of the monarchy, resulting in widespread violence and social upheaval.
• Reign of Terror (France, 1793-1794): The French Revolutionary government, led by Robespierre, used the military to suppress dissent and execute thousands of perceived enemies of the revolution.
• Napoleonic Wars (1803-1815): Napoleon's rise to power and his military conquests across Europe caused immense suffering and loss of life.
• World Wars I & II: While not directly using a military against its own civilians, both world wars were instigated by governments and resulted in the deaths of millions of soldiers and civilians alike.
• The Holocaust: The Nazi regime's systematic extermination of Jews and other minority groups was carried out with the complicity and support of the German military.
• Indonesian Mass Killings (1965-1966): The Indonesian military, with the support of civilian militias, massacred hundreds of thousands of suspected communists and ethnic Chinese.
• Cambodian Genocide (1975-1979): The Khmer Rouge regime, led by Pol Pot, used the military to implement a brutal social engineering project that resulted in the deaths of an estimated 1.5 to 2 million Cambodians.
• Syrian Civil War: The Syrian military has been accused of widespread human rights abuses, including using chemical weapons against its own civilians.
• Yemeni Civil War: The Saudi-led coalition, backed by the US, has been criticised for airstrikes that have killed civilians and destroyed infrastructure.
• Myanmar's Crackdown on the Rohingya: The Myanmar military has been accused of genocide and crimes against humanity for its campaign of violence against the Rohingya Muslim minority.

Note 27: Constitutional frameworks, (page 179)
• Constitutional and Legal Frameworks: United States Constitution: Article II, Section 2 designated the President as the Commander-in-Chief of the armed forces, establishing civilian control.

• The War Powers Resolution (1973) further delineates the powers of the President and Congress regarding military action.
• United Kingdom's Bill of Rights (1689): It establishes the principle of parliamentary consent for maintaining a standing army, ensuring civilian control over the military.
• Scholarly Works: Samuel P. Huntington, *The Soldier and the State* (1957): This seminal work discusses the concept of objective civilian control, where the military remains professional and apolitical, focusing solely on military affairs.
• Gene Sharp, *From Dictatorship to Democracy* (1993): This book outlines strategies for nonviolent resistance against authoritarian regimes, emphasising the importance of civilian control over the military in democratic transitions.
• International Organisations: NATO (North Atlantic Treaty Organization): NATO's founding principles emphasise democratic values and civilian control of the military. NATO members are committed to upholding these principles within their own armed forces and in their collective defence efforts.
• United Nations: The UN Charter promotes international peace and security, including supporting democratic governance and civilian control over the military in member states.
• Statements by Military Leaders: General Mark Milley, Chairman of the Joint Chiefs of Staff (USA), in testimony before Congress, affirmed that the military's role is to "obey lawful orders from civilian leadership" and that it is "not the place of the military to overturn the will of the people".
• Field Marshal Lord Guthrie (UK): In a lecture, Guthrie emphasised the importance of the military's loyalty to the Crown and the elected government, stating that "it is not for the military to decide who governs'.
• The Universal Declaration of Human Rights (UDHR), adopted by the United Nations in 1948, is the cornerstone of international human rights law. It outlines 30 fundamental rights and freedoms that belong to every person in the world, from birth until death.

Note 28: More religious text about sharing and giving. (page 192)

'Each man should give what he has decided in his heart to give, not reluctantly or under compulsion, for God loves a cheerful giver.' (2 Corinthians 9:7)

'Proclaim liberty throughout the land to all its inhabitants. It shall be a jubilee for you; each of you shall return to his property and each of you shall return to his family.' (Leviticus 25:10)

The Bhagavad Gita: Fulfilling One's Duty (Dharma): 'It is better to perform one's own duty (dharma), however imperfectly, than to excel in another's dharma (duty), which is fraught with danger. Even death in the performance of one's own duty brings one glory; to engage in another's duty is a source of shame. (Bhagavad Gita, Chapter 3, Verse 35)

The Importance of Charity (Dana): 'He who gives gifts, seeking nothing in return, who gives gifts prompted by love, gives gifts in the right place, gives gifts at the right time, that man is endowed with the best gift.' (Bhagavad Gita, Chapter 17, Verse 20)

The Dhammapada: Compassion and Suffering: 'All beings tremble before violence. All fear death. All love life. See yourself in others. Then whom can you hurt? What harm can you do?" (The Dhammapada, Verse 129)

'It is better to give than to receive, for the giver finds happiness, the hoarder finds no happiness.' (The Dhammapada, Verse 226)

The Fruits of Generosity: 'He who gives, who abstains from injuring living beings, who observes the moral law, who is pure in conduct - he walks the path to immortality.' (The Dhammapada, Verse 27)

Zigong asked, 'Is there one word that can serve as a guide to conduct throughout one's life?' The Master replied, 'Perhaps the word reciprocity is that word: Do not do to others what you would not want them to do to you.' (Analects of Confucius, Book XV, Verse 24)

'In a state well governed, poverty is shameful. In a state ill governed, riches are shameful.' (Analects of Confucius, Book VIII, Verse 16)

Christianity: 'But if anyone has the world's goods and sees his brother in need and does not help him, how does God's love abide in him?' (1 John 3:17)

Islam: Zakat is one of the Five Pillars of Islam, a mandatory charitable donation given to the poor and needy. (Quran 2:43)

Judaism: Tzedakah, the act of righteous giving, is a core principle. 'Deeds of giving are the very foundations of the world.' (Jewish saying from the Mishna, Pirkei Avot 1:2)

Hinduism: Dana, the practice of selfless giving, is a central tenet. 'He who gives away what he himself desires ... obtains endless happiness.' (Bhagavad Gita)

Buddhism: Generosity is a core Buddhist practice. 'Giving even a little ... with a clear mind is better than giving a lot with a disturbed mind.' (Dhammapada)

Confucianism: "Perhaps in the world there are no good men who are not benevolent." (Analects of Confucius)

'He who is kind to the poor lends to the Lord, and He will reward him for what he has done.' Proverbs 19:17

'He who gives to the poor will lack nothing, but he who closes his eyes to them receives many curses.' - Proverbs 28:27

'The rich and the poor have this in common: The Lord is the Maker of them all.' - Proverbs 22:2

'Do not neglect to show hospitality to strangers, for by doing so some have entertained angels without knowing it.' Hebrews 13:2

'For I was hungry, and you gave me something to eat; I was thirsty, and you gave me something to drink; I was a stranger, and you invited me in.' Matthew 25:35

'If you want to be perfect, go, sell your possessions and give to the poor, and you will have treasure in heaven.' Matthew 19:21

"Give to the one who asks you, and do not turn away from the one who wants to borrow from you.' Matthew 5:42

'Sell your possessions and give to the poor. Provide purses for yourselves that will not wear out, a treasure in heaven that will not be exhausted, where no thief comes near, and no moth destroys.' - Luke 12:33

Note 29: The companies controlling the news (page 211)

• Alphabet Inc. owns YouTube, the world's most popular video-sharing platform, and Google Search, the dominant search engine worldwide. These platforms have immense power to shape public discourse and influence information access.

• Meta owns Facebook, the largest social media network globally, Instagram and WhatsApp. These platforms have a pervasive presence in people's lives and play a significant role in shaping online communication and information consumption.

• Microsoft owns NBCUniversal, one of the largest media conglomerates in the world, with extensive holdings in television, film, news, and streaming services. Microsoft also owns Azure, a leading cloud computing platform that is widely used by media organisations.

• The Walt Disney Company is a diversified media and entertainment giant with a vast portfolio of assets, including Disney Studios, ESPN, ABC, Hulu, and Pixar. These holdings give Disney significant power over content production and distribution.

• Warner Bros. Discovery is another major media conglomerate with a wide range of assets, including Warner Bros. Studios, HBO, CNN, and Discovery Channel. This company has a strong presence in traditional and new media.

• News Corp owns several prominent news outlets, including The Wall Street Journal, The New York Post, and The Sun. These publications have a significant impact on global news coverage and agenda-setting.

• Bertelsmann is a German media conglomerate with a diverse portfolio of assets, including Penguin Random House, RTL Group, and Gruner + Jahr. These holdings give Bertelsmann a strong presence in both print and broadcast media.

• Comcast is a major telecommunications and media company with extensive holdings in cable television, internet services, and NBCUniversal. Comcast's reach and influence extend across multiple media platforms.

• Sony Corporation is a Japanese multinational conglomerate with a significant media presence. Sony owns Sony Pictures Entertainment, PlayStation, and Columbia Records, giving it influence in film, gaming, and music.

• Tencent Holdings is a Chinese technology and entertainment giant with a vast portfolio of assets, including WeChat, Tencent Video, and Tencent Music. Tencent has a dominant position in the Chinese media market and is expanding globally.

• ByteDance Ltd owns TikTok and Douyin and is also the developer of the news platform Toutiao.

Note 30: Back to serfdom (page 216) - Yanis Varoufakis's technofeudalism

In numerous internet and e-marketing business models, the users are not the primary customers. Instead, their data and attention become the product that is sold to advertisers or other third parties. This paradigm is what Yanis Varoufakis has christened 'technofeudalism' and has become prevalent in the digital age, where platforms can collect vast amounts of user data and leverage it for targeted advertising and other revenue-generating activities.

Key Points and Examples:

• Data as the Commodity: The core value proposition of many online platforms lies not in the direct services they provide to users, but in their ability to gather and analyse user data. This data, encompassing demographics, interests, browsing behaviour, and social connections, is extremely valuable to advertisers who seek to target their messages precisely to relevant audiences.

• Free Services, Hidden Costs: Many online services are offered for free to users, but this "free" model is often subsidised by the collection and monetization of user data. Social media platforms, search engines, and many mobile apps fall into this category.

• Targeted Advertising: The primary revenue stream for many of these platforms is advertising. By analysing user data, they can deliver highly targeted ads, ensuring that users see content that is more likely to be relevant and engaging to them. This increases the effectiveness of advertising for businesses, who are willing to pay a premium for this targeted reach.

• Data Brokerage: In some cases, platforms may sell user data directly to data brokers or other third parties. These entities aggregate and analyse data from multiple sources to create detailed profiles of individuals, which can then be used for various purposes, including marketing, risk assessment, and even surveillance.

• Social Media Platforms (e.g., Facebook, Instagram, Twitter): These platforms offer users a way to connect and share content for free. In exchange, they collect vast amounts of user data, which is then used.

Books to read, for further information and books and reports referred to here.

Political Systems and Democracy:

Anne Applebaum - *Twilight of Democracy*

Applebaum explores the global decline of liberal democracy, focusing on how authoritarianism is gaining ground. She examines the role of elites, media, and conspiracy theories in fueling polarization and undermining democratic institutions, drawing on personal experiences and global case studies to explain why some intellectuals embrace autocratic ideologies.

Anne Applebaum - *Autocracy, Inc: 8 e Dictators Who Want to Run the World*

Applebaum investigates how modern autocracies—Russia, China, and others—collaborate to undermine democracy. She reveals how dictators share tactics, from propaganda to corruption, to maintain power and weaken liberal institutions. Through insightful analysis, she exposes the networks of influence that threaten democratic governance worldwide.

Ian Dunt - *How Westminster Works...and Why It Doesn't*

Dunt provides a deep dive into the UK's political system, exposing inefficiencies, outdated traditions, and systemic failures. He examines Parliament, media, civil service, and lobbying, revealing how dysfunction hinders effective governance. With wit and sharp analysis, he argues for reforms to create a more accountable and competent system.

Will Hutton - *8 is Time No Mistakes: How Can We Remake a Better Britain*

Hutton presents a bold vision for a renewed Britain, emphasizing economic fairness, institutional reform, and social justice. He critiques past political failures and offers practical solutions for sustainable growth, democratic accountability, and an equitable society, urging decisive action to avoid repeating historical mistakes.

Naomi Klein - *8 e Shock Doctrine: 8 e Rise of Disaster Capitalism*

Klein argues that neoliberal economists exploit crises—wars, natural disasters, financial collapses—to push free-market policies benefiting elites. She traces this pattern from Chile under Pinochet to post-Katrina New Orleans, showing how privatization and austerity are imposed in times of chaos, reshaping economies and societies for corporate gain.

Terrorism and Conflict:

Thomas Barfield - *Afghanistan: A History*

Barfield provides a comprehensive history of Afghanistan, tracing its political, cultural, and social evolution. He examines its tribal dynamics, foreign invasions, and internal conflicts, explaining how historical patterns shape modern instability. The book offers deep insights into Afghanistan's resilience and the challenges of governance in a fractured landscape.

J.M. Berger & Jessica Stern - *ISIS: 8 e State of Terror*

This book examines the origins, ideology, and tactics of ISIS, detailing how it emerged from Al-Qaeda and used propaganda and brutality to gain power. Berger and Stern analyze the group's recruitment strategies, global influence, and military operations, offering insights into counterterrorism efforts and the broader fight against extremism.

Martha Crenshaw - *Terrorism in Context*

Crenshaw presents a comprehensive analysis of terrorism's historical, political, and psychological dimensions. Using case studies from various regions and time periods, she explores how terrorist movements emerge, evolve, and sustain themselves. The book provides a nuanced understanding of motivations, strategies, and counterterrorism approaches within different sociopolitical contexts.

Alistair Horne - *8 e Battle of Algiers*

Horne chronicles the brutal urban warfare between French forces and Algerian insurgents (FLN) in 1956–57. He examines the use of guerrilla tactics, torture, and counterinsurgency, highlighting its role in Algeria's eventual independence. The book is a gripping account of colonial struggles and the ethical dilemmas of asymmetric warfare.

Global Economics and Inequality:

Javier Blas & Jack Farchy - *8 e World for Sale: Money, Power, and the Traders Who Barter the Earth's Resources*

Blas and Farchy expose the secretive world of commodity traders who control global markets for oil, metals, and food. They reveal how these traders amass fortunes, shape geopolitics, and thrive in crises, often operating beyond government oversight while influencing economies and conflicts worldwide.

Bruce Bueno de Mesquita & Alastair Smith - *8 e Dictator's Handbook*

This book argues that political leaders—whether dictators or democrats—act primarily to maintain power. The authors use game theory to show how elites secure loyalty through patronage, corruption, and selective repression. They challenge conventional wisdom, revealing how self-interest, not ideology, drives governance across different political systems.

Paul Collier - *8 e Bottom Billion*

Collier examines why the world's poorest billion people remain trapped in poverty despite global economic growth. He identifies key "poverty traps" such as conflict, bad governance, and resource dependence. Using data-driven analysis, he proposes targeted interventions—including aid, military intervention, and trade reforms—to help struggling nations escape economic stagnation.

Thomas Piketty - *Capital in the Twenty-First Century*

Piketty analyzes historical data to argue that wealth inequality is a structural feature of capitalism. He shows how returns on capital outpace economic growth, leading to ever-increasing concentration of wealth. Advocating for progressive taxation and wealth redistribution, he challenges traditional economic assumptions about meritocracy and social mobility.

Gabriel Zucman - *8 e Hidden Wealth of Nations*

Zucman exposes how the global elite hide trillions in offshore tax havens, undermining economic fairness. Using innovative research, he quantifies tax evasion's impact on inequality and government revenues. He proposes international cooperation and financial transparency reforms to combat this hidden wealth system that weakens public services and social stability.

Society and Philosophy:

Howard Bloom - *8 e Lucifer Principle*

Bloom explores how violence, competition, and hierarchy are fundamental to human progress. He argues that human history is shaped by biological and cultural forces driving conflict and dominance. Blending psychology, history, and evolutionary theory, he challenges conventional morality, showing how "evil" is an intrinsic part of civilization's development.

Rutger Bregman - *Utopia for Realists*

Bregman argues for radical yet achievable ideas like universal basic income, a shorter workweek, and open borders. Using historical examples and data, he shows how bold social policies can reduce poverty, improve well-being, and create a fairer society. He challenges conventional economic thinking, advocating for a more progressive future.

Jonathan Haidt - *8 e Happiness Hypothesis*

Haidt blends psychology, philosophy, and neuroscience to explore timeless wisdom about happiness. He examines ancient teachings alongside modern science, revealing how meaning, relationships, and resilience shape well-being. The book offers insights into how people can cultivate happiness by balancing reason and emotion, embracing adversity, and finding purpose.

Bertrand Russell - *Common Sense and Nuclear Warfare*

Russell warns of the catastrophic risks of nuclear weapons and argues for global disarmament. He critiques Cold War policies, advocating for diplomacy and rational decision-making to prevent annihilation. With logical clarity, he calls for an end to militaristic thinking, urging world leaders to prioritize peace over destructive power struggles.

Carl Sagan - *8 e Demon-Haunted World*

Sagan defends scientific skepticism against pseudoscience, conspiracy theories, and superstition. He explains the scientific method's importance in fostering critical thinking and rational inquiry. Using real-world examples, he warns against the dangers of ignorance and promotes science as humanity's best tool for understanding the universe and safeguarding democracy.

Sustainability and Future Trends:

David Graeber - *Bullshit Jobs*

Graeber argues that many modern jobs are meaningless, providing no real value to society. Through worker testimonies and economic analysis, he explores how pointless employment damages mental health and wastes human potential. He critiques capitalism's inefficiencies, proposing ways to create more fulfilling and socially beneficial work.

Kate Raworth - ***Doughnut Economics***

Raworth challenges traditional economic models, proposing a framework that balances human well-being with environmental sustainability. The "doughnut" model sets a safe space between essential social foundations and planetary boundaries. She advocates for regenerative, distributive economies that prioritize equity, resilience, and long-term prosperity over endless growth.

Kim Stanley Robinson - ***8 e Ministry for the Future***

This speculative novel envisions a near-future world grappling with climate catastrophe. Following a UN agency's radical efforts to combat climate change, Robinson blends fiction and policy ideas to explore geoengineering, financial reform, and political activism. The book offers a hopeful yet urgent vision for addressing the climate crisis.

Elizabeth Kolbert - ***8 e Sixth Extinction***

Kolbert examines how human activity is driving the planet's sixth mass extinction. Through case studies of disappearing species, she explains the science behind biodiversity loss and its long-term consequences. Blending field reporting with historical context, she highlights the urgency of addressing climate change and environmental destruction.

Yuval Noah Harari - ***21 Lessons for the 21st Century***

Harari explores pressing global issues—AI, nationalism, misinformation, and climate change—offering insights into how societies can navigate uncertainty. He examines technology's impact on work, politics, and personal meaning, urging individuals to develop critical thinking and adaptability in a rapidly changing world. The book offers a broad perspective on modern challenges.

Behavioral Economics:

Daniel Kahneman - *8 inking, Fast and Slow*

Kahneman explores two modes of human thinking: fast, intuitive, and emotional (System 1) versus slow, deliberate, and logical (System 2). He reveals cognitive biases that shape decision-making, from overconfidence to loss aversion, offering insights into how our minds work and how we can make better choices.

Richard Thaler - *Misbehaving: 8 e Making of Behavioral Economics*

Thaler recounts the development of behavioral economics, challenging classical economic theories that assume rational decision-making. Through real-world examples and personal anecdotes, he shows how human biases, emotions, and irrational behaviors influence markets, policy, and everyday life, shaping a field that revolutionized economics and public policy.

Major Reports:

World Inequality Report: World Inequality Lab
Website: https://wir2022.wid.world/
World Bank Website: https://data.worldbank.org/ or https://wir2022.wid.world/

Oxfam Inequality Reports: Oxfam publishes annual reports on global inequality, highlighting the growing gap between the rich and poor and advocating for policy changes to address this issue : https://www.oxfam.org/en/research/inequality-inc

World Economic Forum Global Risks Report: This annual report identifies and analyses the most pressing global risks, including economic, environmental, geopolitical, societal, and technological risks. https://www.weforum.org/publications/global-risks-report-2024/

This report tracks progress towards achieving the 17 Sustainable Development Goals (SDGs), which aim to end poverty, protect the planet, and ensure prosperity for all.
https://unstats.un.org/sdgs/report/2024/

International Monetary Fund (IMF) World Economic Outlook: This report provides analysis and forecasts of global economic developments, including trends in income inequality and the impact of economic policies.
https://www.imf.org/en/Publications/WEO

AFL-CIO
https://aflcio.org/paywatch/highest-paid-ceos

Other Reports

2020 Edelman Trust Barometer:
https://www.edelman.com/trust/2020-trust-barometer

2023 Medscape Physician Compensation Report:
https://www.medscape.com/sites/public/physician-comp/2023

American Association of University Professors (AAUP) 2023 survey: https://www.aaup.org/article/final-2022-2023-faculty-compensation-survey-results

American Bureau of Labor Statistics (BLS) 2023 survey:
https://www.bls.gov/opub/mlr/2023/

Departmental Overview 2022-23, National Audit Office:
https://www.nao.org.uk/overviews/cabinet-office-2022-23/
Global Risks Report 2024, World Economic Forum:
https://www.weforum.org/publications/global-risks-report-2024/

Global Wealth Report 2023, Credit Suisse:
https://www.google.com/search?q=Global+Wealth+Report+2023%2C+Credit+Suisse&oq=Global+Wealth+Report+2023%2C+Credit+Suisse&gs_lcrp=EgZjaHJvbWUyBggAEEUYOdIBCDQ5MTRqMGo0qAIAsAIA&sourceid=chrome&ie=UTF-8

How to Engage with Companies on Executive Compensation, Council of Institutional Investors:
https://www.cii.org/corp_gov_policies

Inequality Kills, Oxfam:
https://www.oxfam.org/en/research/inequality-kills

OECD Economic Surveys: United Kingdom 2023:
https://www.oecd-ilibrary.org/economics/oecd-economic-surveys-united-kingdom_19990502

The Student Campaigns of 1972-3 and 2010-11: Defending the Right to Higher Education:
https://journals.openedition.org/osb/3087

Trends in Income Inequality and its Impact on Economic Growth, OECD: https://www.oecd.org/en/publications/trends-in-income-inequality-and-its-impact-on-economic-growth_5jxrjncwxv6j-en.html

UBS Billionaire Ambitions Report 2024 https://www.ubs.com/global/en/wealthmanagement/family-office-uhnw/reports/billionaire-ambitions-report.html

World Employment and Social Outlook: Trends 2023, International Labour Organization:
https://www.ilo.org/publications/flagship-reports/world-employment-and-social-outlook-trends-2023

APPENDIX 3

Examples of letters to send, **the response rate from representatives in parliament, the Senate, or other G-7 governments** can vary widely and are not consistently documented across all countries. However, **United States**: According to a study by the Congressional Management Foundation (CMF), approximately 42% of people who contacted their congressional representative reported receiving a response. **United Kingdom**: A 2015 survey by the Hansard Society indicated that about 50% of constituents who contacted their MP received a response.

As an investor in a pension fund, you generally have the right to communicate with other investors and make suggestions about the fund's governance. This right stems from your ownership stake in the fund and your vested interest in its responsible and effective management.

However, the specific extent of your rights and the mechanisms for exercising them can vary depending on the jurisdiction and the specific rules and regulations governing the pension fund. In most cases, pension funds have established channels for communication and engagement with their investors, such as:

Shareholder Meetings: These meetings provide an opportunity for investors to voice their concerns, ask questions, and vote on important matters related to the fund's governance.

Written Communication: Investors can often submit written inquiries or suggestions to the fund's management or board of directors.

Investor Advocacy Groups: Some investors may choose to join or form investor advocacy groups to collectively voice their concerns and advocate for changes in the fund's governance or investment practices.

It's important to note that while you have the right to communicate and make suggestions, the fund's management and board of directors have the ultimate responsibility for making decisions about the fund's governance and investment strategies. However, your voice as an investor can still be influential in shaping these decisions, especially when combined with the voices of other concerned investors.

There will be a full set of letters/email templates that you can send that you can send available from our linked website. (February 2025)

1. **Letter to Bank Manager/Director:**
2. **Letter to Company Chairman:**
3. **Letter to Fund Manager of, Pension Fund/Insurance Company:**
4. **Template Letter to the Prime Minister/President:**
5. **Dear, [Minister/Senator/Representative]:**
6. **Letter to a Pension Fund Chairman/Directors:**
7. **Template Letter to a Bishop:**
8. **Template Letter to an Imam:**
9. **Template Letter to a Rabbi:**
10. **Letter to the directors of new technology companies.**

Response rates can vary greatly, these are rough estimates.

High-Profile Figures (Low Expected Response Rates):

Prime Minister/President:

Post: "*[Title], I am concerned about the rising cost of living and its impact on families.* Sincerely, A concerned voter." Expected Response: **Very Low (0-5%)** - These individuals receive an immense volume of messages. A direct response is unlikely, but it may be seen by staff or contribute to broader awareness. There are in some cases websites to communicate directly to the Prime Minister or president.

Cabinet Ministers/Senators:

Post: *"Dear Secretary [Last Name], I am concerned about the lack of affordable housing in our community.* Thank you for your time, A concerned voter." Expected Response: **Low (5-15%)** - They are also busy but may be more likely to respond or have staff acknowledge the message, especially if it's about a local or specific issue.

Religious & Community Leaders (Moderate Response Rates):

Bishops/Imams/Rabbis:

Post: *"Your Grace/Dear Imam/Rabbi [Last Name], I am concerned about the rise in hate speech and discrimination.* Respectfully, A member of your community." Expected Response: **Moderate (20-40%)** - These leaders often engage with their communities on social media. A thoughtful and respectful message may receive a direct response or acknowledgement.

Business Leaders (Variable Response Rates):

Chairpersons of Public Companies/Pension Fund Chairman:

Post: *"Dear Mr./Ms. Chairperson, I am concerned about the company's environmental impact and lack of transparency on sustainability efforts.* Sincerely, A shareholder." Expected Response: **Highly Variable (10-60%)** - Depends heavily on the company's size, culture, the specific issue, and the individual leader. Some companies are very active on social media and responsive to shareholder concerns, others much less so.

Letter to Public Company.

<table>
<tr><td>Chairman/Company Secretary's Name
Company Name
Company Address
City,
State,
ZIP Code</td><td>Your Name
Your Address,
City,
State,
ZIP Code
Email Address</td></tr>
</table>

Dear [Chairman/Company Secretary's Name],

I hope this letter finds you well. I am writing to you as a shareholder in [Company Name], or on behalf of my pension fund which has Invested in [Company Name].

I wish to express my concern regarding the company's Environmental, Social, and Governance (ESG) policies. ESG considerations are increasingly critical to Investors and stakeholders who are looking for transparency and sustainability in business operations.

In particular, I would like to request detailed Information on how the company reviews and determines the remuneration of the CEO, board members, and other key managers. Understanding the rationale and criteria for these compensation packages Is vital to assessing the alignment between executive incentives and long-term shareholder value.

Additionally, I am Interested In the ratio of pay between the CEO or the highest-paid executive and the average salary paid to the workers within the company. This Information Is essential for evaluating the company's commitment to equitable and fair compensation practices.

Lastly, I seek reassurance that [Company Name] has genuinely independent directors and individuals who ensure that ESG matters are given real attention and are not merely a facade. Independent oversight Is critical to integrity and effectiveness of the company's ESG Initiatives. I appreciate your attention to these matters and look forward to your response. Transparency In these areas will not only enhance shareholder trust but also contribute to the long-term success and sustainability of [Company Name].

Thank you for your time and consideration.

Yours sincerely,

[Your Name]
[Shareholder/Beneficiary of Pension Fund]

Also written by the author:

The History of FMCG

Storewars

E-Retail

www.moralmoney.co

Index

A

B

C

D

E

F

G

H

I

J

K

L

M

N

O

P

Q

R

S

T

U

V

W

X

Y

Z

www.ingramcontent.com/pod-product-compliance
Lightning Source LLC
LaVergne TN
LVHW052222200926
848481LV00001B/183
9798349202018